80|81

graphis annual

The International Annual of Advertising and Editorial Graphics

Das internationale Jahrbuch der Werbe-graphik und der redaktionellen Graphik

Le répertoire international de l'art graphique publicitaire et rédactionnel

Edited by / Herausgegeben von / Réalisé par:

Walter Herdeg

Graphis Press Corp., Zurich (Switzerland)

graphis annual 80|81

THE INTERNATIONAL ANNUAL OF ADVERTISING AND EDITORIAL GRAPHICS

This is the 29th annual edition of the original cornerstone of the "Graphis trilogy" which, for more than two decades, has richly earned its world-wide reputation as the standard work reflecting the latest international trends in all design fields. This year's collection continues its survey of graphics in advertisements, booklets, editorial design, annual reports, book jackets, trade magazines and magazine covers, calendars, trade marks, letterheads, packaging, record covers. "It is like a garden of international commercial art, and a delight to both professionals and lay browsers. The quality of reproduction is superb." – *Los Angeles Free Press.* "No matter what the creative climate, the *Graphis Annuals* make the best of things." – *Art Direction.* "A splendid art show in print, exciting and provocative." – *Publishers Weekly.* "*Graphis Annual* offers inspiration to everyone in advertising and visual communication and provides a ready reference for ideas." – *Creative Magazine.* "A must for all graphic collections!" – *Umbrella.* "This international survey of advertising and editorial art, in the nearly three decades of its publication, has undoubtedly become the most influential trend setter of all . . . Its superbly printed pages overflow with fresh conceptions and technical solutions for design problems." – *American Artist.*

Other important GRAPHIS Books:

GRAPHIS POSTERS
THE INTERNATIONAL ANNUAL OF POSTER ART

"Simply wonderful." – *Art Direction.* "More than a lavish volume of fascinating designs, the pages of the book are virtually a mirror of the present moment in time, reflecting ideas and the appearance of people, places and things with extraordinary intensity." – *School Arts.* "New ideas, approaches and standards of excellence can be studied and enjoyed." – *Inland Printer/American Lithographer.* Each edition offers visual evidence of the world's best posters arranged in four major categories: Advertising posters, Cultural posters, Social posters, Consumer posters. Published each year in early Spring.

PHOTOGRAPHIS
THE INTERNATIONAL ANNUAL OF ADVERTISING, EDITORIAL AND TELEVISION PHOTOGRAPHY

In this annual are outstanding world-wide achievements in Advertising; Annual Reports; Book Jackets; Editorial Photography; Magazine Covers; Packaging; Calendars; House Organs; Booklets; Television. ". . . eclectic in more than a historical sense, for they present a vast range of artistic styles." – *Publisher's Weekly.* "For anyone working with the photo-image, for any conceivable purpose involving persuasion and communications, this annual is a visual index to the many creative ways, to the changing visual techniques, and to the shifts in emphasis and style apparent in the work of top notch photographers and production people in the Western world." – *Technical Photography.* "This annual becomes more exciting every year." – *American Artist.* Published each year in late Spring.

"Square Books" format (9½" × 9¾")

ARCHIGRAPHIA
ARCHITECTURAL AND ENVIRONMENTAL GRAPHICS

FILM AND TV GRAPHICS 2
AN INTERNATIONAL SURVEY OF THE ART OF FILM ANIMATION

Distributed in the United States by

Hastings House
Publishers
10 East 40th Street, New York, N.Y. 10016

PUBLICATION No. 160 [ISBN 3-85709-180-0]

Contents   Inhalt   Sommaire

Abbreviations

Abkürzungen

Abréviations

Argentina	ARG	Argentinien	ARG	Allemagne occidentale	GER
Australia	AUS	Australien	AUS	Argentine	ARG
Austria	AUT	Belgien	BEL	Australie	AUS
Belgium	BEL	Brasilien	BRA	Autriche	AUT
Brazil	BRA	Dänemark	DEN	Belgique	BEL
Canada	CAN	Deutschland (West)	GER	Brésil	BRA
Cuba	CUB	Finnland	FIN	Canada	CAN
Czechoslovakia	CSR	Frankreich	FRA	Cuba	CUB
Denmark	DEN	Grossbritannien	GBR	Danemark	DEN
Finland	FIN	Iran	IRN	Espagne	SPA
France	FRA	Israel	ISR	Etats-Unis	USA
Germany (West)	GER	Italien	ITA	Finlande	FIN
Great Britain	GBR	Japan	JPN	France	FRA
Iran	IRN	Jugoslawien	YUG	Grande-Bretagne	GBR
Israel	ISR	Kanada	CAN	Iran	IRN
Italy	ITA	Kuba	CUB	Israël	ISR
Japan	JPN	Kuweit	KUW	Italie	ITA
Kuweit	KUW	Mexiko	MEX	Japon	JPN
Mexico	MEX	Niederlande	NLD	Koweit	KUW
Netherlands	NLD	Norwegen	NOR	Mexique	MEX
Norway	NOR	Österreich	AUT	Norvège	NOR
Poland	POL	Polen	POL	Pays-Bas	NLD
Rumania	RUM	Rumänien	RUM	Pologne	POL
Spain	SPA	Schweden	SWE	Roumanie	RUM
Sweden	SWE	Schweiz	SWI	Suède	SWE
Switzerland	SWI	Spanien	SPA	Suisse	SWI
Uruguay	URU	Tschechoslowakei	CSR	Tchécoslovaquie	CSR
USA	USA	Uruguay	URU	Uruguay	URU
Yugoslavia	YUG	USA	USA	Yougoslavie	YUG

Designers are often restricted in their work—as the author of our preface writes—which has a negative effect on quality in general. This edition nevertheless shows that many illustrators and designers still manage to produce convincing designs full of originality and artistic quality. We would like to thank all those who, year by year, make it possible for us to present this international cross-section.

Wie der Autor unseres Vorwortes schreibt, ist der Designer in seiner Arbeit oft eingeschränkt, was sich negativ auf die Qualität im allgemeinen auswirkt. Diese Ausgabe zeigt, dass sich viele Illustratoren und Designer nicht einschränken lassen und Arbeiten schaffen, die durch Originalität und künstlerische Qualität überzeugen. Wir danken all jenen, die uns jedes Jahr ermöglichen, diesen internationalen Querschnitt zu präsentieren.

Comme l'écrit l'auteur de notre préface, le designer est souvent restreint dans son travail, ce qui se répercute aussi sur la qualité en générale. Ce volume montre cependant qu'il n'y a pas mal d'illustrateurs et de designers qui ne se laissent pas faire, qui créent des travaux appréciés par leur originalité et leur qualité artistique. Nous remercions tous de nous faire parvenir régulièrement leur travaux pour nous mettre à même de présenter ce compendium international.

YOSHI KURI's cover illustration symbolizes the work of the artist, whose creations seem to grow out of the escaping paint so as to be carried out into the world after coming to fruition. He was born in 1928 in Japan, and after completion of his art studies, worked as a cartoonist for newspapers and magazines and produced animated films on the side, many of which won awards at international film festivals. Yoshi Kuri heads an art gallery and an animated film studio in Tokyo.

YOSHI KURIs Umschlagillustration symbolisiert die Arbeit des Künstlers, dessen Werke aus der auslaufenden Farbe zu wachsen scheinen, um nach ihrer Vollendung in die Welt hinausgetragen zu werden. Er wurde 1928 in Japan geboren. Nach Abschluss des Kunststudiums arbeitete er als Karikaturist für Zeitungen und Zeitschriften, daneben produzierte er Trickfilme, die an internationalen Filmfestspielen preisgekrönt wurden. In Tokyo leitet er eine Kunstgalerie und ein Trickfilmstudio.

YOSHI KURI, l'illustrateur de notre couverture, nous donne une vue symbolique du travail de l'artiste, dont les idées s'accumulent en une flaque de peinture, d'où semble naître ses œuvres d'art, qui, une fois achevées, sont emportées dans les quatre coins du monde. Né au Japon en 1928. Après des études des beaux-arts, il travaille comme caricaturiste pour divers journaux et magazines et produit des dessins animés qui lui ont valu nombre de médailles de festivals internationaux de cinéma. Il a sa propre galerie d'art et son studio cinématographique à Tokyo.

Paul Rand

Politics of Design

PAUL RAND, designer, teacher and painter, studied at the Pratt Institute, the Parsons School of Design and with George Grosz at the Art Students League. He has been a professor at the Yale University School of Art since 1956 and he is working as a consultant for IBM, Westinghouse and the Cummins Engine Co. Apart from various awards for his work, he has also been accorded honorary titles. Paul Rand has illustrated a number of books, written articles for design and art magazines and has published various works, including *Thoughts on Design, The Trademarks of Paul Rand* and *Design and the Play Instinct*.

It is no secret that the real world in which the designer functions is not the world of art, but the world of buying and selling. For sales, and not design, are the *raison d'être* of any business organization. Unlike the salesman, however, the designer's overriding motivation is art: art in the service of business, art which enhances the quality of life and deepens appreciation of the familiar world.

Design is a problem-solving activity. It provides a means of clarifying, synthesizing and dramatizing a word, a picture, a product, or an event. A serious barrier to the realization of good design, however, is the layers of management inherent in any bureaucratic structure. For aside from sheer prejudice or simple unawareness, one is apt to encounter such absurdities as second guessing, kow-towing, posturing, nit-picking and jockeying for position, let alone such buck-passing institutions as the committee meeting and the task force. At issue, it seems, is neither malevolence nor stupidity, but, simply, human frailty.

The smooth functioning of the design process may be thwarted in other ways: by the imperceptive executive who, in matters of design, understands neither his proper role nor that of the designer; by the eager but cautious advertising man whose principal concern is pleasing his client; and by the insecure client who depends on informal office surveys and pseudo-scientific research dealing with questions that are unanswerable and answers that are questionable.

Unless the design function in a business bureaucracy is so structured that direct access to the ultimate decision-maker is possible, trying to produce good work is very often an exercise in futility. Ignorance of the history and methodology of design—how work is conceived, produced and reproduced—adds to the difficulties and misunderstandings. Design is a way of life, a point of view. It involves the whole complex of visual communication: talent, creative ability, manual skill, and technical knowledge. Aesthetics and economics, technology and psychology are intrinsically related to the process.

One of the more common problems which tend to create doubt and confusion is caused by the inexperienced and anxious executive who innocently expects, or even demands, to see not one but many solutions to a problem. These may include a number of visual and/or verbal concepts, an assortment of layouts, a variety of pictures and colour schemes, as well as a choice of type styles. He needs the reassurance of numbers and the opportunity to exercise his personal preferences. He is also most likely to be the one to insist on endless revisions with unrealistic deadlines, adding to an already wasteful and time-consuming ritual. Theoretically, a great number of ideas assures a great number of choices, but such choices are essentially quantitative. This practice is as bewildering as it is wasteful. It discourages spontaneity, encourages indifference and, more often than not, produces results which are neither distinguished, interesting nor effective. In short, good ideas rarely come in bunches.

The designer who voluntarily presents his client with a batch of layouts often does so not out of prolificacy, but out of uncertainty or fear. He thus encourages the client to assume the role of referee. In the event of genuine need, however, the skilful designer is able to produce a reasonable number of good ideas. But quantity by demand is quite different from quantity by choice. Design is a time-consuming occupation. Whatever his working habits, the designer fills many a waste-basket in order to produce one good idea. Advertising agencies can be especially guilty in this "numbers game". Bent on impressing the client with their ardour, they present a welter of layouts, many of which are superficial interpretations of potentially good ideas, or slick renderings of trite ones.

Frequent job reassignments within an active business are additional impediments about which management is often unaware. Persons unqualified to make design judgements are frequently shifted into design-sensitive positions. The position of authority is then used as evidence of expertise. While most people will graciously accept and appreciate criticism when it comes from a knowledgeable source, they will resent it (openly or otherwise) when it derives solely from a power position, even though the manager may be highly intelligent or have self-professed "good taste". At issue is not the right, or even the duty, to question, but the right to make design judgement. Such misuse of privilege is a disservice to management and counter-productive to good design. Expertise in business administration, journalism, accounting or selling, though necessary in its place, is not expertise in problems dealing with visual appearance. The salesman who can sell you the most sophisticated computer typesetting equipment is rarely one who appreciates fine typography or elegant proportions. Actually, the plethora of bad design that we see all around us can probably be attributed as much to good salesmanship as to bad taste.

Deeply concerned with every aspect of the production process, the designer must often contend with inexperienced production personnel and time-consuming purchasing procedures, which stifle enthusiasm, instinct and creativity. Though peripherally involved in making aesthetic judgements (choosing printers, papermakers, typesetters and other suppliers), purchasing agents are, for the most part, ignorant of design practices, insensitive to subtleties that mean quality, and unaware of marketing needs. Primarily, and rightly, concerned with cost-cutting, they mistakenly equate elegance with extravagance and parsimony with wise business judgement.

These problems are by no means confined to the bureaucratic corporation. Artists, writers and others in the fields of communication and visual arts, in government or private industry, in schools or churches, must constantly cope with those who do not understand and are, therefore, unsympathetic to their ideas. The designer is especially vulnerable because design is grist for anybody's mill. "I know what I like" is all the authority one needs to support one's critical aspirations.

Like the businessman, the designer is amply supplied with his own frailties. But unlike him, he is often inarticulate, a serious problem in an area in which semantic difficulties so often arise. This is more pertinent in graphic design than in the industrial design or architectural fields, because graphic design is more open to aesthetic rather than functional preferences.

Stubbornness may be one of the designer's admirable or notorious qualities (depending on one's point of view): a principled refusal to compromise, or a means of camouflaging inadequacy. Design clichés, meaningless patterns, stylish illustrations and predetermined solutions are signs of such weakness. An understanding of the significance of modernism and familiarity with the history of design, of painting, of architecture and other disciplines, which distinguish the educated designer and make his role more meaningful, are not always his strong point.

The designer, however, needs all the support he can muster, for his is a unique but unenviable position. His work is subject to every imaginable interpretation and to every piddling piece of fault-finding. Ironically, he seeks not only the applause of the connoisseur, but the approbation of the crowd.

A salutary working relationship is not only possible but essential. Designers are not always intransigent, nor are all purchasing agents blind to quality. Many responsible advertising agencies are not unaware of the role that design plays as a communication force. And the man who pays the piper, the businessman who is sympathetic and understanding, is not altogether illusory. He is professional, objective, and alert to new ideas. He places responsibility where it belongs, and does not feel insecure enough to see himself as an expert in a field other than his own. He is, moreover, able to provide an harmonious environment in which goodwill, understanding, spontaneity, and mutual trust, qualities so essential to the accomplishment of creative work, may flourish.

Similarly, the skilled graphic designer is a professional whose world is divided between lyricism and pragmatism. He is able to distinguish between trendiness and innovation, between obscurity and originality. He sees freedom of expression not as licence for abstruse ideas, and tenacity not as bullheadedness, but as evidence of his own convictions. His is an independent spirit guided more by an "inner artistic standard of excellence" [1] than by some external influence. At the same time he realizes that good design must withstand the rigours of the marketplace, he believes that without good design the marketplace would be a showcase of visual vulgarity.

The creative arts have always laboured under adverse conditions. Subjectivity, emotion, and opinion seem to be concomitants of "artistic" questions. The layman feels insecure and awkward about making design judgements, even though he pretends to make them with a certain measure of know-how. But, like it or not, business conditions compel many to get inextricably involved with problems in which design plays some role. For the most part, the creation or the effects of design, unlike science, are neither measurable nor predictable, nor are the results necessarily repeatable. If there is any assurance, besides faith, a business-man can have, it is in choosing talented, competent and experienced designers.

Meaningful design (as demonstrated by so many of the examples in this book), design of quality and wit, is no small achievement, even in an environment in which good design is understood, appreciated and ardently accepted, and in which profit is not the only motive. At best, work that has any claim to distinction is the exception, even under the most ideal circumstances. After all, our epoch can boast of only one Cassandre.

[1] The Dynamics of Creation, by Anthony Storr, p. 189, Atheneum, 1972.

Paul Rand

Design-Politik

PAUL RAND, Designer, Lehrer und Maler, absolvierte
seine Studien am Pratt Institute, der Parsons School
of Design und mit George Grosz an der Art Students
League. Seit 1956 ist er Professor an der Yale University School of Art, daneben arbeitet er als Berater
für IBM, Westinghouse und die Cummins Engine Co.
Neben verschiedenen Auszeichnungen für seine
Arbeiten, wurden ihm auch Ehrentitel verliehen. Paul
Rand illustrierte mehrere Bücher, schrieb Artikel für
Design- und Kunstzeitschriften und veröffentlichte
verschiedene Werke, u. a. *Thoughts on Design, The
Trademarks of Paul Rand* und *Design and the Play
Instinct.*

Es ist kein Geheimnis, dass die reale Welt, in welcher der Designer arbeitet, nicht die Welt der Kunst ist, sondern die Welt des Kaufens und Verkaufens. Denn Verkauf und nicht Design ist der Daseinszweck eines jeden Unternehmens. Anders als der Verkäufer wird jedoch der Designer vor allem von der Kunst motiviert: von der Kunst im Dienste eines Geschäftes, von Kunst, die Lebensqualität erhöht und das Verständnis für die uns vertraute Welt vertieft.

Das Design stellt sich die Lösung von Problemen zur Aufgabe. Es stellt eine Möglichkeit der Klärung, Synthese und Dramatisierung eines Wortes, eines Bildes, eines Produkts oder eines Ereignisses zur Verfügung. Vor der Verwirklichung guten Designs stehen als ernsthafte Barrieren jedoch die Managementebenen, die jeder bürokratischen Struktur zu eigen sind. Denn neben glattem Vorurteil und schlichter Unkenntnis kann man dort so absurden Dingen begegnen wie Besserwisserei, Unterwürfigkeit, Herauskehren des Vorgesetzten, kleinlicher Krittelei und festgefahrenen Positionsstrategien, einmal ganz abgesehen von Institutionen wie der Komiteesitzung und irgendwelcher Sonderabteilungen, die zur Weitergabe des Schwarzen Peters da sind. Aber, wie es scheint, geht es hier nicht um Bosheit oder Dummheit, sondern ganz einfach um menschliche Schwächen.

Der glatte Ablauf des Design-Vorganges kann auch auf andere Weise gestört werden: von wahrnehmungsunfähigen Geschäftsführern, die, in Fragen des Designs, weder ihre eigene Rolle noch die des Designers verstehen; vom eifrigen aber vorsichtigen Werbemanager, dessen Hauptinteresse es ist, seinen Kunden zufriedenzustellen; und vom unsicheren Kunden, der von inoffiziellen Büroumfragen und pseudowissenschaftlicher Forschung abhängig ist, die sich mit Fragen beschäftigen, die nicht zu beantworten sind, und Antworten liefern, die fragwürdig bleiben.

Wenn die Funktion eines Designers in einer Firmenbürokratie nicht so strukturiert ist, dass ein direkter Zugang zu demjenigen, der letztendlich entscheidet, möglich ist, bleibt der Versuch, gute Arbeit zu leisten, oft vergebene Liebesmühe. Unkenntnis der Entwicklung und Methodologie des Designs — wie eine Arbeit konzipiert, produziert und reproduziert wird — trägt zusätzlich zu Schwierigkeiten und Missverständnissen bei. Design ist eine Lebensweise, eine Weltanschauung. Es umschliesst den ganzen Komplex visueller Kommunikation: Talent, kreatives Können, handwerkliche Fähigkeiten und technisches Wissen. Ästhetik und Wirtschaftlichkeit, Technologie und Psychologie sind aufs engste mit diesem Prozess verknüpft.

Eines der gewöhnlicheren Probleme, das für Zweifel und Verwirrung sorgt, wird von dem unerfahrenen und besorgten Geschäftsführer verursacht, der ganz arglos erwartet oder sogar verlangt, dass ihm mehr als eine Lösung eines Problems präsentiert wird. Diese Lösungen können eine Anzahl visueller und/oder verbaler Konzepte, eine Vielzahl Layouts, zahlreiche Bilder und Farbmuster und ein Sortiment von Schriftarten einschliessen. Er braucht die Absicherung durch Quantität und die Gelegenheit, seine persönlichen Vorlieben auszuspielen. Er ist wahrscheinlich auch derjenige, der endlos Abänderungen mit unrealistischen Terminen fordert und somit ein bereits verschwenderisches und Zeit kostendes Ritual noch verlängert. Theoretisch sorgt eine Vielzahl von Ideen für vielfältige Auswahlmöglichkeiten, aber diese sind im wesentlichen nur quantitativ. Dieser Vorgang ist so verwirrend wie er verschwenderisch ist. Er ermutigt Spontaneität, ermutigt Gleichgültigkeit und führt häufig genug zu Resultaten, die weder bemerkenswert, noch interessant oder wirkungsvoll sind. Kurz gesagt, gute Ideen gibt es nicht wie Sand am Meer.

Der Designer, der seinem Kunden freiwillig mehrere Layouts präsentiert, tut das oft nicht, weil er so produktiv wäre, sondern weil er unsicher oder ängstlich ist. Er ermutigt so den Kunden, in die Rolle des Schiedsrichters zu schlüpfen. Falls es wirklich erforderlich ist, kann der fähige Designer im vernünftigen Rahmen auf verschiedene gute Ideen kommen, aber Quantität auf Anforderung ist etwas ganz anderes als freiwillig erbrachte Quantität. Gutes Design zu realisieren ist sehr zeitaufwendig. Welche Arbeitsmethode ein Designer auch haben mag, er füllt viele Papierkörbe, ehe er eine gefundene Idee für gut befindet. Werbeagenturen tragen zu diesem «Zahlenlotto» in besonderem Masse bei. Da sie ihren Kunden mit ihrem Fleiss beeindrucken wollen, präsentieren sie ihm einen Schwung Layouts, von denen viele nur oberflächliche Interpretationen potentiell guter Ideen sind, oder aber auf Hochglanz gebrachte Ausführungen abgedroschener Einfälle.

Häufige Neubesetzung eines Arbeitsplatzes innerhalb einer Firma stellt eine zusätzliche Behinderung dar, deren sich das Management oft nicht bewusst ist. Oft werden Personen, die nicht für Design-Entscheidungen qualifiziert sind, auf Posten befördert, in denen sie eben diese Entscheidungen treffen müssen. Die berufliche Stellung wird dann als Beweis für Fachkenntnis benützt. Während die meisten Menschen Kritik annehmen, wenn sie sachverständiger Kenntnis der Probleme entspringt, lehnen sie sie (offen oder sonstwie) ab, wenn sie nur aufgrund einer Machtposition erfolgt, selbst wenn der betreffende Manager noch so intelligent ist oder behauptet, «guten Geschmack» zu haben. Fraglich ist hier nicht das Recht oder die Pflicht, Fragen zu stellen, sondern das Recht, eine das Design betreffende Entscheidung zu fällen. Solch ein Privilegienmissbrauch leistet dem Unternehmen als solches einen Bärendienst und verhindert überdies gutes Design. Fachkenntnis in Geschäftsverwaltung, Journalismus, Buchhaltung oder Verkauf ist, obwohl an seinem Platz notwendig, noch nicht gleichbedeutend mit Fachkenntnis in Fragen visueller Gestaltung. Der Verkäufer, der einem die fortschrittlichste Computersatzmaschine verkaufen kann, ist selten jemand, der sich sonderlich für typographische Feinheiten und elegante Proportionen interessiert. Wahrscheinlich lässt sich die Überfülle schlechten Designs, das wir überall sehen, ebenso oft auf gute Verkäufer wie auf schlechten Geschmack zurückführen.

Um jeden Aspekt des Produktionsablaufs sehr bemüht, muss sich der Designer oft mit unerfahrenem Produktionspersonal und zeitintensiven Einkaufsvorgängen herumschlagen, die Enthusiasmus, Instinkt und Kreativität ersticken. Obwohl am Rande in ästhetische Entscheidungen (Auswahl von Druckern, Papierlieferanten, Setzerei oder ähnlichem) verwickelt, haben die Einkäufer meist keine Ahnung von Designpraktiken und haben kein Gespür für die Kleinigkeiten, die Qualität bedeuten. Ihre Hauptaufgabe ist, zu Recht, Sparsamkeit walten zu lassen, und aus diesem Grund verwechseln sie irrtümlicherweise Eleganz mit Extravaganz und Knauserigkeit mit klugen Geschäftsentscheidungen.

Diese Probleme beschränken sich keinesfalls nur auf bürokratische Firmen. Künstler, Autoren und andere im Bereich der Kommunikation und der visuellen Künste tätige Personen müssen sich bei Regierung und Privatindustrie, Schulen und Kirchen ständig mit jenen herumschlagen, die ihre Ideen nicht verstehen und ihnen deshalb ablehnend gegenüberstehen. Der Designer ist besonders verletzlich, weil Design Wasser auf jedermanns Mühle ist. «Ich weiss, was mir gefällt», ist die ganze Autorität, die jemand braucht, um sein kritisches Trachten zu untermauern.

Wie der Geschäftsmann weist auch der Designer seine Schwächen auf. Anders als er, vermag er sich aber oft nicht auszudrücken, ein ernstes Problem in einem Bereich, in dem sich häufig semantische Schwierigkeiten ergeben. Das ist bei Graphik-Design von grösserer Bedeutung als bei Industrie-Design oder in der Architektur, weil Graphik-Design eher von ästhetischen als von funktionellen Präferenzen geleitet wird.

Je nach Standpunkt, mag Sturheit eine der bewundernswerten oder notorischen Qualitäten des Designers sein. Sie ist die prinzipielle Verweigerung des Kompromisses oder ein Mittel der Verschleierung von Schwächen. Designklischees, sinnlose Muster, modische Illustrationen und vorgefasste Lösungen sind Zeichen solcher Schwäche. Ein Verständnis für die Bedeutung des Modernismus und Vertrautheit mit der Geschichte des Designs, der Malerei, der Architektur und anderer Disziplinen, die den gebildeten Designer kennzeichnen und in seiner Rolle bedeutsamer machen, sind nicht immer seine starke Seite.

Der Designer braucht jedoch jede nur denkbare Unterstützung, weil er eine einzigartige, aber nicht beneidenswerte Position innehat. Seine Arbeit ist jeder denkbaren Interpretation und jeder noch so belanglosen Kritik ausgesetzt. Ironischerweise sucht er nicht nur den Beifall des Kenners, sondern auch Anerkennung bei der Menge.

Eine vernünftige Arbeitsbeziehung ist nicht nur möglich, sondern sogar wesentlich. Designer sind nicht immer unnachgiebig, und nicht alle Einkäufer sind für Qualität blind. Viele verantwortungsbewusste Werbeagenturen kennen die Rolle des Designs als Kommunikationskraft. Und der Geschäftsmann mit Verständnis für die anstehenden Probleme ist nicht gänzlich illusorisch. Er ist geschäftstüchtig, objektiv und neuen Ideen gegenüber aufgeschlossen. Er legt Verantwortung in die richtigen Hände und ist nicht so unsicher, dass er sich in einem anderen als seinem Fachgebiet als Experte aufspielen will. Er sorgt ausserdem für eine harmonische Umgebung, in der guter Wille, Verständnis, Spontaneität und gegenseitiges Vertrauen, die Vorbedingungen kreativer Arbeit, gedeihen.

In ähnlicher Weise ist der fähige Graphik-Designer ein echter Profi, dessen Welt zwischen Gefühl und Pragmatismus aufgeteilt ist. Er kann zwischen aufgesetztem Trend und Neuerung, zwischen Obskurem und Originellem unterscheiden. Er sieht Freiheit der Meinungsäusserung nicht als Freibrief für abstruse Ideen und hält Beharrlichkeit nicht für Dickköpfigkeit, sondern für einen Beweis für seine eigene Grundsatztreue. Sein unabhängiger Geist wird mehr von einem «inneren künstlerischen Leistungsstandard» [1] geleitet als von irgendwelchen äusseren Einflüssen. Gleichzeitig erkennt er, dass gutes Design den harten Anforderungen des Marktes standhalten muss, und glaubt, dass der Markt ohne gutes Design ein Schauplatz visueller Vulgarität wäre.

Die kreativen Künste haben immer unter widrigen Umständen zu schaffen gehabt. Subjektivität, Emotion und Meinung scheinen die Begleiter «künstlerischer» Fragen zu sein. Der Laie fühlt sich unsicher und hilflos, wenn er Design-Entscheidungen treffen soll, auch wenn er vorgibt, dass er diese Entscheidungen mit einem gewissen Mass an Sachkenntnis trifft. Aber viele werden, ob sie es nun wollen oder nicht, durch die Geschäftslage gezwungen, sich mit Problemen zu beschäftigen, bei denen Design eine Rolle spielt. Meistenteils sind die Entstehung oder die Wirkung von Design, anders als physikalische Vorgänge, weder messbar noch vorherzusagen. Auch lässt sich ein einmal gewonnenes Ergebnis nicht notwendigerweise wiederholen. Der Geschäftsmann kann sich, ausser durch guten Glauben, einzig dadurch absichern, dass er talentierte, kompetente und erfahrene Designer wählt.

Sinnvolles Design (wie es die Beispiele in diesem Buch demonstrieren), Design von Qualität und Witz ist keine geringe Leistung, auch nicht in einer Umgebung, in der gutes Design verstanden, anerkannt und hoch geschätzt wird, und in der Profit nicht das einzige Motiv des jeweiligen Tuns ist. Bestenfalls ist aber Arbeit, die den Anspruch des Herausragenden erheben kann, die Ausnahme, selbst unter den idealsten Voraussetzungen. Denn immerhin kann sich unsere Epoche nur *eines* Cassandre rühmen.

[1] The Dynamics of Creation, von Anthony Storr, S. 189, Atheneum, 1972.

Paul Rand

Business et design

PAUL RAND, designer, professeur et peintre, a fait ses études au Pratt Institute, à la Parsons School of Design et avec George Grosz à l'Art Students League. Depuis 1956 il est professeur à la Yale University School of Art; à part cela, il travaille comme conseiller pour IBM, Westinghouse et la Cummins Engine Co. Ses travaux lui ont valu de nombreuses distinctions et plusieurs titres honorifiques. Paul Rand est illustrateur de livres, il écrit des articles pour des magazines d'art et d'arts graphiques et a publié divers ouvrages, entre autres *Thoughts on Design, The Trademarks of Paul Rand* et *Design and the Play Instinct.*

Il n'est guère sensé de se dissimuler que le réel où le designer est appelé à fonctionner n'a rien à faire avec le monde de l'art, mais représente un monde terre à terre, dominé par les principes de la vente et de l'achat. C'est que le chiffre d'affaires, et non pas le design, est la raison d'être de toute organisation industrielle ou commerciale. Toutefois, la motivation sine qua non du designer est tout autre que celle du vendeur. Elle le porte à mettre l'art au service des affaires, un art qui enrichit la qualité de vie et approfondit la vision du réel qui nous est familier.

Le design est une activité consistant à résoudre des problèmes en ce sens qu'il procure les moyens de clarifier, de synthétiser, de dramatiser un mot, une image, un produit, un événement. Le design de qualité se heurte en cours de réalisation à un obstacle majeur: la hiérarchie du management qui caractérise toute structure bureaucratique. Sans parler des préjugés ou des incompréhensions pures et simples, on rencontre des absurdités telles que la pédanterie, l'obséquiosité, l'affectation, la chicanerie, l'intrigue visant le pouvoir, et bien entendu le rejet des responsabilités sur autrui via les comités et les sous-groupes. Ce qui semble en jeu ici, ce n'est pas tellement la malveillance ou la stupidité, mais l'inévitable faiblesse humaine.

Le déroulement approprié du processus de design peut être contrecarré d'autre manière: par un responsable qui, ne connaissant rien au design, ne perçoit pas correctement ni son propre rôle ni celui de l'artiste; par un publicitaire certes enthousiaste, mais prudent dont le principal souci est de satisfaire son client; par un client peu sûr de lui qui s'appuie sur des sondages occasionnels faits par ses bureaux et sur des résultats de recherches pseudo-scientifiques portant sur des questions insolubles et des réponses contestables.

Dans la mesure où la fonction du design au sein d'une structure bureaucratique d'entreprise n'est pas conçue de manière à permettre l'accès au vrai décideur, les tentatives en vue d'une création de qualité s'avèrent trop souvent de simples exercices en futilité. Qui plus est, l'incompétence en ce qui concerne l'histoire et la méthodologie du design – la manière dont un travail se conçoit, se produit et se reproduit – vient s'ajouter aux difficultés et aux malentendus constatés. Le design est un mode de vie, un type de vision du réel qui englobe la totalité complexe des communications visuelles, le talent, l'aptitude à créer, le doigté et le savoir-faire manuel, les connaissances techniques. L'esthétique et l'économie, la technologie et la psychologie participent intimement au processus de création.

L'un des problèmes les plus souvent rencontrés et qui tend à semer le doute et la confusion surgit par la faute du responsable sans expérience et redoutant de s'engager qui s'aventure à réclamer en toute innocence non pas une seule, mais toute une série de solutions à un problème donné, ou tout au moins s'attend à se les voir proposer. Il peut s'agir d'un certain nombre de concepts visuels et/ou verbaux, d'un assortiment de layouts, d'un choix d'illustrations et de schèmes couleurs, d'une sélection de caractères typo. Un tel responsable entend appuyer son jugement sur un élément statistique, le nombre de données parmi lesquelles, pour se sécuriser, il pourra faire son marché en ayant l'impression de formuler des préférences qui lui sont personnelles. Ce sera très probablement aussi le même qui insistera sur d'innombrables révisions dans des délais impossibles, en un rituel irraisonné gaspillant le temps et l'énergie disponibles. En bonne théorie, une kyrielle d'idées est garante d'un choix assez large, mais ce genre de choix est essentiellement d'allure quantitative, une pratique aussi déroutante que dilapidatrice. On bloque ce faisant la spontanéité, favorise l'indifférence et la production de résultats ternes, sans intérêt ni efficacité réelle. C'est que les bonnes idées ne sont pas foison et ne surgissent généralement qu'une à une.

Le designer qui présente de son propre gré toute une série de projets à son client ne le fait souvent pas par jaillissement créateur, mais mû par l'incertitude, voire la crainte. Il encourage par-là son client à tenir le rôle de l'arbitre. Lorsqu'un besoin réel le commande, un designer expert est tout à fait capable de produire un certain nombre d'excellentes idées, mais la quantité résultant de la demande est autre chose que celle qui résulte du choix. Le design est une activité coûteuse en termes de temps investi. Quelles que soient ses habitudes de travail, il arrive à tout designer de remplir sa corbeille à papier avant de mettre au point une idée qui fait tilt. Les agences publicitaires sont enclines à porter une lourde responsabilité dans ce «jeu des grands nombres». Pour faire de l'épate, elles présentent une masse de layouts témoignant de leur «créativité» et qui ne sont pour la plupart que des resucées de quelques bonnes idées fondamentales ou des interprétations habiles du déjà-dit et déjà-vu.

Les mutations intervenant au sein du management constituent des goulots d'étranglement supplémentaires dont la direction de l'entreprise ne se rend guère compte. Des personnes non qualifiées sont promues à des postes où il s'agit de porter des jugements compétents sur des questions de design. L'autorité qu'elles exercent leur semble suffisamment tenir lieu de compétence. Alors que l'être humain est ainsi fait qu'il accepte et apprécie assez facilement les critiques émanant de source autorisée, il s'insurgera ouvertement ou indirectement lorsque ces mêmes critiques sont émises en fonction de la seule autorité hiérarchique d'un individu même doté en principe d'une bonne intelligence ou affirmant disposer d'un goût affiné. Ce qui est ici en cause, ce n'est pas le droit, voire le devoir de critiquer, mais le droit de porter un jugement en matière de design. Cet abus du privilège que confère la position dans la hiérarchie est nuisible à l'entreprise et préjudiciable à la mise au point d'un design de qualité. La compétence acquise dans les domaines de la gestion, du journalisme, de la comptabilité ou des ventes, aussi respectable soit-elle dans la spécialité en question, ne saurait être étendue aux problèmes touchant à l'aspect visuel. Le vendeur capable de vous faire acheter la composeuse électronique la plus perfectionnée est rarement à même d'apprécier la beauté de la typographie ou l'équilibre des proportions. Et l'on peut en effet attribuer sans risque d'erreur le foisonnement des solutions de design ratées dans le paysage visuel actuel aussi souvent à un talent poussé de la vente qu'au mauvais goût tout simplement.

Le designer, qui porte attention à tous les aspects de la production, doit souvent s'expliquer avec du personnel de production inexpérimenté et des procédures d'achat interminables qui étouffent dans l'œuf tout enthousiasme, instinct et créativité. Bien qu'ayant à porter des jugements d'ordre esthétique en choisissant l'imprimeur, le fabricant de papier, l'atelier de composition et d'autres fournisseurs, les préposés aux achats n'en sont guère conscients; ignares pour la plupart en matière de procédés de design et insensibles aux questions de qualité, ils en viennent à méconnaître les exigences du marketing. Leur rôle veut qu'ils soient surtout attachés à réduire les coûts; à leurs yeux, l'élégance est synonyme d'extravagance; en serrant la vis à outrance, ils croient obéir aux impératifs d'une saine morale économique.

Ces problèmes ne se rencontrent pas seulement dans les contacts du designer avec l'entreprise bureaucratique. Les artistes, les rédacteurs et autres spécialistes des arts de la communication et des arts visuels se heurtent partout, dans les bureaux de l'administration d'Etat comme dans ceux de l'industrie privée, dans les milieux scolaires comme dans les Eglises à des gens qui ne les comprennent pas et ne réagissent donc pas avec sympathie aux idées qu'ils émettent. Le designer est d'autant plus vulnérable que tout le monde croit avoir son mot à dire quand il s'agit de création visuelle. Souvent, un laconique «je sais parfaitement ce que je veux» coupera court à un embryon de dialogue.

Tout comme l'homme d'affaires, le designer est amplement pourvu de faiblesses. Mais alors que le premier sait s'exprimer avec volubilité, l'artiste est souvent empêtré dans la verbalisation de son art, ce qui pèse lourd dans une relation où les difficultés sont si souvent d'ordre sémantique. Je pense ici surtout à l'art graphique, plus souvent l'objet de préférences esthétiques que l'esthétique industrielle ou l'architecture, dont le caractère fonctionnel s'impose plus aisément.

L'entêtement, cette qualité admirable ou détestable du designer, se traduit par le refus des compromissions. Mais que cache-t-il? La grandeur d'âme ou une faiblesse savamment camouflée? On ne saurait assez recommander à chaque artiste de s'informer pleinement de l'histoire et des tendances modernes de son art et des arts parallèles pour tenir bon, entêté ou simplement sur la défensive, dans la situation unique, mais peu enviable qui est la sienne. Le projet qu'il soumet risque d'être débattu et interprété interminablement, d'être examiné à la loupe grossissante. Fort de son art, capable de recourir à une verbalisation suffisante pour faire apparaître l'étendue de sa culture, il doit néanmoins tabler sur le dialogue plus que sur l'obstination. Le designer n'est pas toujours intransigeant ni le client ou son chef des achats intraitable et réfractaire à la qualité du travail créateur. Après tout, le design est un art de la communication. Il n'est pas illusoire d'envisager de la part de l'homme d'affaires une attitude dictée par la sympathie et la compréhension en même temps que le coup d'œil professionnel, objectif et l'ouverture aux idées nouvelles. Nous attendons de lui qu'il exerce sa responsabilité là où il le faut et ne pousse pas l'erreur de jugement jusqu'à se considérer comme un expert dans un domaine où manifestement il ne l'est pas. C'est au client de mettre à disposition de la relation qu'il entretient avec l'artiste un environnement harmonieux où la bonne volonté, la compréhension, la spontanéité et la confiance réciproque peuvent s'épanouir et assurer le plein succès de l'entreprise commune.

Le graphiste rompu à son métier sait trouver la juste voie entre l'envolée lyrique et les considérations pragmatiques. Il sait distinguer la mode passagère de l'innovation réelle, l'obscurité de l'originalité. La liberté d'expression ne signifie pas pour lui le champ libre aux idées farfelues, et s'il se montre tenace, ce n'est pas parce qu'il a l'esprit obtus, mais parce qu'il a un pas d'avance sur son client en matière de création et que sa conviction s'est forgée en cours d'élaboration de la solution proposée. Cet esprit indépendant est guidé bien plus par un «étalon intérieur d'excellence artistique» [1] que par des influences extérieures. En même temps, il est conscient de ce que le design de qualité doit pouvoir affronter victorieusement les intempéries du marché et s'y imposer pour éviter à ce dernier de sombrer dans la médiocrité, voire la vulgarité au point de vue visuel.

Les arts de création ont de tout temps eu à s'exprimer dans des conditions peu favorables. La subjectivité, l'émotion, l'opinion personnelle semblent accompagner les questions artistiques. Il est donc inévitable que le non-spécialiste ne se sente pas à son aise en abordant la difficile question du jugement d'une œuvre d'art appliqué, même s'il prétend le contraire. Mais qu'il le veuille ou non, le businessman ne peut échapper à l'explication continue evec les arts visuels, si difficiles à quantifier quant à leur impact. Dans ce domaine, les succès ne sont ni prévisibles ni objectivables et donc reproductibles à volonté. Le mieux qu'un homme d'affaires avisé ait à faire, c'est encore de s'entourer de designers de talent, ayant fait leurs preuves et dont la compétence est indiscutable.

Le design significatif (dont témoignent tant d'exemples rassemblés dans le présent volume), soit le design qui allie qualité et esprit, n'est pas une mince affaire, même dans un environnement favorable où le design de qualité se voit compris, apprécié, voire accepté avec enthousiasme, et où la motivation du profit ne règne pas en seule maîtresse. Les travaux méritant le plus haut qualificatif ne sont pas légion, tant s'en faut, même dans les circonstances les plus propices à l'éclosion du génie. Après tout, il n'y a eu à notre époque qu'un seul Cassandre!

[1] The Dynamics of Creation, par Anthony Storr, p. 189. Ed. Atheneum, 1972.

Index to Artists and Designers
Verzeichnis der Künstler und Gestalter
Index des artistes et maquettistes

Index to Art Directors
Verzeichnis der künstlerischen Leiter
Index des directeurs artistiques

Index to Agencies and Studios
Verzeichnis der Agenturen und Studios
Index des agences et studios

Index to Publishers
Verzeichnis der Verleger
Index des Editeurs

Index to Advertisers
Verzeichnis der Auftraggeber
Index des clients

ERRATUM – GRAPHIS ANNUAL 79/80

■ In the last volume of GRAPHIS ANNUAL wrong credits were given for a
concertina-type folder for a newly opened shopping centre, shown as Nos 133,
134 on page 67. The designer was Julia Alldridge and not Paul Anthony.

■ In der letzten Ausgabe von GRAPHIS ANNUAL haben wir für einen Leporello-
prospekt für ein neu eröffnetes Einkaufszentrum (Abb. 133, 134 auf Seite 67) als
Gestalter einen falschen Namen genannt. Der Prospekt wurde von Julia Alldridge
und nicht von Paul Anthony gestaltet.

■ Dans la dernière édition de GRAPHIS ANNUAL nous avions reproduit à la
page 67, fig. 133, 134 un dépliant en accordéon pour un nouveau centre commercial. Ce dépliant a été conçu par Julia Alldridge et non pas par Paul Anthony
comme nous l'avions indiqué.

■ Entry instructions may be requested by anyone interested in submitting
samples of exceptional graphics or photography for possible inclusion in our
annuals. No fees involved. Closing dates for entries:
GRAPHIS ANNUAL (advertising and editorial art and design): 31 January
PHOTOGRAPHIS (advertising and editorial photography): 30 June
GRAPHIS POSTERS (an annual of poster art): 30 June
Write to: Graphis Press Corp., Dufourstrasse 107, 8008 Zurich, Switzerland

■ Einsendebedingungen können von jedermann angefordert werden, der uns
Beispiele hervorragender Photographie oder Graphik zur Auswahl für unsere
Jahrbücher unterbreiten möchte. Es werden keine Gebühren erhoben.
Einsendetermine:
GRAPHIS ANNUAL (Werbe- und redaktionelle Graphik): 31. Januar
PHOTOGRAPHIS (Werbe- und redaktionelle Photographie): 30. Juni
GRAPHIS POSTERS (ein Jahrbuch der Plakatkunst): 30. Juni
Adresse: Graphis Verlag AG, Dufourstrasse 107, 8008 Zürich, Schweiz

■ Tout intéressé à la soumission de travaux photographiques et graphiques
recevra les informations nécessaires sur demande. Sans charge de participation.
Dates limites:
GRAPHIS ANNUAL (art graphique publicitaire et rédactionnel): 31 janvier
PHOTOGRAPHIS (photographie publicitaire et rédactionnelle): 30 juin
GRAPHIS POSTERS (annuaire sur l'art de l'affiche): 30 juin
S'adresser à: Editions Graphis SA, Dufourstrasse 107, 8008 Zurich, Suisse

Editor and Art Director: Walter Herdeg
Assistant Editors: Stanley Mason, Vreni Monnier
Project Manager: Vreni Monnier
Designers: Martin Byland, Ulrich Kemmner
Art Assistants: Willy Müller, Peter Wittwer

1

Magazine Advertisements

Newspaper Advertisements

Zeitschriften-Inserate

Zeitungs-Inserate

Annonces de revues

Annonces de presse

Advertisements
Anzeigen
Annonces

ARTIST / KÜNSTLER / ARTISTE:

1 Charles Santore
2 Robert Byrd
3 Jaye Carlson
4 Haruo Miyauchi
5, 6 Heather Cooper

DESIGNER / GESTALTER / MAQUETTISTE:

1, 2, 5, 6 Elmer Pizzi
3 Sidjakov & Berman Assoc.
4 Richard Mantel

ART DIRECTOR / DIRECTEUR ARTISTIQUE:

1, 2, 5, 6 Elmer Pizzi
3 Jerry Berman
4 Seymour Chwast

AGENCY / AGENTUR / AGENCE – STUDIO:

1, 2, 5, 6 Gray & Rogers, Inc.
3 Sidjakov & Berman Assoc.
4 Push Pin Studios, Inc.

1, 2, 5, 6 Spreads from a long-standing advertising campaign for *Grit*, the national small-town weekly newspaper. Fig. 1 refers to a film entitled *The Prisoner of Alcatraz*; Fig. 2 refers to Count Dracula and Fig. 6 is an allusion to Andersen's fairy-tale *The Ugly Duckling*. (USA)
3 Black-and-white *First National Bank* advertisement offering a water filter at a reduced price as a reward for increased savings. (USA)
4 Magazine advertisement for *Haber Typographers*. (USA)

1, 2, 5, 6 «Der grosse Frosch in kleinen Städten.» Aus einer seit Jahren laufenden Kampagne einer Zeitung mit Lokalausgaben für Kleinstädte. Abb. 1 «Der Froschmann von Alcatraz» spielt auf den Film «Der Gefangene von Alcatraz» an, Abb. 2 auf Dracula und Abb. 6 «Das hässliche Fröschlein» auf das Andersen-Märchen *Das hässliche Entlein*. (USA)
3 Schwarzweiss-Anzeige einer Bank, die als Prämie für Spareinlagen einen Wasserfilter zu einem günstigen Preis anbietet. (USA)
4 Zeitschriftenanzeige für eine Schriftsetzerei. (USA)

1, 2, 5, 6 «La grande grenouille dans les petites villes.» Campagne auto-promotionnelle d'un journal avec des éditions locales pour des petites villes rurales. Fig. 1: «L'homme-grenouille d'Alcatraz» se réfère au film «L'évasion d'Alcatraz», la fig. 2 au Comte Dracula et la fig. 6, «La vilaine petite grenouille», au conte d'Andersen *Le vilain petit canard*. (USA)
3 Annonce noir-blanc d'une banque qui offre un filtre à eau à un prix avantageux à ceux qui ouvre un compte de dépôt. (USA)
4 Annonce de magazine d'un atelier de typographie. (USA)

7

8

ARTIST / KÜNSTLER / ARTISTE:

7, 8 Fred Otnes
9 R.O. Blechman
10 Dietrich Ebert
11, 12 Alan E. Cober

DESIGNER / GESTALTER / MAQUETTISTE:

7, 8, 11, 12 Jerry Demoney
9 Howard Title

9

Advertisements / Anzeigen / Annonces

7, 8, 11, 12 Examples from a prestige campaign by *Mobil* already looking ahead into the future. Fig. 7 is entitled "Imagine tomorrow 1,000 feet deep. And awfully wet". All illustrations are printed in full colour on silver ground. (USA)
9 Newspaper advertisement for *Sony* tape recorders that pick up the slightest nuance. (USA)
10 Magazine advertisement for *Metabowerke*, comparing old, proven things made in Swabia with its own ingenious Swabian products. In full colour. (GER)

7, 8, 11, 12 «Stellen Sie sich das Morgen 3000 Meter tief vor. Und entsetzlich nass.» – «Stellen Sie sich das Morgen weder flüssig noch fest vor. Wir tun es.» – «Stellen Sie sich das Morgen ohne Auseinandersetzung vor. Wie unangenehm!» Beispiele aus einer Prestige-Kampagne von *Mobil*, die heute schon an morgen denkt. Mehrfarbig auf Silber gedruckt. (USA)
9 Zeitungsanzeige für *Sony*-Tonbänder, die auch die kleinsten Nuancen aufzeichnen. (USA)
10 Zeitschriftenanzeige der *Metabowerke*, die alte, in Schwaben ausgetüftelte Gegenstände mit den eigenen, ebenso ausgeklügelten schwäbischen Produkten vergleicht. Mehrfarbig. (GER)

7, 8, 11, 12 «Assumez que l'avenir aura une profondeur de 3000 m, qu'il sera affreusement mouillé.» – «Assumez que l'avenir ne sera ni liquide ni solide. Nous connaissons sa consistence.» «Assumez qu'il n'y aura pas de discussions. Quel domage!» Exemples figurant dans une campagne de prestige lancée par *Mobil* qui pense déjà aujourd'hui à ce qu'il faut faire demain. Illustrations en couleurs imprimées sur fond argenté. (USA)
9 Annonce pour les bandes magnétiques *Sony*, qui enregistrent toutes les nuances. (USA)
10 Cette annonce de magazine des *Metabowerke* présente des objets anciens de la Souabe qui sont créés de façon aussi subtile que les produits souabes de cette entreprise. (GER)

ART DIRECTOR / DIRECTEUR ARTISTIQUE:

7, 8, 11, 12 Jerry Demoney
9 Howard Title
10 Achim Sommer

AGENCY / AGENTUR / AGENCE – STUDIO:

7, 8, 11, 12 Mobil Public Affairs
9 Waring & LaRosa
10 Leonhardt & Kern

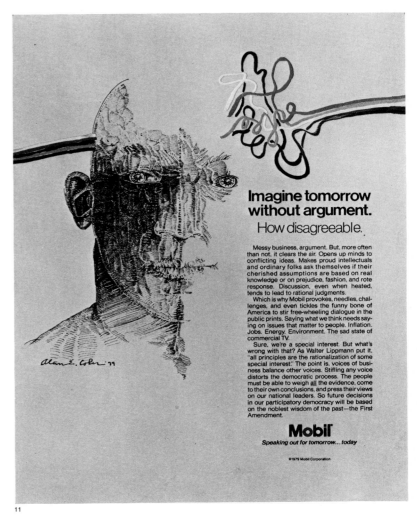

11

10

12

Advertisements
Anzeigen
Annonces

13, 14 From a newly-launched series of advertisements for *Nocona Boots*. Full-colour illustrations in photo-realistic style. (USA)
15 "France qualified twice for the Argentine." Full-colour advertisement for the football boots worn by the French team at the last World Cup Finals in the Argentine. The cockerel is the French national symbol. (FRA)
16–18 Examples from a series of advertisements for a pharmaceutical company, for an antibiotic for babies and the prematurely born and a medicament for vascular diseases. (ARG)
19, 20 Double-spread magazine advertisements for *American Medical International*, a company which has specialized in the field of health care services and whose technical equipment and own services are constantly geared to current conditions (Fig. 19) so that nothing remains standing where it started (Fig. 20). Full colour. (USA)

13, 14 Aus einer neu lancierten Anzeigenserie für Cowboy-Stiefel. Photorealistische Illustrationen in Farbe. (USA)
15 «Frankreich hat sich zweimal für Argentinien qualifiziert.» Mehrfarbige Anzeige für Fussballschuhe, die die französische Mannschaft in Argentinien trug. Der Hahn ist das Wahrzeichen von Frankreich. (FRA)
16–18 Beispiele aus einer Anzeigenserie einer pharmazeutischen Fabrik, hier für ein Antibiotikum für Frühgeborene und Babies und ein Medikament gegen Gefässkrankheiten. (ARG)
19, 20 Doppelseitige Zeitschriftenanzeigen eines Unternehmens, das sich auf dem Sektor des Gesundheitswesens spezialisiert hat und dessen Dienste und technische Einrichtungen auf die jeweiligen Bedingungen abgestimmt sind (Abb. 19) und das auch nicht dort stehen bleibt, wo es angefangen hat (Abb. 20). Mehrfarbig. (USA)

ARTIST / KÜNSTLER / ARTISTE:

13, 14 Alex Ebel
15 Bernard Durin
16 Omar Tracogna
17, 18 Javier Cafaro
19, 20 Dick Drayton

DESIGNER / GESTALTER / MAQUETTISTE:

13, 14 Angus McQueen/Mark Keller
16–18 Eduardo A. Cánovas
19, 20 Dick Drayton

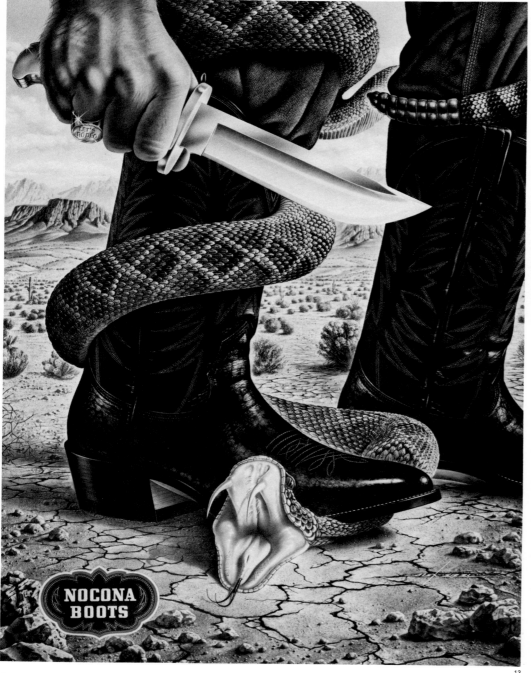

13

14

15

13, 14 Exemples d'une nouvelle série d'annonces lancée en faveur d'une marque de bottes Western. Illustrations couleurs réalisées dans la manière du photo-réalisme. (USA)

15 Cette annonce fait allusion à la Coupe du monde de football en Argentine, où la France était représentée deux fois, une fois par son équipe et une fois par les chaussures françaises *Patrick*. Le coq est l'un des emblèmes de la France. (FRA)

16–18 D'une série d'annonces pour les produits pharmaceutiques des Laboratoires *Bagò*, ici pour un antibiotique destiné aux prématurés et aux nouveau-nés et un médicament pour le traitement des maladies vasculaires. (ARG)

19, 20 Annonces doubles pages d'une entreprise, dont les installations techniques et le service sanitaire offerts tiennent compte des circonstances actuelles (fig. 19) et sont développés continuellement. En polychromie. (USA)

19

16

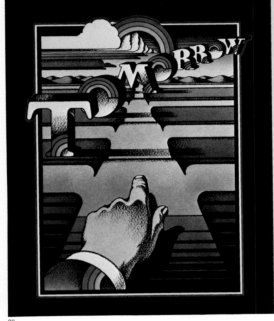

20

17

18

21 Magazine advertisement for the *Gut reisen* ("Good travelling") travel bureau that eliminates accidents beforehand which could occur on holiday. In black and white. (GER)
22, 25 From a series of double-spread magazine advertisements for a new *Saba* video recorder. (GER)
23 Black-and-white advertisement for a typographers which is constantly developing new type. Stylised compositors' case. (ITA)
24 Magazine advertisement for *Dioressence*, a "barbaric" perfume by *Dior*. Red dress, green palm-leaves. (FRA)
26, 27 Illustration in actual size and corresponding magazine advertisement for *Cerruti*, a fashion designer. (FRA)

21 Zeitschriften-Anzeige des Reisebüros *Gut reisen*, das auch an eventuelle Pannen denkt und sie bereits vor dem Urlaub aus dem Wege räumt. (GER)
22, 25 Aus einer Serie von doppelseitigen Zeitschriftenanzeigen für ein neues Videogerät von *Saba*. (GER)
23 Schwarzweiss-Anzeige einer Schriftsetzerei, die immer wieder neue Schriften entwickelt. Stylisierter Setzkasten. (ITA)
24 Zeitschriften-Anzeige für *Dioressence*, das «barbarische» Parfum von *Dior*. Rotes Kleid, grüne Palmblätter. (FRA)
26, 27 Illustration in Originalgrösse und entsprechende Zeitschriftenanzeige des Modeschöpfers *Cerruti*. (FRA)

21 «Que faut-il faire que les mouches ne se déguisent pas en éléphants.» Annonce d'une agence de voyage qui pense déjà avant le départ à toutes les éventualités. Noir-blanc. (GER)
22, 25 Exemples d'un série d'annonces de magazines doubles pages pour un nouveau magnétoscope de *Saba*. (GER)
23 Annonce de magazine (noir-blanc) d'un atelier de typographie qui cherche toujours des alternatives. Case stylisée. (ITA)
24 Annonce de magazine pour *Dioressence*, le parfum «barbare» de *Dior*. Robe rouge, feuilles vertes. (FRA)
26, 27 Illustration (grandeur nature) et annonce de magazine correspondante du créateur de modes *Cerruti*. (FRA)

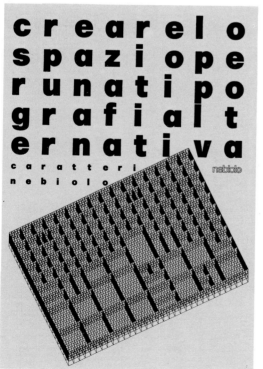

21

22

23

ARTIST / KÜNSTLER / ARTISTE:

21 Norman Junge
22 Peter Kretzmann
24 Gruau
25 Ursula Becker
26, 27 Jörg Hermle

DESIGNER / GESTALTER / MAQUETTISTE:

21 Norman Junge
23 Sergio Nepote
26, 27 Philippe Martignoni

ART DIRECTOR / DIRECTEUR ARTISTIQUE:

21 Norman Junge
22 Helmut Vandenberg
23 Gianni Parlacino
25 Reiner Held/Jürgen Heymen
26, 27 Philippe Martignoni

AGENCY / AGENTUR / AGENCE – STUDIO:

21 Acon
22, 25 Doyle Dane Bernbach GmbH
23 Centroune
24 Claude Michel
26, 27 Mandarine

DIORESSENCE

le parfum "barbare"
de Christian Dior

24

25

25

26

27

37

28, 29, 31 Illustrations and double-spread magazine advertisement from a series by *Siegwerk*, printing inks, a company which for many years has had a rainbow as its symbol. (GER)
30 Magazine advertisement for an art gallery, offering an original lithography by an artist. Cream-coloured Rolls Royce, olive-coloured wall, ochre hard brick floor. (USA)
32 Double-spread magazine advertisement for the *Schoellershammer* paper company, praising its quality of paper with Homeric songs. In black and white. (GER)

28, 29, 31 Illustrationen und doppelseitige Zeitschriftenanzeige aus einer Serie der Druckfarben-fabrik *Siegwerk*, die seit Jahren den Regenbogen als Signet hat. (GER)
30 Zeitschriftenanzeige einer Kunstgalerie, die hier eine Originallitho eines Künstlers anbietet. Cremefarbener Rolls Roys, olivefarbene Wand, braunroter Klinkerboden. (USA)
32 Doppelseitige Zeitschriftenanzeige der Papierfabrik *Schoellershammer*, die hier mit homerischen Gesängen ihre Papiere lobt. Schwarzweiss. (GER)

28, 29, 31 Illustrations et annonce de magazine double page figurant dans une série pour les encres d'imprimerie *Siegwerk*, dont le symbole est l'arc-en-ciel. (GER)
30 Annonce de magazine d'une galerie d'art qui offre une lithographie originale d'un artiste. Rolls Royce beige, parois olive, carreaux rouge-brun. (USA)
32 Annonce de magazine double page d'une papeterie, qui chante une hymne «homérique» sur ses produits. Illustration en noir et blanc. (GER)

ARTIST / KÜNSTLER / ARTISTE:

28, 29, 31 Braldt Bralds
30 Bob Bidner
32 Horst H. Erbelding

DESIGNER / GESTALTER / MAQUETTISTE:

28, 29, 31 Braldt Bralds
30 Bob Bidner
32 Olaf Gaumer

ART DIRECTOR / DIRECTEUR ARTISTIQUE:

28, 29, 31 Robert Pütz
30 Bob Bidner
32 Olaf Gaumer

AGENCY / AGENTUR / AGENCE – STUDIO:

28, 29, 31 Robert Pütz GmbH & Co
30 Bob Bidner
32 Art + Act

29

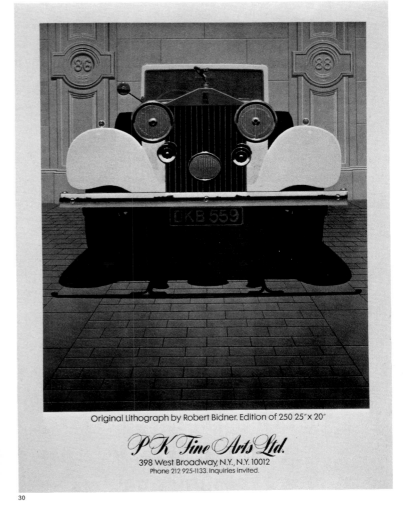

Original Lithograph by Robert Bidner. Edition of 250 25"x 20"

PK Fine Arts Ltd.
398 West Broadway, N.Y., N.Y. 10012
Phone 212 925-1133. Inquiries invited.

30

Auf
Wind und Wogen
reimt sich Bogen.

In stürmischen Zeiten
muß man sich als Drucker auf
seine Druckfarben und
Druckhilfsmittel verlassen
können. Regenbogendrucker
haben sich ihren eigenen
Reim darauf gemacht.

31

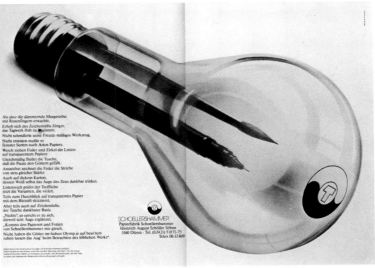

32

39

Fête:

A continental description of an elaborate party or dinner. A perfect description of a function held at the unique and personal facilities of the Kingsmill Golf Club Restaurant. Birthdays, weddings, anniversaries, Bar Mitzvahs, business meetings, club or organizational affairs. The list is endless. Our experienced staff will be happy to show you how to take advantage of our exquisite facilities and unique menus. Simply call, 220-2600.

33

Menufique!

This Tuesday could be your night to savor mandarin walnut chicken peaked by snow peas that capture the joy of oriental cuisine.
The James River can become the Tiber as delectable manicotti shells overflow with rich cheeses and seasoned meats. What special menu will grace this Tuesday night's buffet at the Kingsmill Golf Club Restaurant? Call. Ask. Reserve a place for yourself. 220-2600. Bon appetit!

34

Riverdine.

A very special word for a very special experience. The James River in an atmosphere you can never get enough of. Culinary delights so varied, you can make Kingsmill Golf Club Restaurant a constant source of dining pleasure.
Come savor oysters on the half shell, succulent shrimp, steaming hot loaves of bread, veal Oscar, rack of lamb or crab imperial fit for royalty. Riverdine. Tonight. Call 220-2600.

35

33–35 From a series of uniform, small-format advertisements explaining some culinary specialities from the restaurant of the *Kingsmill Golf Club*. In black and white. (USA)
36 Double-spread magazine advertisement for a special risk insurance offered by the Continental Insurance Co. Black and white, uniform in blue and white. (USA)
37, 38 Illustration and corresponding magazine advertisement for *Golden Skillet* fried chicken. (USA)

33–35 Aus einer Serie von einheitlich gestalteten, kleinformatigen Anzeigen, die einige kulinarische Köstlichkeiten des *Kingsmill Golf Club* Restaurants aufzählen. Schwarzweiss. (USA)
36 Doppelseitige Zeitschriftenanzeige für die spezielle Risikoversicherung einer Versicherungsgesellschaft. Schwarzweiss, Uniform in Blau und Weiss. (USA)
37, 38 Illustration und entsprechende Zeitschriftenanzeige einer Restaurantkette, die ausschliesslich Brathähnchen serviert. (USA)

33–35 D'une série d'annonces à petit format, de conception uniforme, vantant les délices culinaires du restaurant *Kingsmill Golf Club*. Dessins en noir et blanc. (USA)
36 Annonce de magazine double page pour une assurance spéciale contre les risques mis au point par une compagnie d'assurances. Noir-blanc, uniforme en bleu et blanc. (USA)
37, 38 Illustration et annonce de magazine où elle figure. Publicité pour les poulets rôtis d'une chaîne de restaurants. (USA)

WE HAVE A SPECIAL RISK SERVICE.
OUR COMPETITORS HAVE A SPECIAL RISK SERVICE.
AND THAT'S WHERE THE SIMILARITY ENDS.

Continental Special Risk Underwriters (CSRU) is a better service than our competitors' because:
First, our service is a network of in-house services, unparalleled in the industry.
Here's what we offer:
A complete range of coverages including primary, excess and umbrella.
Tailor-made financial plans including spread premium payments for qualified accounts, large and small deductibles, and self-insured retentions.

Flexible cash management using compensating balances, premium cash flow and wire transfers (within 48 hours).
Additional services including countrywide claims service, loss control and engineering plus industrial hygiene, ocean marine and commercial inland marine insurance, data processing, international, reinsurance, accident and health, and life insurance.
For captive insurance companies:
In addition to making all our normal services available to captives, CSRU offers specialized services including general management, accounting, underwriting, actuarial and policy issuance.
All of our services have been programmed so they can be customized and selectively applied to meet your clients' particular needs. And each client only has to buy the services he or she wants.
Finally, every risk program is handled through a single contact: a Continental Risk Planner from one of 4 cities spanning the U.S. Helped by a team of specialists, our Risk Planner works with you to analyze requirements, set up a program to meet them, and provide year-round service to keep things running smoothly.

For more information please contact the CSRU representative nearest you:
Frank Hofstatter, 100 Pine Street, San Francisco, CA 94111.
(415) 576-8155.
Gerald Tetzman, 360 West Jackson Boulevard, Chicago, IL 60606.
(312) 341-2747.
Ray Micucci, 1810 Commerce Street, Dallas, TX 75201.
(214) 748-7351.
Sara Roblin, 80 Maiden Lane, New York, NY 10038.
(212) 374-4344.

FOR EVERY SPECIAL RISK NEED: A SERVICE THAT'S PROGRAMMED TO WORK.

CONTINENTAL SPECIAL RISK UNDERWRITERS
A facility of
The Continental Insurance Companies
subsidiaries of The Continental Corporation

36

37

38

ARTIST / KÜNSTLER / ARTISTE:

37, 38 Robert Grossman

DESIGNER / GESTALTER / MAQUETTISTE:

33–35 Hal Tench
36 Lee Epstein
37, 38 Anita Rose

ART DIRECTOR / DIRECTEUR ARTISTIQUE:

33–35 Dick Athey
36 Lee Epstein
37, 38 Anita Rose

AGENCY / AGENTUR / AGENCE – STUDIO:

33–35, 37, 38 Webb & Athey, Inc.
36 Doyle Dane Bernbach, Inc.

Advertisements / Anzeigen / Annonces

ピーチケント

㊀ 株式会社 竹月

Advertisements /Anzeigen /Annonces

ARTIST / KÜNSTLER / ARTISTE:
39—41 Kazumasa Nagai

DESIGNER / GESTALTER / MAQUETTISTE:
39—41 Kazumasa Nagai

ART DIRECTOR / DIRECTEUR ARTISTIQUE:
39—41 Kazumasa Nagai

AGENCY / AGENTUR / AGENCE – STUDIO:
39—41 Nippon Design Center

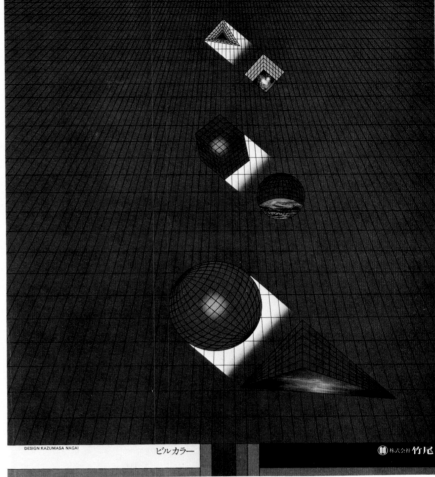

40

41

39—41 Examples from a series of uniform magazine advertisements for the Takeo Paper Co. Fig. 40: dark blue ground, graphic elements in red, green and yellow; Fig. 41: the colours of the triangle vary from yellow to orange, red and violet to dark blue, full-colour elements on a black ground, foreground in yellow. (JPN)

39—41 Beispiele aus einer Serie von einheitlich gestalteten Zeitschriftenanzeigen für eine Papierfabrik. Abb. 40: dunkelblauer Grund, graphische Elemente in Rot, Grün und Gelb; Abb. 41: die Farben des Dreiecks wechseln von Gelb über Orange, Rot, Violett ins Dunkelblau, mehrfarbige Elemente auf schwarzem Grund, Vordergrund in Gelb. (JPN)

39—41 Exemples d'une longue série d'annonces de magazines, de conception uniforme, lancée en faveur d'une papeterie. Fig. 40: fond en bleu foncé, éléments graphiques en rouge, vert et jaune; fig. 41: les couleurs du triangle passent du jaune et l'orange au rouge, violet et bleu foncé, divers éléments graphiques en couleurs sur fond noir, bande jaune au bas de la page. (JPN)

42

43

Advertisements / Anzeigen / Annonces

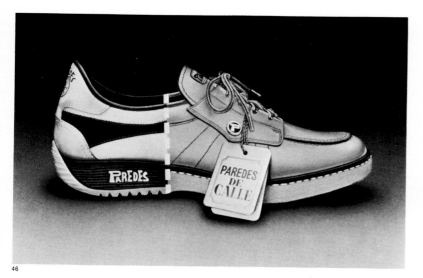

46

47

42 Full-colour magazine advertisement for the Metropolitan Printing Service. (USA)
43 In the State of Louisiana the carving of decoy-birds is an old tradition which has been carefully preserved until the present day, and just as much care is taken by the *Phillips Petroleum* company as regards the protection of wildfowl during its drilling operations. Brownish green duck. (USA)
44 Magazine advertisement for the Advertising Council of Rochester, an organization for visual and verbal communication serving public institutions. The illustrations symbolize the various institutions helped by the council in this sole capacity. (USA)
45 Magazine advertisement for the Citizens First National Bank of Tyler. (USA)
46 Illustration for an advertisement for *Paredes* bad-weather shoes. One half of the shoe is in blue and white, the other one in brown. (SPA)
47 Thanks to the good delivery service of the *Dixie/Marathon* company, customers need not keep a large stock of goods. Brown boxes and full-colour stripes. (USA)
48 Magazine advertisement for the Continental Insurance Co., with a policy covering all imaginable risks in one insurance document. (USA)

42 Mehrfarbige Zeitschriftenanzeige einer Druckerei. (USA)
43 Im Staate Louisiana ist das Schnitzen von Lockvögeln eine uralte Tradition, die heute noch sorgfältig gepflegt wird – mit ebensolcher Sorgfalt geht *Phillips Petroleum* vor, wenn es bei Bohrarbeiten um den Schutz von Wildhühnern geht. Bräunlich-grüne Ente. (USA)
44 Zeitschriftenanzeige einer Organisation für visuelle und verbale Kommunikation, die ausschliesslich für im Dienste der Öffentlichkeit stehende Institutionen arbeitet. Die Illustrationen symbolisieren die verschiedenen Institutionen, denen geholfen wurde. (USA)
45 Zeitschriftenanzeige eines alteingesessenen Bankinstituts am Tyler Square. (USA)
46 Illustration einer Anzeige für Schlechtwetterschuhe, erschienen unter dem Motto: wechseln Sie die Schuhe, aber nicht *Paredes*. Hinten blau-weiss gestreift, vorne braun. (SPA)
47 Dank dem guten Lieferdienst dieser Firma für Wegwerfartikel, brauchen sich die Kunden nicht mit Bergen von Vorräten einzudecken. Braune Schachteln, mehrfarbige Streifen. (USA)
48 Zeitschriftenanzeige einer Versicherungsgesellschaft, die alle nur erdenklichen Risikodeckungen in einer Police einschliesst. (USA)

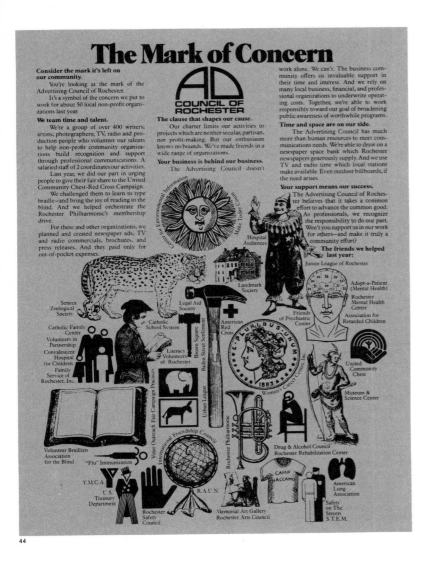

The Mark of Concern

Consider the mark it's left on our community.

You're looking at the mark of the Advertising Council of Rochester.

It's a symbol of the concern we put to work for about 50 local non-profit organizations last year.

We team time and talent.

We're a group of over 400 writers, artists, photographers, TV, radio and production people who volunteer our talents to help non-profit community organizations build recognition and support through professional communications. A salaried staff of 2 coordinates our activities.

Last year, we did our part in urging people to give their fair share to the United Community Chest-Red Cross Campaign.

We challenged them to learn to type braille—and bring the joy of reading to the blind. And we helped orchestrate the Rochester Philharmonic's membership drive.

For these and other organizations, we planned and created newspaper ads, TV and radio commercials, brochures, and press releases. And they paid only for out-of-pocket expenses.

AD COUNCIL OF ROCHESTER

The clause that shapes our cause.

Our charter limits our activities to projects which are neither secular, partisan, nor profit-making. But our enthusiasm knows no bounds. We've made friends in a wide range of organizations.

Your business is behind our business.

The Advertising Council doesn't work alone. We can't. The business community offers us invaluable support in their time and interest. And we rely on many local business, financial, and professional organizations to underwrite operating costs. Together, we're able to work responsibly toward our goal of broadening public awareness of worthwhile programs.

Time and space are on our side.

The Advertising Council has much more than human resources to meet communications needs. We're able to draw on a newspaper space bank which Rochester newspapers generously supply. And we use TV and radio time which local stations make available. Even outdoor billboards, if the need arises.

Your support means our success.

The Advertising Council of Rochester believes that it takes a common effort to advance the common good. As professionals, we recognize the responsibility to do our part. Won't you support us in our work for others—and make it truly a community effort?

The friends we helped last year:

Junior League of Rochester
Adopt-a-Patient (Mental Health)
Rochester Mental Health Center
Association for Retarded Children
Friends of Psychiatric Center
United Community Chest
Museum & Science Center
Drug & Alcohol Council Rochester Rehabilitation Center
American Lung Association
Safety on The Streets S.T.E.M.
Memorial Art Gallery Rochester Arts Council
R.A.U.N.
CAMP MACCAMO
Rochester Philharmonic
"Flu" Immunization
Volunteer Braillists Association for the Blind
Y.M.C.A.
U.S. Treasury Department
International Friendship Council
Voter Outreach Fair Campaign Practices
Urban League
Women's Career Center, Inc.
Literacy Volunteers of Rochester
Baden Street Settlement
Brown Square
American Red Cross
Catholic School System
Legal Aid Society
Landmark Society
Hospital Audiences
Make Today Count
Center for Environmental Information
Seneca Zoological Society
Catholic Family Center
Volunteers in Partnership
Convalescent Hospital for Children
Family Service of Rochester, Inc.

44

We've been around the square a long time.

When the trolleys ran. And the cotton bloomed. And the streets were brick. And the circus came. Citizens First National was there! Helping that's really what it is all about today. They're kinda old-fashioned, that way. For they still remember when the square was a square. You see ...Citizens First National was there! First place in the hearts of their many friends. You might say.

CITIZENS FIRST

45

We're the Linus Yale of packaged insurance. If anybody can lock every kind of coverage you need into one secure policy, it's us.

Continental invented the first Comprehensive Business Policy (CBP) in 1963. And we've been improving it ever since. ☐ *In one admirably flexible multi-peril package, you can get every kind of property and liability protection that the average business needs (except for workers' compensation which must be written separately). You can also get many kinds of specialized protection that your business might need. Such as inland marine. And boiler and machinery with its exacting inspection service requirements.* ☐ *CBP is highly cost-efficient. So your multiple coverages are less expensive in our package than they would be if you tried to buy them separately.* ☐ *Continental is uniquely qualified to create a protection package for any business.* ☐ *First, we have more experience writing this kind of policy than any other company.* ☐ *Second, we handle so many kinds of insurance, and write so much of each, that we've become expert in every phase. (Including accident and health, bad debt insurance, and even surety and fidelity bonds.)* ☐ *Third, more than 10,000 independent agents and countless brokers work with our 36 Continental branch offices, each of which handles the underwriting, pricing and claims service for its own area.* ☐ *Finally, we're a multi-national company, completely familiar with international insurance and its multitude of regulations. And capable of protecting your business interests anywhere in the world.* ☐ *Packaged insurance can improve risk management efficiency for most businesses. See if yours is one of them. Send for our free informative booklet.*

The pin tumbler lock, invented by Linus Yale in 1848.

The Continental Insurance Companies
Inventors of the Comprehensive Business Policy

GET THIS FREE 32-PAGE BOOKLET: "WHAT YOU SHOULD KNOW ABOUT MADE TO ORDER BUSINESS INSURANCE PACKAGES"

Please send me your free booklet on business insurance packages.

Name
Company
Street
City
State _____ ZIP

Mail to: Corporate Communications, Dept 106 The Continental Insurance Companies 80 Maiden Lane, New York, N.Y. 10038

48

ARTIST / KÜNSTLER / ARTISTE:

42 Seymour Chwast/Haruo Miyauchi
43 Don Ivan Punchatz
44 Evelyn Esch/Stock Art
45 Christy Mull
46 Ramon Gonzalez Teja
47 Siegbert Reinhard
48 Ed Acuna

DESIGNER / GESTALTER / MAQUETTISTE:

42 Richard Mantel
44 John Kuchera
45 Don Trousdell
47 Victor Della Barba
48 Lee Epstein

ART DIRECTOR / DIRECTEUR ARTISTIQUE:

42 Seymour Chwast
43 Frank Rizzo
44 John Kuchera
45 James Wilkens
46 Roberto Pascual
47 Victor Della Barba
48 Lee Epstein

AGENCY / AGENTUR / AGENCE – STUDIO:

42 Push Pin Studios, Inc.
43 Tracy-Locke
44 Hutchins/Young & Rubicam Inc.
45 William Finn Advertising
46 Dos Puntos S.A.
47 Lewis & Gilman
48 Doyle Dane Bernbach, Inc.

42 Annonce de magazine en couleurs pour une imprimerie. (USA)
43 La sculpture de leurres en bois est un métier de longue tradition en Louisiane qui est cultivée soigneusement encore aujourd'hui – c'est avec le même soin que *Phillips Petroleum* protège le habitat des canards sauvages menacés par les travaux de forage. (USA)
44 Annonce de magazine d'une organisation de communication visuelle et verbale qui travaille exclusivement pour des institutions publiques non-profitables. Les illustrations symbolisent les institutions auxquelles cette organisation avait offert ses services. (USA)
45 Annonce de magazine pour une vieille banque située au Tyler Square. (USA)
46 Pour les chaussures *Paredes*. La chaussure, à moitié brune, à moitié rayée en bleu et blanc, fait allusion au slogan: changez les chaussures, mais ne changez pas *Paredes*. (SPA)
47 Grâce au service de livraison mis au point par cette fabrique d'articles à jeter, les clients ne doivent pas combler leurs caves d'articles en réserve. Boîtes brunes, bande couleur. (USA)
48 Annonce de magazine d'une compagnie d'assurance qui offre la couverture de toutes sortes de risques imaginables par une seule police. Noir et blanc. (USA)

49 Newspaper advertisement for a new exciting roller coaster in an amusement park in Williamsburg. (USA)
50 Newspaper advertisement announcing a new fashion collection by Sue Wong, presented at *Joseph Magnin's*. (USA)
51, 52 From a series of newspaper advertisements dealing with mountaineering and advising climbers only to drink *Busch* beer after a mountain has been scaled. (USA)
53, 54 Illustration and complete newspaper advertisement from the *Village Voice* paper, inviting people to a teach-in against atomic power. The same motive was used for a poster. (USA)
55–57 Examples from a series of small-format newspaper advertisements for various *Kikkoman Shoyu* sauces. Each advertisement is presenting a different Japanese saying on the subject of cooking. (JPN)

49 «Das Lock Ness Monster lebt.» Zeitungsanzeige für eine neue Berg- und Talbahn in einem Vergnügungspark. (USA)
50 Diese Zeitungsanzeige kündigt die neue Modekollektion von Sue Wong an, die bei *Joseph Magnin* vorgeführt wird. (USA)
51, 52 «Güte-Test.» – «Sagen und Legenden.» Aus einer Serie von Zeitungsanzeigen, hier zum Thema Bergsteigen; man rät den Bergsteigern, *Busch*-Bier erst nach dem Erklimmen eines Berges zu trinken. (USA)
53, 54 Illustration und vollständige Zeitungsanzeige der Zeitung *Village Voice*, die hier zu einem Teach-In gegen Atomkraft einlädt. Das selbe Motiv wurde auch als Plakat verwendet. (USA)
55–57 Aus einer Serie von kleinformatigen Zeitungsanzeigen für verschiedene Saucen von *Kikkoman Shoyu*. Jede Anzeige bringt ein japanisches Sprichwort zum Thema Kochen. (USA)

49 «Le monstre du Lock Ness vit.» Annonce de journal pour un nouveau toboggan excitant et sensationnel dans un parc d'attraction de Williamsburg. (USA)
50 *Joseph Magnin* annonce que la nouvelle collection de Sue Wong sera présentée dans ses magasins. (USA)
51, 52 «Test de qualité.» – «Mythes et légendes.» D'une série d'annonces de journaux, ici au sujet de l'alpinisme, conseillant de ne boire la bière *Busch* qu'après l'arrivée au sommet. (USA)
53, 54 Illustration et annonce correspondante du journal *Village Voice* qui invite les gens à participer à un teach-in contre l'énergie nucléaire. A paru aussi sous forme d'affiche. (USA)
55–57 Exemples d'une série d'annonces de journaux à petit format pour les sauces de *Kikkoman Shoyu*. Chaque annonce présente un proverbe concernant la cuisine. (JPN)

49

50

ARTIST / KÜNSTLER / ARTISTE:

49 Rick Lovell/Whole Hog Studios
50 Karen Johnson
53, 54 Brad Holland
55–57 Tadashi Ohashi

Advertisements

Anzeigen

Annonces

51

52

53

55

56

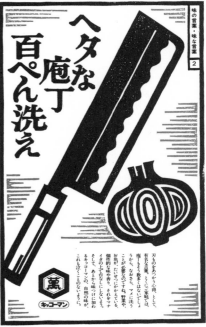

57

Village Voice Teach-In Against Nuclear Power
Saturday, May 5, at Riverside Memorial Church, 10 am to 7 pm, free

Speakers Include:
Ralph Nader, Barry Commoner, Elizabeth Holtzman, Tony Mazzocchi,
William Sloane Coffin, Joe Brown, Joe Bruno, Paul DeBriul, John Gofman,
Michael Harrington, Charles Komanoff, Ruth Messinger, Ernest Sternglass,
Sam Lovejoy, master of ceremonies

Sunday, May 6: March on Washington
Sponsored by the May 6th Coalition, 924-1210 for further information

54

DESIGNER / GESTALTER / MAQUETTISTE:

49   Don Trousdell
50   Don Clark
55–57 Tadashi Ohashi

ART DIRECTOR / DIRECTEUR ARTISTIQUE:

49   Steve Magee
50   Don Clark
51, 52 John Chepelsky
53, 54 Brad Holland
55–57 Tadashi Ohashi

AGENCY / AGENTUR / AGENCE – STUDIO:

49   McDonald & Little
51, 52 Needham, Harper & Steers

58 The insupportable traffic conditions in California, aggravated by huge cars, are enough to make one commit suicide . . . unless, of course, one buys a *Volkswagen*. (USA)
59, 60 From a series of newspaper advertisements for ready-mixed Louis & Gilbert Hotel Cocktails. (USA)
61 The traditional fashion house of Montreal, *Eaton*, congratulates *The Gazette* newspaper on the occasion of its 200th anniversary, and points out that both spread fashion in their own way. (CAN)
62, 63 From a series of full-colour advertisements for a cleaning agent for dirty, scaly ovens. (BRA)
64 Black-and-white newspaper advertisement of a studio for visual communication and market analysis. (MEX)
65 Double-spread magazine ad showing various cow breeds, in particular the *Suchard* chocolate cow called *Milka*. (GER)

58 Die unhaltbaren Verkehrsverhältnisse in Kalifornien, hervorgerufen durch riesige Strassenkreuzer, treiben einen zum Selbstmord . . «ausser man kaufe sich einen VW». (USA)
59, 60 Aus einer Serie von Zeitungsanzeigen für fertig gemixte Cocktails, die sich für Hotels gut eignen. (USA)
61 Das alteingesessene Montrealer Modehaus *Eaton* gratuliert der Zeitung *The Gazette* zum 200jährigen Bestehen, denn beide arbeiten auf ihre Weise an der Verbreitung der Mode. (CAN)
62, 63 Aus einer Serie von mehrfarbigen Anzeigen für ein Mittel zur Reinigung verkrusteter Backöfen. (BRA)
64 Zeitungsanzeige eines Studios für visuelle Kommunikation und Marktanalysen. Schwarzweiss. (MEX)
65 Doppelseitige Zeitschriftenanzeige, die verschiedene Kuhrassen zeigt, unter anderem die *Milka*-Schokolade-Kuh von *Suchard*. *Milka*-Kuh in lila. (GER)

58 En Californie, les conditions de circulation, dues aux immenses voitures, sont aussi insupportables qu'on est poussé au suicide . . . «si l'on ne s'achète pas une VW». (USA)
59, 60 D'une série d'annonces de journaux pour des cocktails déjà préparés qui sont très pratiques pour les hôtels. (USA)
61 La vieille maison de mode *Eaton* de Montréal félicite le journal *The Gazette* de son 200e anniversaire, parce que les deux s'occupent depuis longtemps de la «diffusion» de la nouvelle mode. En noir et blanc. (CAN)
62, 63 D'une série d'annonces polychromes lancées en faveur d'un produit pour nettoyer les fours incrustés. (BRA)
64 Annonce de journal d'un studio de communication visuelle et d'études du marché. En noir et blanc. (MEX)
65 Double page présentant les différentes éspèces de vaches, entres autres la vache au chocolat *Milka* de *Suchard*. (GER)

59

60

Or buy a Volkswagen.

58

ARTIST / KÜNSTLER / ARTISTE:

58 Charles Piccirillo
59, 60 Robert Miller
61 Eugenie Groh
62, 63 Brasílio
64 Ruben Padova
65 Erna de Vries

DESIGNER / GESTALTER / MAQUETTISTE:

58 Charles Piccirillo
59, 60 Robert Miller
61 Charlotte Rawstron
62, 63 Wilson Pereira da Nobraga
64 Arie J. Geurts

ART DIRECTOR / DIRECTEUR ARTISTIQUE:

58 Charles Piccirillo
59, 60 Paul Hodges
61 Harriet Santroch
62, 63 Bernd Michael Misske
64 Arie J. Geurts
65 Maria-Christina Sennefelder

AGENCY / AGENTUR / AGENCE – STUDIO:

58 Doyle Dane Bernbach, Inc.
59, 60 F. William Free & Co., Inc.
61 T. Eaton Co. Ltd.
62, 63 Young & Rubicam do Brasil
64 Laboratorio de Diseño y Análisis de Mercado/ Cartón y Papel de Mexico
65 Young & Rubicam GmbH

61

Torta de morangosta?

Olhe só o que um forno mau cuidado pode fazer com a sua comida. Easy-Off significa "Limpa fácil" e é o prático e moderno limpa fornos que garante a sua família o gostinho autêntico da deliciosa comida que você faz.
Conserve o seu fogão sempre limpinho com Easy-Off. Assim o seu marido não vai ficar sem graça, disfarçar, dar outra mordidinha e afirmar:
— Já sei! É torta de morangosta?

COM EASY-OFF LIMPANDO O FORNO, SUA FAMÍLIA LIMPA O PRATO.

62

Leitango à lusitana?

Olhe só o que um forno mau cuidado pode fazer com a sua comida. Easy-Off significa "Limpa fácil" e é o prático e moderno limpa fornos que garante a sua família o gostinho autêntico da deliciosa comida que você faz.
Conserve o seu fogão sempre limpinho com Easy-Off. Assim o seu marido não vai ficar sem graça, disfarçar, dar outra mordidinha e afirmar:
— Já sei! É um leitango à lusitana?

COM EASY-OFF LIMPANDO O FORNO, SUA FAMÍLIA LIMPA O PRATO.

63

64

Advertisements /Anzeigen /Annonces

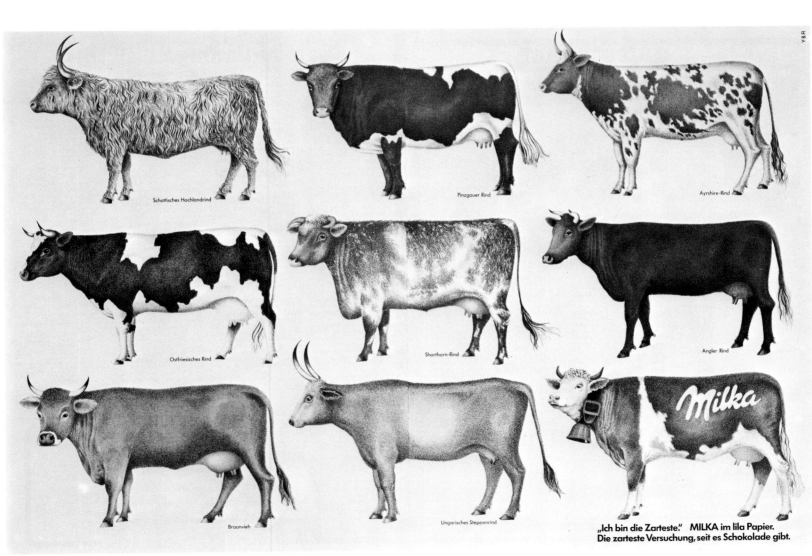

Schottisches Hochlandrind   Pinzgauer Rind   Ayrshire-Rind

Ostfriesisches Rind   Shorthorn-Rind   Angler Rind

Braunvieh   Ungarisches Steppenrind

„Ich bin die Zarteste."   MILKA im lila Papier.
Die zarteste Versuchung, seit es Schokolade gibt.

65

49

彫刻するような楽しさが お料理にもあるんですね

66

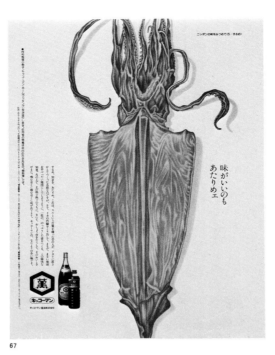

味がいいのも
あたりめェ

67

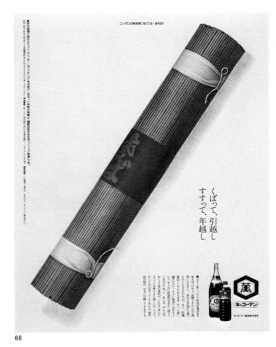

くばって、引越し
すすて、年越し

68

積み重ねてきた味

●京都の冬の味覚といえば千枚漬。
あの、ひとかかえもある聖護院か
ぶらを、薄い一片ずつに切って、
タルの中へ散きつめていくのです
が。"積み重ねて出てくる味"とは、
まさに、これを言うのでしょう。
かぶのまわりへ緑の、みぶ菜をも
して漬くのは、"配色"への心づかい
も入っています。そして、お皿づかい
むらさき色のキッコーマンを。
こちらも、四〇〇年という歴史を、
積み重ねてきた味の、持ち味です。

●月刊料理小冊子〈キッコーマン・ホームクッキング〉をお送りします。2月号の特集は堀江ひろこ先生の〝鶏肉料理〟です。
甘所・氏名・年令を明記の上、年間購読料800円をそえて右記へお申し込みください。現金書留=〒103 東京都中央区日本橋茅場町1-3キッコーマンHC係へ。郵便振替=口座番号=東京5-96667・キッコーマン東京支店へ。

キッコーマン
キッコーマン醤油株式会社

69

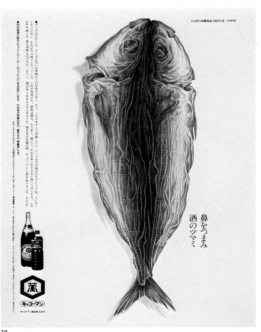

鼻をつまみ
酒のツマミ

70

ARTIST / KÜNSTLER / ARTISTE:

66–70 Tadashi Ohashi
71–73 Kenji Sumura
74, 75 Marc Boss

DESIGNER / GESTALTER / MAQUETTISTE:

66–70 Tadashi Ohashi
74, 75 Atelier Jaquet

ART DIRECTOR / DIRECTEUR ARTISTIQUE:

66–70 Tadashi Ohashi
71–73 Opit s.r.l.
74, 75 Jeanette Vuillemin

AGENCY / AGENTUR / AGENCE – STUDIO:

71–73 Opit S.r.l.
74, 75 Atelier Jaquet

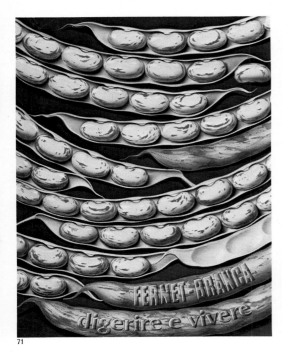

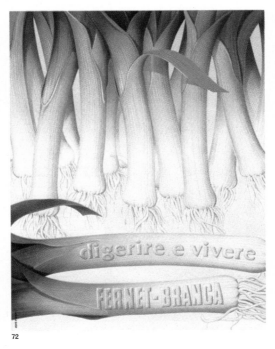

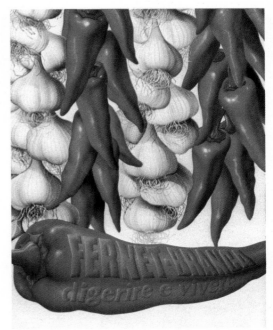

71

72

73

66 From a long-standing series of magazine advertisements for *Kikkoman Shoyu* sauces. Red radishes, green leaves. (JPN)

67–70 Examples from a series of newspaper advertisements entitled "The tastes of Japan." Fig. 67 shows dried squid, in light brown shades, called *Surume*; Fig. 68 shows *Soba*, dried buckwheat noodles (lilac-coloured strip with yellow lettering); Fig. 69: *Tsukemono*, Japanese pickled vegetables (green vegetables, red pepper); Fig. 70: *Himono*, dried fish illustrated by a greyish-blue fish. (JPN)

71–73 Magazine advertisements from a series for the digestive *Fernet-Branca*. Red and white speckled beans. (ITA)

74, 75 Magazine advertisements for *Schweppes*—best drunk on all occasions, but particularly in festive company or on bleak, rainy Sundays. (SWI)

66 Aus einer Serie von Zeitschriftenanzeigen für Saucen von *Kikkoman Shoyu*. Rote Radieschen, grüne Blätter. (JPN)

67–70 Beispiele aus einer Serie von Zeitungsanzeigen, die unter dem Titel «Die schmackhaften Essensgewohnheiten Japans» erschien. Abb. 67: *Surume* – getrockneter Tintenfisch (hellbraun); Abb. 68: *Soba* – getrocknete Buchweizennudeln (lila Band mit gelber Schrift); Abb. 69: *Tsukemono* – japanische Essiggemüse (grünes Gemüse, rote Pfefferschote); Abb. 70: *Himono* – getrockneter Fisch (graublauer Fisch). (JPN)

71–73 Zeitschriftenanzeigen aus einer Serie für *Fernet-Branca*, der verdauen hilft. Rot-weiss gesprenkelte Bohnen. (ITA)

74, 75 Zeitschriftenanzeigen für *Schweppes*, das sich in fröhlicher Gesellschaft oder an regnerischen Sonntagen bestens trinken lässt. (SWI)

66 D'une longue série d'annonces de magazine pour les sauces de *Kikkoman Shoyu*. Radis rouges, feuilles vertes. (JPN)

67–70 Exemples d'une série d'annonces de magazine, parue sous le titre «Les saveurs du Japon». Fig. 67: *Surume* – seiche sèche (en tons bruns pâle); fig. 68: *Soba* – nouilles de blé noir, sèches (bande lilas, symboles japonais jaunes); fig. 69: *Tsukemono* – légumes japonais au vinaigre (légumes verts, piment rouge); fig. 70: *Himono* – poisson sec (poisson en tons bleus grisâtre). (JPN)

71–73 Annonces de magazine figurant dans une série pour *Fernet-Branca*, un liqueur digestif. Haricots mouchetés. (ITA)

74, 75 Annonces de magazine pour *Schweppes*, qui se boit tant qu'il y aura de bons moments ou pendant les affreux dimanches pluvieux. (SWI)

Advertisements/Anzeigen/Annonces

74

75

As a business advertiser, you've got to get the attention of the world's toughest audience. Have you ever thought of using a club?

Sometimes it takes a club to get their attention.

76

Some people think it's just industrial advertising. We think you face the toughest audience in communications.

If you're responsible for your company's business and professional advertising, you've got one of the toughest jobs in communications.

Your audience is probably the most sophisticated, well-educated and demanding audience any advertiser ever had to face. They have highly specialized needs, and highly specialized knowledge to match. They're a lot tougher when they're buying for their companies than they are when they're buying for themselves. And they have to be. Because if they buy the wrong product, it may cost their companies a great deal of money. It may even cost them their jobs.

But you not only face one of the world's toughest audiences. You also face a management that probably doesn't appreciate how tough your job really is.

Which is why you should consider using a club. The Business/Professional Advertising Association. We offer our members a host of services, from planning guides and seminars that can help you communicate more effectively to helping you find a job if you need one.

But more importantly, we can help you increase your professionalism and find ways to make your job more important to your management.

To find out the details and the city nearest you, just call (212) 661-0222. The Business/Professional Advertising Association. The toughest audience in communications looks even tougher without it.

Business · Professional Advertising Association

Sometimes it takes a club to get their attention.

78

77

76–78 Illustration and complete advertisements for the Business/Professional Advertising Association. (USA)
79, 80 From a long-standing series of magazine advertisements for the *Aviation Insurance Agency*. (USA)
81 Double-spread magazine advertisement with full-colour illustrations for the *Rosenbaum* printing company. (AUT)

76–78 «Manchmal braucht's einen Club, um ihre Aufmerksamkeit zu wecken.» Illustration und vollständige Anzeigen für einen Werbeclub, der in verschiedenen Städten Seminare und Fortbildungskurse für Werbeleute organisiert. (USA)
79, 80 Aus einer langjährigen Serie von Zeitschriftenanzeigen der *Aviation Insurance Agency*, die Linienpiloten gegen Verdienstausfall versichert, wenn sie aus medizinischen Gründen den Beruf nicht mehr ausüben können. (USA)
81 Doppelseitige Zeitschriftenanzeige mit farbigen Illustrationen zum Thema «Rolle». Ankündigung der Druckerei *Brüder Rosenbaum*, dass sie eine neue Rollenoffset-Maschine angeschafft haben. (AUT)

76–78 «Des fois il faut un club afin de susciter leur attention.» Illustration et annonces complètes pour un club publicitaire qui organise des séminaires et des cours spéciaux pour des publicitaires. (USA)
79, 80 Exemples d'une longue série d'annonces de magazine d'une compagnie d'assurance auprès de laquelle les pilotes de ligne peuvent s'assurer contre la perte du salaire s'ils sont empêcher de travailler pour des raisons médicales. En noir et blanc. (USA)
81 Annonce de magazine double page avec des illustrations en couleurs accompagnant des jeux de mots sur «Rolle», qui signifie en allemand rôle ou rouleau. C'est ainsi qu'une imprimerie annonce qu'elle a acheté une nouvelle rotative. (AUT)

ARTIST / KÜNSTLER / ARTISTE:

76–78 Don Ivan Punchatz
79 Bill Myer
80 Rick Meyerowitz
81 Wilfried Gebhard

DESIGNER / GESTALTER / MAQUETTISTE:

81 Fritz Haubmann

ART DIRECTOR / DIRECTEUR ARTISTIQUE:

79, 80 Dick Henderson
81 Fritz Haubmann

AGENCY / AGENTUR / AGENCE – STUDIO:

76–78 Sketch Pad Studio
79, 80 Cole Henderson Drake, Inc.
81 Demner & Merlicek

IF YOU COULDN'T FLY, COULD YOU HACK IT?

If you were permanently grounded, earning a living could drive you to distraction. That's why we offer "lump sum" insurance. It's designed to make it possible for pilots who are permanently prevented from flying for their airlines for medical reasons (other than pre-existing) to pay off their heavy bills in one big "lump" —after the specified waiting period, of course. So living comfortably on a limited income would be a whole lot easier. For details, write to Harvey W. Watt, P.O. Box 20787, Atlanta Airport, Atlanta, Ga. 30320. Or call 767-7501. Outside Georgia, call toll-free: (800) 241-6103. Someday you just might need a financial lift.
Aviation Insurance Agency

79

Junk food for thought.

Part of the problem with too much soda pop, pizza, potatoes, cream puffs, pie and popcorn is that they take the place of more nutritious foods. Which is one of the things we're concerned about: everyday good health. If you're interested in your total physical well-being, get in touch with us. We offer airline pilot occupational disability coverage and a relicensing program (which is available to policy holders only). Just write to Harvey W. Watt, P.O. Box 20787, Atlanta Airport, Atlanta, Georgia 30320. Or call 767-7501. Outside Georgia, call toll-free: (800) 241-6103. It's worth a thought.

Aviation Insurance Agency

80

(Aus aktuellem Anlaß:)
Die beste Rolle ist die, die man sich aussuchen kann:

Schaumrolle · Spielt keine Rolle mehr · Rolling Stones
Rolle rückwärts · Hechtrolle · Schinkenrolle
Gemeiner Roller · Edelroller · Rollenoffset-Rolle (jetzt beim happy printer)

Kleine Rolle · Große Rolle · Traumrolle
Hosenrolle (Rosenbaum-Kavalier) · Ohne-Hosen-Rolle · Rolle vorwärts
Ro(u)lett · Ro(u)lett russisch · Wolln's mich rollen?

Wenn es gilt, hohe Auflagen schnell und günstig zu drucken, ist die beste Rolle für Ihren Druckauftrag die Offsetrolle.
Und wenn Sie Schnelligkeit und Preis allein nicht beeindrucken können, und Sie auf beste Qualität (be)stehen, dann sollten Sie sich jetzt die Offsetrolle von Rosenbaum aussuchen.

(Daß wir auch Aufträge mit kleineren Auflagen in der bekannten Rosenbaum-Qualität drucken, dürfte sich in den letzten 100 Jahren schon herumgesprochen haben.)

Langsam spricht es sich herum: Rosenbaum hat Rollenoffset. Bitte weitersagen!

1051 Wien, Margaretenstr. 94
Tel. (0 22 2) 55 56 01
Druckerei Brüder Rosenbaum (the happy printer)

Demner & Merlicek

Unsere neue Rollenoffsetanlage ist ein Spitzenprodukt von König & Bauer, Würzburg, BRD

81

53

82

83

84

85

Advertisements
Anzeigen
Annonces

SURVIVORS. AN AMERICAN ORIGINAL.

Tough. Rugged. Good-looking. These are the boots that have what it takes to survive in America: the original Herman Survivors®. And, like most originals, they're often copied but never duplicated.

We think that's because, after 101 years of boot-making, we're still paying attention to the little things. Like fastening real brass eyelets on our boots. Lining them with leather that's soft as a glove. Padding them for extra comfort and protection. And vowing that, no matter how high the price of leather, we won't cut down on quality to cut down on cost.

Things like that add up to a boot that's built to stay around for awhile.

And maybe that's why, in an age of fleeting imitations, we're practically part of the landscape.

HERMAN SURVIVORS

Boots that never say die.

For stores nearest you, and a complimentary copy of the Old Farmer's Almanac, write: Joseph M. Herman Shoe Co., Dept. 79, Millis, MA 02054.

86

We've spent 50 years helping all kinds of clients to solve outlandish dyeing problems.

Since 1929 (some year to launch a new company!), we've been a leading supplier of hydrosulphites to the textile industry.

But we didn't develop our business, and our reputation, by being just a supplier. We're leaders because our technical staff works with you to develop innovative new reducing systems, and we can often save you money doing it.

Our product line of reducing agents is so extensive there should already be a Royce product that's ideal for your operation. If we don't have what you need, our R&D staff will develop a product specifically for your requirements.

And when you give us an order, we deliver. Because we're basic in many of our raw materials. We have our own production plants, sales force and our own fleet of trucks.

These are just some of the reasons why Royce has rolled ahead over the past 50 years. Now watch while Royce rolls ahead for the next 50 years.

Royce

Royce Chemical Co. E. Rutherford, N.J. 07073 Telex: 133-385 • Cable: Royco • 201 438-5200

87

goosedown

What's good for the goose is good for you in outerwear from Pacific Trail.

For who knows more about goosedown than the geese themselves. Even silly geese are warm geese, because they never go out in the cold without a warm layer of down. So what's good for the goose and what's good for you (and the gander, too) is down filled outerwear from Pacific Trail. Like fluff-puffed jackets. Flashy trimmed vests. Or deep down parkas. Each one stuffed with 100% prime northern down for comfort and warmth. Trimmed for fun. Colored in just about as many shades as

there are snowflake patterns. And there's goosedown outerwear to fit men, women, boys and girls. Good for the goose. Good for everyone. Men's basic and fashion jackets, 55.00 to 90.00. Men's vests, 33.00 to 53.00. All sizes S-M-L-XL. Assorted styles in either highloft nylon taffeta or chambray poplin.

Boys' basic and fashion vests, sizes 10 to 20, 26.00 to 36.00. Boys' basic jacket, sizes 8 to 20, 50.00. Boys' fashion jacket, sizes 12 to 20, 50.00 to 60.00. See the entire collection of Men's and Boys' Outerwear. Learn more about down. Meet representatives from Pacific Trail and see their slide show and special "down" demonstration in Men's Outerwear.

Wednesday, November 9 at Brookdale and Rosedale from 6:30 to 8 p.m. Thursday, November 10 in Downtown Minneapolis from 11:30 a.m. to 1:30 p.m. St. Paul and Burnsville from 2:30 to 4 p.m. Southdale and Ridgedale from 6:30 to 8:00 p.m.

DAYTON'S FOR MEN

88

What to wear on your way to the top.

Two that are new from **PEEPLES**

a. The Randy shoe in brown, chocolate, khaki or taupe pigsuede; taupe, cherry brown, chocolate or oyster calf. (Available in August.)

b. The Loop boot in taupe, burgundy, rust or cherry brown calf.

FLAIRS EDGE

110 Orchard St. (Delancy and Orchard), New York, N.Y. 10002. Phone 212/673-3001. Open Monday through Friday, 9:00 a.m. to 5:30 p.m.; Sunday, 9:00 a.m. to 6:00 p.m.

ILLUSTRATION AND DESIGN BY JOSEPH SELLARS

89

Advertisements
Anzeigen
Annonces

ARTIST / KÜNSTLER / ARTISTE:

90, 91 John Matthews
92, 93 Joseph Sellars
94, 95 Mark Hess

DESIGNER / GESTALTER / MAQUETTISTE:

90, 91 John C. Jay
92, 93 Joseph Sellars
94, 95 Mark Hess/Richard Silverstien

ART DIRECTOR / DIRECTEUR ARTISTIQUE:

90, 91 John C. Jay
92, 93 Joseph Sellars
94, 95 Richard Silverstien

AGENCY / AGENTUR / AGENCE – STUDIO:

90, 91 Bloomingdale's

90, 91 Newspaper advertising campaign launched by *Bloomingdale's* to promote the latest *Yves Saint Laurent* jeans and trousers which are all named after an animal. Black-and-white illustrations. (USA)
92, 93 Examples from a series of black-and-white magazine advertisements for the latest models in the *Soldati* shoe-fashion range. (USA)
94, 95 Full-colour illustration and complete advertisement for *Levi Strauss* jeans, giving details of a competition organized by this company with the Olympics in mind. (USA)

90, 91 Mit einer Anzeigenkampagne in Zeitungen lanciert *Bloomingdale's* die neue Jeans- und Hosenmode von *Yves Saint Laurent*, der jedem Modell einen Tiernamen gab. Illustrationen in Schwarzweiss. (USA)
92, 93 Beispiele aus einer Serie von Zeitschriftenanzeigen, die die neuen Schuhmodelle von *Soldati* vorstellt. Schwarzweiss. (USA)
94, 95 «Im Geiste der Olympiade veranstaltet *Levi Strauss* den aussergewöhnlichsten Wettbewerb.» Illustration (mehrfarbig) und vollständige Anzeige eines Jeansfabrikanten, der den Wettbewerbsgewinnern entweder eine Summe in bar ausbezahlt oder einen Teil an die Realisierung eines lange gehegten Wunsches zahlt. (USA)

90, 91 C'est par moyen de cette campagne d'annonces que *Bloomingdale's* lance la nouvelle gamme de jeans et de pantalons créés par *Yves Saint-Laurent*, gamme dont chaque modèle porte le nom d'un animal. Les illustrations sont en noir et blanc. (USA)
92, 93 Exemples d'une série d'annonces de magazine qui présente les nouveaux modèles des chaussures *Soldati*. Illustrations en noir et blanc. (USA)
94, 95 «Dans l'esprit des Jeux Olympiques, *Levi Strauss* lance le concours le plus extraordinaire.» Illustration (en couleurs) et annonce complète. *Levi Strauss* offre aux gagnants de payer une certaine somme à la réalisation de n'importe quel «rêve» ou bien de payer une somme comptant. (USA)

94

95

2

Booklets

Folders

Catalogues

Invitations

Programmes

Broschüren

Faltprospekte

Kataloge

Einladungen

Programme

Brochures

Dépliants

Catalogues

Invitations

Programmes

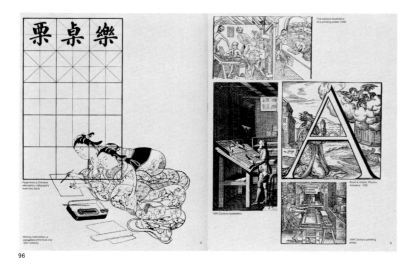

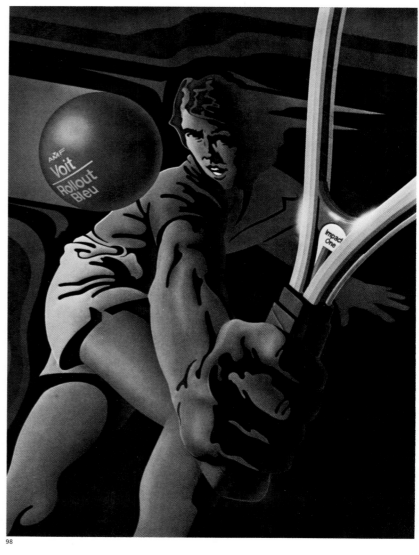

96

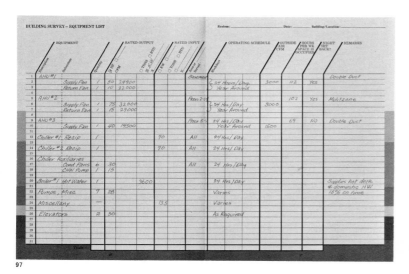

97

98

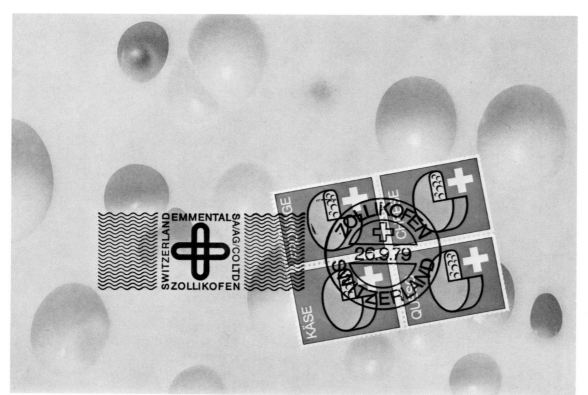

99

100

103

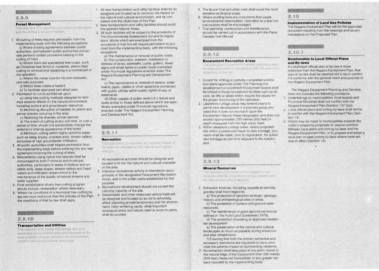

101

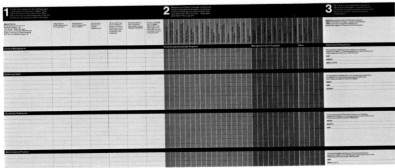

102

96 From a series of brochures called *The Printing Salesman's Herald*, regularly produced by *Champion Papers*, dealing here with black-and-white printing. (USA)
97 Double spread from a *Honeywell* handbook about an introduction to energy conservation with comfort. Border in various colours. (USA)
98 Full-colour illustration from a prospectus for AMF Voit raquetball products. (USA)
99 A slice of Emmental cheese with red stamps serves as a cover for a small-format brochure for the Emmental Ltd. cheese company. (SWI)
100, 101 Cover illustration and double spread from a brochure dealing with the proposed plan for the Niagara Escarpment. (CAN)
102 Double spread with gatefolds (black and white, yellow, red and green) from a folder dealing with a *Pepsi-Cola* human resources planning and development guide. (USA)
103 Cover of the catalogue for the exhibition "Typography and Graphics with Letraset" organized by the Institute for new technical forms and Letraset Germany. In black and white. (GER)

96 Aus einer regelmässig erscheinenden Broschüre einer Papierfabrik, hier mit Artikeln zum Thema des Schwarzweiss-Drucks. Die Abbildungen zeigen: eine Seite aus einem chinesischen Kalligraphieheft, Japanerinnen beim Schreibunterricht, Druckerei im Jahre 1499, Schriftsetzer im 18. Jh., Initial aus einem Messbuch und Druckpresse aus dem 16. Jh. (USA)
97 Doppelseite aus einem von *Honeywell* herausgegebenen Handbuch über bessere Nutzung und Speicherung von Energie in Geschäftshäusern. Umrandung in verschiedenen Farben. (USA)
98 Mehrfarbige Illustration aus einem Prospekt für Tennisschläger. (USA)
99 Ein Stück Emmentalerkäse mit aufgeklebten roten Marken dient als Titelbild einer kleinformatigen Broschüre der Käsehandelsfirma Emmental AG. (SWI)
100, 101 Diese Broschüre enthält Vorschläge zur Erhaltung der archäologisch, geologisch und naturhistorisch interessanten Niagara-Flusslandschaft. Titelbild und Doppelseite. (CAN)
102 Doppelseite mit Auslegern (schwarzweiss, gelb, rot, grün) aus einem Faltprospekt über einen von *Pepsi-Cola* organisierten Management-Kurs. (USA)
103 Titelblatt des Katalogs für die Ausstellung «Schrift und Graphik mit Letraset», die vom Institut für neue technische Form und von Letraset Deutschland organisiert wurde. Schwarzweiss. (GER)

96 D'une brochure publiée régulièrement par une papeterie. Ce numéro est consacré à l'impression en noir et blanc. Les illustrations montrent une page d'un cahier de calligraphie chinois, des japonaises apprenant à écrire, une imprimerie de l'année 1499, un typographe du 18e siècle, initiale d'un missel et une presse d'imprimerie du 16e siècle. (USA)
97 Page double figurant dans un manuel de *Honeywell* sur l'utilisation et l'accumulation d'énergie dans les immeubles commerciaux. Encadrement en diverses couleurs. (USA)
98 Illustration en polychromie d'un prospectus pour des raquettes de tennis. (USA)
99 Un morceau d'emmenthal avec des timbres rouges collés dessus sert de couverture de la brochure d'une maison de commerce et d'exportation de fromages. (SWI)
100, 101 Cette brochure contient un projet pour la protection de l'escarpement du Niagara, région intéressante du point de vue archéologique, géologique et d'histoire naturelle. (CAN)
102 Page double avec replis (noir-blanc, jaune, rouge et vert) d'un dépliant consacré à un cours de management organisé par *Pepsi-Cola*. (USA)
103 Couverture du catalogue d'une exposition intitulée «Typographie et art graphique avec Letraset». En noir et blanc. (GER)

104

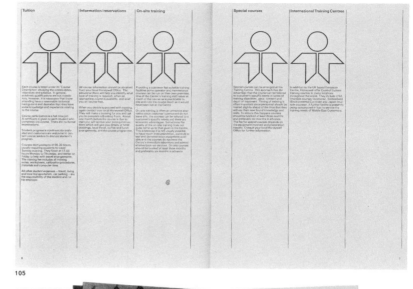

105

106

107

104, 105 Cover and inside spread of a brochure for a *Honeywell* educational centre for computer experts. Title page: design in blue and green, red point; inside spread: symbols in green and red, blue lettering. (GBR)
106–108 Opened cover (pink, blue, yellow and white) and inside spreads (Fig. 107 with narrow inserted sheets) in blue, pink and white from a brochure for the *Isetan Department Store* dealing with babies' various stages of growth. (JPN)
109–111 The *Warren* paper company gives tips about what to look out for when betting on the horses, and comes to the conclusion that the same criteria can be applied whether betting on a horse or on *Warren Patina Coated Matte* paper—a new product. Cover in red, yellow and black. The inside spreads of this small-format brochure are printed in brilliant colours. (USA)
112 Illustration from a folder in which various tinned vegetables produced by the *Bonduelle* company are introduced to the public. (GER)

104, 105 Titelblatt und Innenseite einer Broschüre über ein von *Honeywell* geleitetes Ausbildungszentrum für Computerfachleute in England. Titelblatt: Design in Blau und Grün, roter Punkt, blaue Schrift; Innenseite: Symbole in Grün und Rot, blaue Schrift. (GBR)
106–108 Geöffneter Umschlag (rosa, blau, gelb und weiss) und Innenseiten (Abb. 107 mit schmäleren eingefügten Zwischenseiten) in Blau, Rosa und Weiss aus einer Broschüre mit Angaben über Wachstumsstadien von Babies. (JPN)
109–111 Die Papierfabrik *Warren* gibt hier einige Tips, worauf bei Pferdewetten geachtet werden muss, und kommt dabei zum Schluss, dass dieselben Kriterien ausschlaggebend sind, ob nun auf ein Pferd oder das neue matte Kunstdruckpapier von *Warren* gesetzt wird. Umschlag (rot, gelb und schwarz) und Innenseiten (in bunten Farben) einer kleinformatigen Broschüre. (USA)
112 Illustration aus einem Prospekt, in welchem die verschiedenen Gemüsekonserven von *Bonduelle* vorgestellt werden. (GER)

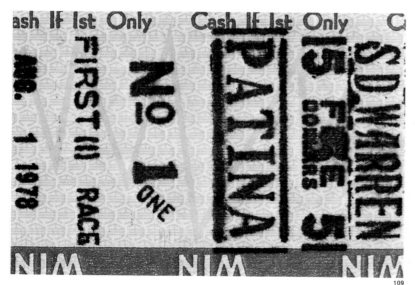

109

110

ARTIST / KÜNSTLER / ARTISTE:

106—108 Kumiko Nagasaki/Hiro Nobuyama
109—111 Bill Gunn/Gene Lemery/Holmes Hurll/
        John Gatie/Murry Huber/Mark Bellerose
112 Braldt Bralds

DESIGNER / GESTALTER / MAQUETTISTE:

104, 105 Gavin Healey
106—108 Kenzo Nakagawa/Satch Morikami
109—111 Jim Witham/Kayo Burman
112 Robert Pütz

108

112

104, 105 Couverture et page intérieure d'une brochure sur un centre de forma-
tion de *Honeywell* pour des spécialistes de l'électronique. Fig. 104: bleu et vert,
point rouge, typo verte; fig. 105: symboles en vert et rouge. (GBR)
106—108 Recto et verso de la couverture (rose, bleu, jaune, blanc) et pages intérieures (fig. 107 avec des pages intercalées) en bleu, rose et blanc d'une brochure
contenant des indications sur la croissance des bébés. (JPN)
109—111 La papeterie *Warren* donne ici quelques renseignements concernant les
tiercés et en tire la conclusion que les même critères sont déterminants qu'on
mise sur un cheval ou le nouveau papier couché de *Warren*. Couverture (rouge,
jaune, noir) et pages (en couleurs vives) d'une petite brochure. (USA)
112 Illustration figurant dans un prospectus qui présente les conserves de légumes *Bonduelle*. (GER)

ART DIRECTOR / DIRECTEUR ARTISTIQUE:

104, 105 Gavin Healey
106—108 Kenzo Nakagawa
109—111 Jim Witham/Kayo Burman
112 Robert Pütz

AGENCY / AGENTUR / AGENCE – STUDIO:

104, 105 Gavin Healey Design
106—108 Nippon Design Center
109—111 Humphrey Browning MacDougall
112 Robert Pütz GmbH & Co.

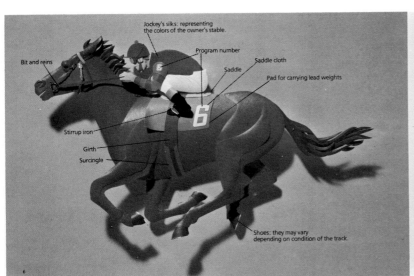

111

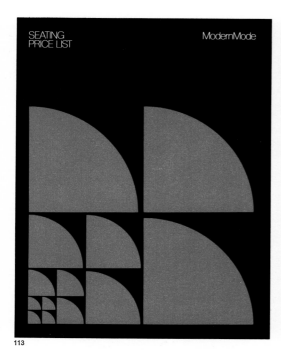

113

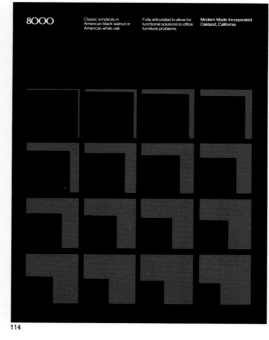

114

115

113–115 Covers of folders taken from a thick, spiral-bound brochure of a furniture company. (USA)
116, 117 Double spread and illustration in actual size from a publication by the *American Forest Institute* stating its case for the preservation of forests and the reforesting of areas where many trees have been cut down due to the increasing use of wood in many branches of industry. (USA)
118 Full-colour illustration in Magritte-style on the front cover of a folder for *Hamilton Rentals*, a company that leases business machines. (USA)
119 Inside spread of an opened folder for IBM typewriters. The typewriter is in blue. (FRA)

113–115 Umschläge von Faltprospekten, die alle aus einem dicken Ringhefter einer Möbelfabrik stammen. (USA)
116, 117 Doppelseite und Illustration (in Originalgrösse) aus einer Publikation des amerikanischen Forstinstituts, das hier für die Erhaltung der Wälder und die Wiederaufforstung plädiert, da der Baumbestand durch die Verarbeitung von Holz in verschiedenen Industriezweigen zurückgeht. (USA)
118 «Was stimmt hier nicht?» Mehrfarbige, Magritte nachempfundene Illustration auf der Vorderseite der Faltmappe einer Firma, die Büromaschinen vermietet. (USA)
119 Geöffneter Faltprospekt (Innenseite) für IBM-Schreibmaschinen. Blaue Maschine. (FRA)

113–115 Couvertures de dépliants volants contenus dans un livre d'une fabrique de meubles. (USA)
116, 117 Page double et illustration (grandeur nature) d'une publication de l'Administration américaine des Eaux et Forêts en faveur de la protection des forêts et le reboisement de régions déboisées par les différentes industries auxquelles le bois sert de matière première. (USA)
118 «Qu'est-ce qui ne joue pas ici?» Illustration (en polychromie) évoquant les tableaux de Magritte. Couverture du portfolio d'une maison qui loue des machines de bureau. (USA)
119 Dépliant (panneaux intérieurs) pour les machines à écrire de l'IBM. Machine bleue. (FRA)

ARTIST / KÜNSTLER / ARTISTE:

116, 117 Richard Hess
118 John Martin
119 René Nettler

DESIGNER / GESTALTER:

113–115 Michael Vanderbyl
118 David Wymann

ART DIRECTOR:

113–115 Michael Vanderbyl
118 David Wyman
119 Michel Adam

AGENCY / AGENTUR / AGENCE:

113–115 Vanderbyl Design
116, 117 Van Dyke, McCarthy & Tavernor, Inc.
118 Stephenson, Ramsay, O'Donnell Ltd.

116

Booklets / Prospekte / Brochures

118

119

BOLIDEN INTERTRADE

120

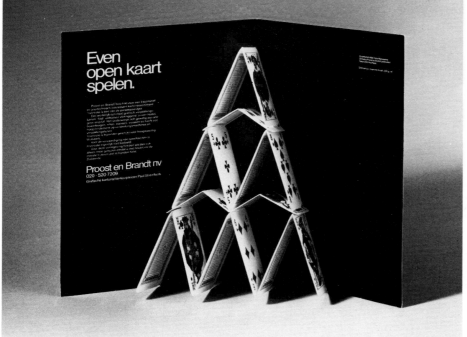

121

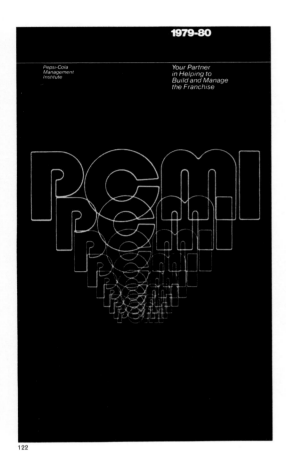

122

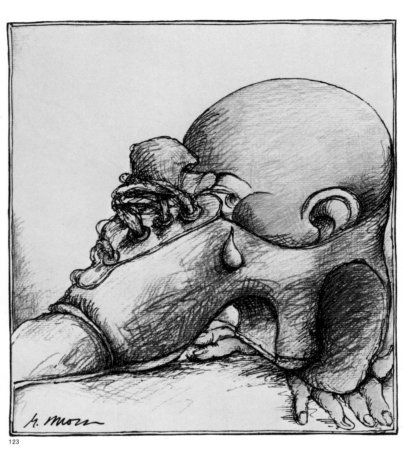

123

ARTIST / KÜNSTLER:

120 Ch. Broutin
123 Geoffrey Moss

DESIGNER / GESTALTER:

121 Hans Manusama
122 Russel Tatro
123 Larry Stires
124, 125 Manfred Schipper

ART DIRECTOR:

120 Jan A. Nyman
122 Frank Rupp
123 Larry Stires
124, 125 Manfred Schipper

AGENCY / AGENTUR:

120 Arbman & Lenskog
122 Pepsi-Cola
       Graphic Arts Dept.
123 Geigy Pharmaceuticals
124, 125 Parker Pen/
       Marketing Services

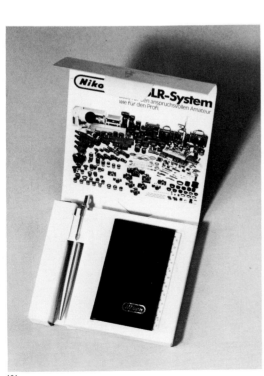

124

125

Allergy relief: taking a different approach

Different ways to defy spring allergies

126

127

Booklets / Prospekte / Brochures

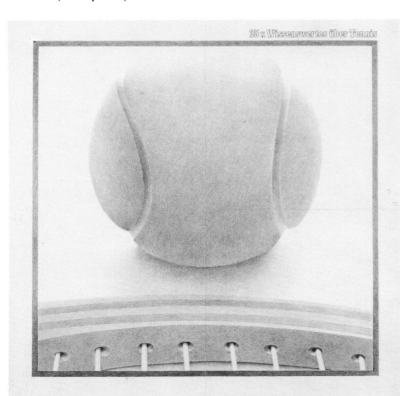

25 x Wissenswertes über Tennis

25 x Wissenswertes über Fussball

129

130

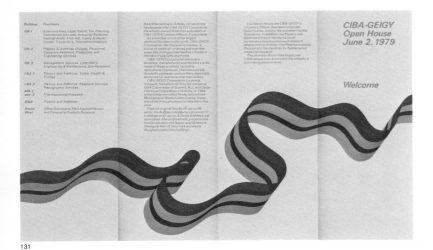

131

ARTIST / KÜNSTLER / ARTISTE:

126–128 Ray Domingo
129, 130 Walter Lienert
133 Eduardo A. Cánovas

DESIGNER / GESTALTER / MAQUETTISTE:

126–128 Larry Stires
129, 130 Walter Lienert
131 Sigrid Geissbühler
132 August Maurer
133 Eduardo A. Cánovas

ART DIRECTOR / DIRECTEUR ARTISTIQUE:

126–128 Larry Stires
129, 130 Emil Häsler
131 Sigrid Geissbühler
132 August Maurer
133 Eduardo A. Cánovas

AGENCY / AGENTUR / AGENCE – STUDIO:

126–128 Geigy Pharmaceuticals
129, 130, 132 Ciba-Geigy/Zentrale Werbung
131 Ciba-Geigy/Corporate Art Service
133 Estudio Cánovas

128

132

126–128 Examples from a series of folders distributed by *Ciba-Geigy* for a new anti-allergy medi-cament. Full-colour cover illustrations and inside spread. (USA)
129, 130 Opened front covers of folders for *Tanderil*, a medicament used mostly for injuries in sport. On the verso, 25 points deal with rules and other interesting facts about various kinds of sport, here about tennis and football. The illustrations are in black and white. (SWI)
131 *Ciba-Geigy* invites people to visit its new building complex at the Ardsley headquarters. Ribbon in blue, green, yellow and red, lettering in blue. (USA)
132 Advertising for *Hemeran* cream and jelly manufactured by *Geigy*, a medicament that makes tired legs young and vigorous again—as symbolized on the blue and green boxes. (SWI)
133 Cover of a folder for a lung medicament. The lungs are portrayed as being composed of gram-positive and gramnegative bacteria colouring (named after the Danish doctor Gram). (ARG)

126–128 Beispiele aus einer von *Ciba-Geigy* verschickten Serie von Faltprospekten für ein neues Antiallergikum. Mehrfarbige Umschlagillustrationen und Innenseite. (USA)
129, 130 Geöffnete Vorderseiten von Faltprospekten für *Tanderil*, ein Medikament, das vor allem bei Sportverletzungen angewendet wird. Auf der Rückseite werden jeweils in 25 Punkten Spiel-regeln und andere wissenswerte Fakten über verschiedene Sportarten – hier Tennis und Fussball – aufgezählt. Illustrationen in Schwarzweiss. (SWI)
131 *Ciba-Geigy* lädt zu einer Besichtigung der neuen Gebäudekomplexe am Hauptsitz in Ardsley ein. Band in Blau, Grün, Gelb und Rot, blaue Schrift. (USA)
132 Werbung für *Hemeran* Crème und Gel von *Geigy*, ein Medikament, das müde Beine wieder springlebendig macht, was durch die Beine auf den Schachteln (Weiss auf blauem, resp. grünem Grund) symbolisiert wird. (SWI)
133 Titelblatt eines Prospektes für ein Lungenmittel. Die Lunge wurde stilisiert durch gram-positive und gramnegative Bakterienfärbung dargestellt (nach dem Arzt Gram benannt). (ARG)

126–128 Exemples d'une série de dépliants distribués par *Ciba-Geigy* pour introduire un nouveau médicament contre les allergies. Illustrations de couverture et page intérieure. (USA)
129, 130 Rectos dépliés d'une série de feuilles à grand format pour *Tanderil*, un médicament utilisé dans le traitement de blessures de sport. Au verso on trouve des informations sur les règles de jeu et d'autres faits intéressants de divers sports – ici sur le tennis et le football. Illustrations en noir et blanc. (SWI)
131 *Ciba-Geigy* invite les intéressés à visiter les nouveaux immeubles du siège central à Ardsley. Bande en bleu, vert, jaune et rouge, typographie bleue. (USA)
132 Elément publicitaire pour la crème et le gel *Hemeran* de *Geigy*, un médicament qui fait «cou-rir» les jambes fatiguées, ce que symbolisent les jambes sur les boîtes. (SWI)
133 Pour un médicament, utilisé dans le traitement de maladies des poumons. Poumons stylisés par coloration gram positif et gram négatif de bactéries. (Gram: médecin danois) (ARG)

133

SEHEN
DER
ERSTE
SINN

Das Sehen dient dem Menschen mehr als alle anderen Sinne. Mit dem Auge erfaßt er seine Umwelt und macht mehr aus ihr. Die Natur beobachten, die Perspektive begreifen, die Technik verstehen, die Schönheit erleben, Farben und Formen erkennen, Geschwindigkeit und Gefahr einschätzen, Kunst und Illusion genießen – das alles und noch mehr ist Sehen →

134

135

136

ARTIST / KÜNSTLER / ARTISTE:

135 Fernando Alvarez Cozzi
136 Kim Milnazik
137 James Hill
138–140 Lynda Fishbourne

DESIGNER / GESTALTER / MAQUETTISTE:

134 Udo Wüst
135 Fernando Alvarez Cozzi
136 Barry Atkinson
137 Johannes Kastner
138–140 John Milligan

70

Booklets / Prospekte
Brochures

134 Double spread from a publication of the *Rodenstock* optical works entitled *Sehen* (Looking). Full-colour illustration. (GER)
135 Recto and verso of a folder for *Glyvenol*, a medicament against vein complaints by *Ciba-Geigy*. Yellow legs, blue shoes on green. (URU)
136 Full-colour illustration on the inside panel of an advertising portfolio for Air Products and Chemicals, Inc. (USA)
137 Illustration in actual size from a prestige campaign lanced by the Federation of Pharmaceutical Industries. The brochure lists the results obtained in pharmaceutical research, here the discovery of a hormone for hitherto sterile women. (GER)
138–140 Covers from an advertising portfolio, a folder and a catalogue for Prime Computer, Inc. (USA)

134 Doppelseite aus der von den Optischen Werken *Rodenstock* herausgegebenen Publikation mit dem Titel *Sehen*. Mehrfarbige Illustration. (GER)
135 Vorder- und Rückseite eines Faltprospektes für das Venenmittel *Glyvenol* von *Ciba-Geigy*. Gelbe Beine, blaue Schuhe, grüner Grund. (URU)
136 Illustration auf der inneren Klappe einer Werbemappe, die Informationen über die von Air Products & Chemicals, Inc., hergestellten chemischen Produkte enthält. Mehrfarbig. (USA)
137 Illustration in Originalgrösse aus einer Prestige-Werbekampagne des Bundesverbandes der pharmazeutischen Industrie. Die Broschüre zählt die in der Pharma-Forschung erzielten Resultate auf, hier die Entdeckung eines Hormons für Frauen, die bisher keine Kinder kriegen konnten. (GER)
138–140 Umschläge einer Werbemappe, eines Faltprospektes und eines Katalogs einer Computer-Firma. (USA)

134 Page double figurant dans une publication que *Rodenstock*, maison d'appareils d'optique, a réalisée sous le titre «Voir». (GER)
135 Recto et verso d'un dépliant pour un médicament de *Ciba-Geigy* contre la phlébite. Jambes jaunes, chaussures bleues, fond vert. (URU)
136 Illustration sur le panneau intérieur d'un portfolio contenant des informations sur les produits chimiques fabriqués par Air Products & Chemicals, Inc. En polychromie. (USA)
137 Illustration (en grandeur nature) figurant dans une campagne de prestige de la Fédération de l'Industrie pharmaceutique. La brochure fait état des résultats auxquels on est parvenus grâce aux recherches pharmaceutiques; ici on discute une hormone pour les femmes qui n'ont pas pu avoir des enfants. (GER)
138–140 Couvertures d'un portfolio, d'un dépliant et d'un catalogue publiés par une entreprise de l'électronique. (USA)

ART DIRECTOR / DIRECTEUR ARTISTIQUE:

134 Heinrich Gorissen
136 Barry Atkinson
137 Horst Sambo
138–140 John Milligan

AGENCY / AGENTUR / AGENCE – STUDIO:

136 Mueller & Wister
137 Lintas
138–140 John Milligan Design, Inc.

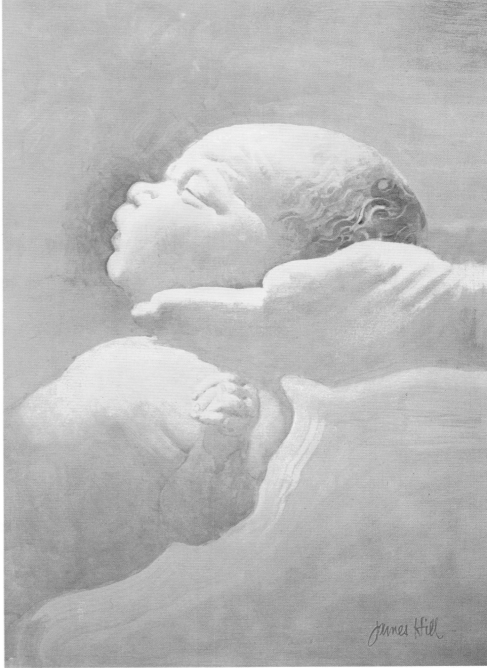

137

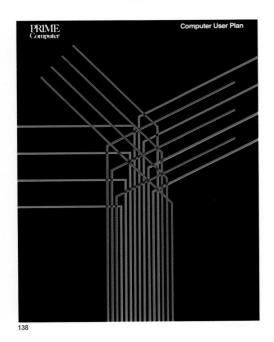

138

139

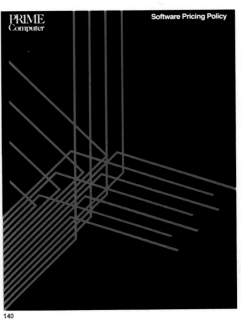

140

141

142

ARTIST / KÜNSTLER / ARTISTE:

141, 142 Christian Lang/Werner Lüthy
143 Jack Davis
144, 145 Tom Evans

DESIGNER / GESTALTER / MAQUETTISTE:

141, 142 Christian Lang
143 Larry Stires

ART DIRECTOR / DIRECTEUR ARTISTIQUE:

141, 142 Christian Lang
143 Larry Stires
144, 145 Tom Poth

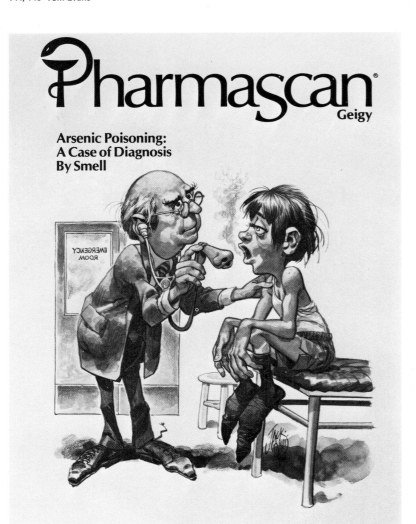

144

141, 142 Opened front spreads of two folders that are part of a series for the antibiotic *Rimaktan* made by *Ciba*. The illustrations portray the effective range of this medicament, here for pneumonia or tuberculosis as well as for purulent skin infections. (SWI)
143 Cover of a publication regularly published by *Geigy* and distributed mostly to chemists. The illustration refers to an article about the provision of a diagnosis for arsenic poisoning. In full colour. (USA)
144, 145 Double spread and illustration in actual size from a brochure for the *Hills Fitness Center*. Fig. 144 symbolizes the daily stress to which modern man is physically and psychically subjected; Fig. 145: individual training programmes in a relaxed atmosphere. (USA)

143

145

Booklets / Prospekte / Brochures

141, 142 Geöffnete Vorderseiten von zwei Faltprospekten, die Teil einer Serie für das Antibiotikum *Rimaktan* von *Ciba* sind. Die Illustrationen zeigen die Anwendungsbereiche dieses Mittels, hier bei Pneumonie oder Tuberkulose und bei eitrigen Hautkrankheiten. (SWI)
143 Titelblatt einer regelmässig von *Geigy* herausgegebenen Publikation, die hauptsächlich für Apotheker bestimmt ist. Die Illustration bezieht sich auf einen Artikel über das Stellen von Diagnosen bei Arsenvergiftungen. Mehrfarbig. (USA)
144, 145 Doppelseite und Illustration in Originalgrösse aus einer Broschüre für ein Fitness-Center. Abb. 144 symbolisiert den täglichen Stress, welcher dem modernen Menschen psychisch und physisch zusetzt; Abb. 145: individuelle Trainings-Programme in erholsamer Atmosphäre. (USA)

141, 142 Rectos dépliés de deux feuilles qui font partie d'une série lancée en faveur d'un antibiotique de *Ciba*. Les illustrations se réfèrent aux rayons d'application de ce médicament, ici pour les pneumonies et la tuberculose et des infections purulentes de la peau. (SWI)
143 Couverture d'une publication de *Geigy* qui paraît régulièrement et qui s'adresse surtout aux pharmaciens. L'illustration se réfère à un article qui discute la diagnostic en cas d'empoisonnements à l'arsenic. En polychromie. (USA)
144, 145 Page double et illustration (en grandeur originale) tirées d'une brochure présentant un nouveau centre de fitness. Fig. 144 symbolise le stress psychique et physique auquel l'homme moderne est soumis chaque jour; fig. 145: programmes d'entraînement individuels. (USA)

146

147

SEND
THIS KIT TO
CAMP!
(and school!)

148

146 Plan from the Swiss-Mosaic leporello folder with which the *Swiss Tourist Office* introduces a series of small museums and private collections in Switzerland. (SWI)
147 Cover illustration from the self-promotional brochure of the graphic designer, photographer and film cartoonist Paul Brühwiler. (SWI)
148 Space-promotion folder published by the *New York Times Magazine* which is said to be more efficient in education advertising than many other publications of this kind. (USA)
149, 150 Double spread and cover from the new catalogue of courses and lectures at *Emory & Henry College*. (USA)
151, 152 Two spreads from a leporello folder and its slip-case. The illustration shows a part of the worldwide *Reuter* network. (GBR)
153 From an *Interface Group* brochure, an employment agency that provides the private sector of business with qualified personnel—above all women, members of minority groups and civil servants. (USA)

146 Situationsplan aus dem Leporello-Prospekt Schweiz-Mosaik, mit welchem die *Schweizerische Verkehrszentrale* eine Reihe kleiner Museen und Liebhabersammlungen in der Schweiz vorstellt. (SWI)
147 Titelbild einer Eigenwerbebroschüre des Graphik-Designers, Photographen und Trickfilmers Paul Brühwiler. (SWI)
148 Mit diesem Faltprospekt preist sich das *New York Times Magazine* an als Werbeträger für Anzeigen auf dem Gebiet Schule und Ferienlager. (USA)
149, 150 Doppelseite und Umschlag des neuen Kurs- und Vorlesungsverzeichnisses des *Emory & Henry College*. (USA)
151, 152 Zwei Seiten aus einem Leporello-Prospekt und dazugehöriger Schuber. Die Illustration zeigt einen Ausschnitt aus dem weltweiten Kommunikationsnetz der Nachrichtenagentur *Reuter*. (GBR)
153 Aus der Broschüre eines Stellenvermittlungsbüros, das qualifiziertes Personal, vor allem Frauen, Angehörige von Minderheitsgruppen und Bundesangestellte an die Privatwirtschaft vermittelt. (USA)

146 Carte d'un dépliant en accordéon intitulé Mosaïque Suisse. *L'Office suisse du tourisme* présente ici toute une série de petits musées et de collections privées en Suisse. (SWI)
147 Couverture d'une brochure autopromotionnelle d'un artiste graphique, photographe et réalisateurs de bandes dessinées. (SWI)
148 C'est avec ce dépliant que le magazine *New York Times* se recommande comme meilleur élément publicitaire pour les écoles et les camps. (USA)
149, 150 Page double et couverture du nouveau programme des cours d'une université. (USA)
151, 152 Deux pages d'un dépliant en accordéon et son enveloppe. L'illustration présente un détail du réseau international de communication de l'agence de presse *Reuter*. (GBR)
153 De la brochure d'un bureau de placement qui procure des emplois dans le secteur privé pour des personnes qualifiées, surtout des femmes, des minorités et des employés de l'Etat. (USA)

To be: making a decision as a high school senior between a career or continuing study at a college is difficult. ■ You may choose to look immediately for a job that eventually will place you in a particular career area, perhaps for many years. ■ You may choose to take a year off before entering college to decide if you wish to continue your education or what course of study you are most interested in following. ■ The last two years of high school are a time of questioning, of inquiry, of examination, of self-evaluation. ■ What am I going to be? ■ What do I want to be? ■

149

EMORY & HENRY COLLEGE 78·79

150

ARTIST / KÜNSTLER / ARTISTE:

148 William Pourdom
149, 150 Tim Girvin/Robert DeGast (Photo)
153 Don Weller

DESIGNER / GESTALTER:

146, 147 Paul Brühwiler
148 Paul Kutil
149, 150 Robin Rickabaugh/ Terry Daline
151, 152 Mervyn Kurlansky/ Laura Starling/Sue Horner
153 Tets Yamashita

ART DIRECTOR:

146, 147 Paul Brühwiler
148 Andrew Kner
149, 150 Robin & Heidi Rickabaugh
151, 152 Mervyn Kurlansky
153 Tets Yamashita

AGENCY / AGENTUR:

146, 147 Paul Brühwiler
151, 152 Pentagram Design
153 Harte Yamashita & Harte

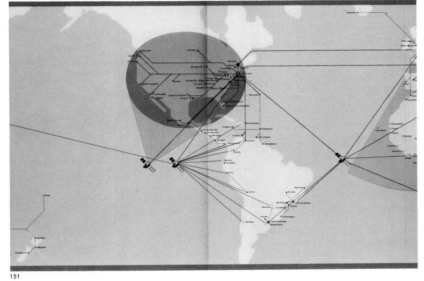

151

REUTERS COMMUNICATIONS

152

153

Booklets / Prospekte

154

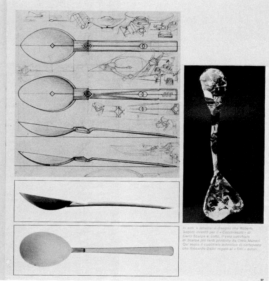

155

156

157

158

154 The illustration is meant to symbolize the efforts of the transport company *Southern Pacific* to encourage commercial contacts and trade between the United States and Mexico. Opened cover of a brochure in black and white. (USA)
155, 156 Spreads from the *Ottagono* magazine for architecture, interior and industrial design. Fig. 155: from an article entitled: The Story of a Spoon and various Sheiks; Fig. 156: the illustration on the copyright page refers to an article about Le Corbusier. (ITA)
157 Brochure published by a European association for the promotion of silk. (ITA)
158 Examples from a series of folders for the *Comfort* company. The company symbol was used throughout the series, whereby only the colours of the horizontal lines were subject to changes and variations. In subdued white. (ITA)
159 Cover of a brochure for an inhaler for people suffering from asthma. (AUS)
160 Brochure published by the *King Baudouin Foundation* on the occasion of the Year of the Child entitled "Children and the City". Brown house façades, full-colour ball. (BEL)
161 Christmas card produced by the artist Wallace Mead. (USA)

154 Die Illustration soll die Bemühungen des Transportunternehmens *Southern Pacific* symbolisieren, die Wirtschaftsbeziehungen und den Warenaustausch zwischen den USA und Mexico zu fördern, was durch die hin- und herfahrenden Transportmittel gezeigt wird. Geöffneter Umschlag einer Broschüre. Schwarzweiss. (USA)
155, 156 Seiten aus der Zeitschrift *Ottagono* für Architektur, Einrichtung und Industrie-Design. Abb. 155: zu einem Artikel mit dem Titel: Die Geschichte eines Löffels und verschiedener Scheiche; Abb. 156: die Illustration auf der Copyrightseite bezieht sich auf einen Artikel über Le Corbusier. (ITA)
157 Umschlag einer Broschüre, die von der Europäischen Kommission zur Förderung des Verkaufs von Seide herausgegeben wurde. (ITA)
158 Beispiel aus einer Serie von Prospekten für die Firma *Comfort*. Als Umschlagillustration wurde durchwegs das Firmensymbol verwendet, wobei nur die Linie in der Farbe variierte. In gebrochenem Weiss. (ITA)
159 Umschlag einer Broschüre für einen Inhalierapparat für Asthmatiker. Vorwiegend in Pastellfarben gehaltene Illustration. (AUS)
160 Zum Jahr des Kindes herausgegebene Broschüre der *Stiftung König Baudouin* mit dem Titel «Die Kinder und die Stadt». Braune Häuserfronten, farbiger Ball. (BEL)
161 Weihnachtskarte des Künstlers Wallace Mead. (USA)

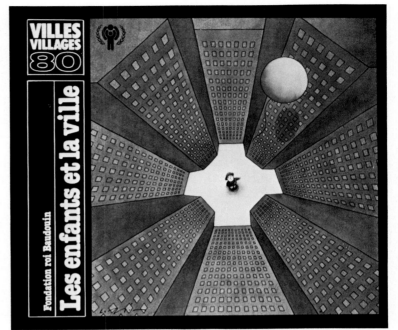
160

EVERYONE HAS A RIGHT TO BREATHE
The preventive approach to asthma therapy with Becotide Inhaler
(beclomethasone dipropionate BP)

Allen & Hanburys

159

161

154 L'illustration devrait symboliser les efforts qu'a pris *Southern Pacific*, une entreprise de transports, afin de stimuler les relations économiques et les échanges de marchandises entre les Etats-Unis et le Méxique. Couverture ouverte d'une brochure. (USA)
155, 156 Pages d'*Ottagono*, magazine d'architecture, d'ameublement et de création industrielle. Fig. 155 accompagne un article intitulé «L'histoire d'une cuillère et de divers cheiks»; fig. 156: cette illustration, accompagnant la table des matières, se réfère à un article sur Le Corbusier. (ITA)
157 Couverture d'une brochure publiée par la Commission européenne pour la promotion de la soie. (ITA)
158 Exemple d'une série de prospectus publiés par la maison *Comfort*. Toutes les couvertures de cette série sont de conception uniforme: on s'est servi de la marque de fabrique de cette entreprise en variant seulement la couleur de la ligne horizontale. (ITA)
159 Couverture d'une brochure pour un inhalateur pour les asthmatiques. (AUS)
160 Cette brochure, intitulée *Les enfants de la ville* a été publiée par la *Fondation Roi Baudouin*. Maisons en tons bruns, ballon en couleurs. (BEL)
161 Carte de Noël de l'artiste Wallace Mead. (USA)

162

163

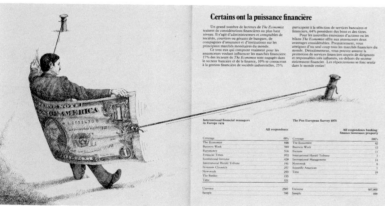

164

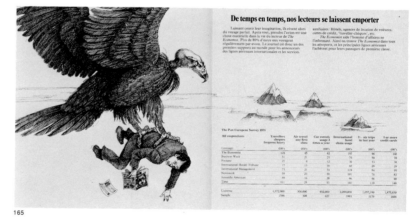

165

162 Self-promotional brochure published by an agency on the occasion of its 10th anniversary. Red title on black, yellow lettering, blue cockerel on a blue ground, red comb. (FRA)
163 Brochure of a Tokyo radio and television company. Red, green, blue and grey. (JPN)
164, 165 Brochures distributed to entice advertising by the French in the English financial newspaper *The Economist*. The subjects in these brochures deal with financial power. (FRA)
166, 167 The signet of Dunbar Corp. is employed in various ways on these covers. (USA)
168 Brochure of Cordis Corp. which produces blood-pressure apparatus for dialysis. (USA)
169 Cover of a WGBH Television brochure. (USA)
170 This small-format, full-colour folder for *Fortune* magazine is aimed at attracting advertising from the gifts industry and travel companies. (USA)

162 Zum 10jährigen Bestehen einer Agentur herausgegebene Eigenwerbebroschüre. Roter Titel auf Schwarz, gelbe Schrift, blauer Hahn auf blauem Grund, roter zehnzackiger Kamm. (FRA)
163 Broschüre einer tokioter Radio- und Fernsehgesellschaft. Rot, Grün, Blau auf Grau. (JPN)
164, 165 Von der englischen Wirtschaftszeitung *The Economist* in Frankreich zur Anzeigenwerbung. Themen: finanzielle Macht; Leser lassen sich zeitweise mitreissen. (FRA)
166, 167 Das Signet der Dunbar Corp. wird auf diesen Umschlägen variiert. (USA)
168 Broschüre einer Firma, die Apparaturen zur Blutdruckregulierung bei Dialysen herstellt. (USA)
169 Umschlag einer Broschüre, die von einer Fernsehgesellschaft herausgegeben wird. (USA)
170 Dieser kleinformatige Prospekt der Zeitschrift *Fortune* ist als Anzeigenwerbung bestimmt und richtet sich an die Geschenkindustrie und Reiseunternehmen. Mehrfarbig. (USA)

162 Brochure autopromotionnelle publiée à l'occasion du 10e anniversaire d'une agence. Titre rouge sur noir, typo jaune, coq bleu sur fond bleu, crête rouge à dix dents. (FRA)
163 Brochure d'une société de radio et télévision. Rouge, vert, bleu sur gris. (JPN)
164, 165 Brochure autopromotionnelle distribuée en France par un journal économique anglais. Thèmes: la puissance financière et les lecteurs qui se laissent emporter des fois. (FRA)
166, 167 Variation de la marque de fabrique de la Dunbar Corp. (USA)
168 En faveur des appareils utilisés pour la dialyse pour compenser la pression. (USA)
169 Couverture d'une brochure publiée par une société de télévision. (USA)
170 Petit prospectus que le magazine *Fortune* a adressé aux entreprises fabricant des cadeaux et des souvenirs et aux sociétés touristiques pour les inciter à placer des annonces. (USA)

Booklets / Prospekte / Brochures

166

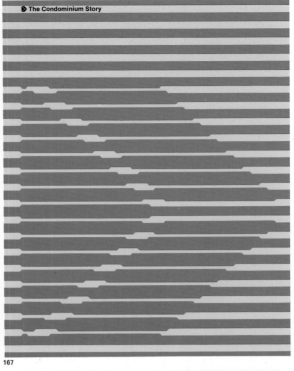

167

168

169

170

171

172

ARTIST / KÜNSTLER / ARTISTE:

171 Bernard Kuh
172 Josse Goffin
174 Chris Bobin
176, 177 Waltraut & Friedel Schmidt

DESIGNER / GESTALTER / MAQUETTISTE:

173 Craig Srebnik/Robin Rickabaugh
174 Walter Lefman
175 Bill Caldwell

ART DIRECTOR / DIRECTEUR ARTISTIQUE:

173 Robin & Heidi Rickabaugh
174 Walter Lefman
175 Bill Caldwell
176, 177 Hanno Rink

AGENCY / AGENTUR / AGENCE – STUDIO:

175 International Communication Agency

Booklets / Prospekte / Brochures

174

171, 172 The brochure "Pro Europe—Opinions and Graphics of young Europeans", realized by the publishing organ of the German savings banks, contains the verbal and visual attitudes expressed by young Common Market Europeans. Cover illustration and Belgian contribution. (GER)
173 Programme of the lunch-time lectures at Portland State University. Dark red rose. (USA)
174 In this brochure, published by *Time Magazine*, the collected radio advertising is commented upon in humorous way. Full-color illustration. (USA)
175 Correspondence card used on the occasion of the *America now* exhibition in Belgrade. (YUG)
176, 177 Illustration in actual size and complete cover of a brochure in which the *Sauerländer* publishing company presents its new books for children and young people. (SWI)

171, 172 Die Broschüre *Pro Europa – Meinungen und Graphiken junger Europäer* vereinigt die verbal und visuell zum Ausdruck gebrachten Stellungnahmen junger, vom *Deutschen Sparkassenverlag* angefragter Europäer aus EG-Ländern. Titelmotiv und belgischer Beitrag. (GER)
173 Programm der Lunch-Vorlesungen der Portland State University. Dunkelrote Rose. (USA)
174 In dieser vom *Time Magazine* herausgegebenen Broschüre wird die gesammelte Radiowerbung für diese Zeitschrift auf humorvolle Weise kommentiert. Mehrfarbige Illustrationen. (USA)
175 Während der Belgrader Ausstellung *America Now* verwendete Korrespondenzkarte. (YUG)
176, 177 Illustration (in Originalgrösse) und vollständiger Umschlag eines Prospektes, in welchem der Verlag *Sauerländer* die neuen Kinder- und Jugendbücher anzeigt. (SWI)

171, 172 Dans cette brochure, publiée sous le patronat des Editions des caisses d'épargne allemandes, des jeunes Européens provenant des Etats-membres de la Communauté Européenne expriment leurs opinions (par écrit et visuellement) au sujet d'une Europe unie. (GER)
173 Programme d'une série de lectures données à l'heure du déjeuner. Rose en rouge foncé. (USA)
174 Dans cette brochure publiée par la magazine d'information *Time* on commente de façon humoristique la publicité lancée à la radio en faveur de ce magazine. En polychromie. (USA)
175 Carte de correspondance utilisée pendant l'exposition *America now* à Belgrade. (YUG)
176, 177 Illustration (en grandeur nature) et couverture complète d'un prospectus distribué par les Ed. *Sauerländer* pour annoncer les nouveaux livres d'enfant et de jeunesse. (SWI)

175

177

176

178

179

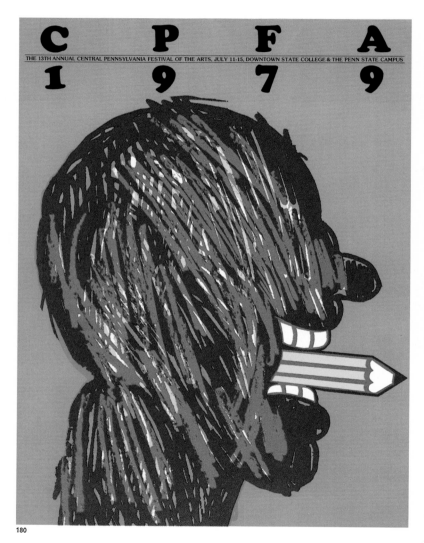

180

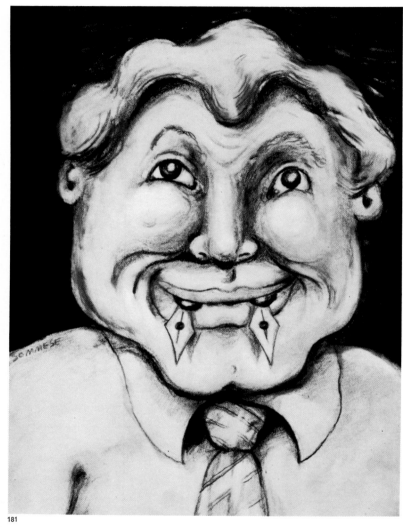

181

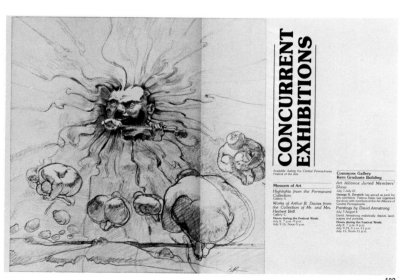

182

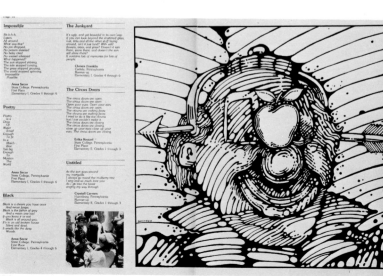

183

ARTIST / KÜNSTLER / ARTISTE:

180, 181, 183 Lanny Sommese
182 Bill Kinser
184 Bill Sanderson
185 Coleen Quinn

DESIGNER / GESTALTER / MAQUETTISTE:

178, 179 Christof Gassner
180–183 Lanny Sommese
184 Mark Biley
185 Sidjakov & Berman Assoc.

ART DIRECTOR / DIRECTEUR ARTISTIQUE:

180–183 Lanny Sommese
184 John McConnell
185 Nicolas Sidjakov

AGENCY / AGENTUR / AGENCE – STUDIO:

178, 179 Christof Gassner
180–183 Lanny Sommese Design
184 Pentagram Design
185 Great Cruz Bay Company

184

178, 179 These two sub-titles were employed in the programme "Plays on German Television, Channel 2." (GER)
180–183 Cover, full-page illustration and double spreads from the 13th Annual Central Pennsylvania Festival of the Arts programme. All illustrations are in black and white. (USA)
184 Six famous English artists have contributed one illustration, each in a certain colour, for the 500 copies of a portfolio printed by a typesetter/compositor. (FRA)
185 Brochure for a new, exclusive housing estate built by the Great Cruz Bay Company on the Caribbean island St. John. Printed in brown on wrapping paper. (USA)

178, 179 Diese beiden Zwischentitel wurden in der Programmbroschüre «Schauspiel im ZDF» verwendet. (GER)
180–183 Umschlag, ganzseitige Illustration und Doppelseiten aus dem Programmheft des Kunstfestivals von Central Pennsylvania. Abb. 181, 182: Programm der im Rahmen des Festivals gezeigten Ausstellungen; Abb. 183: Doppelseite mit Beispielen aus dem Lyrik-Wettbewerb. Alle Illustrationen sind schwarzweiss. (USA)
184 Sechs berühmte englische Künstler haben je eine Illustration in einer bestimmten Farbe zu diesem in 500 Exemplaren gedruckten Portfolio einer Setzerei beigesteuert. (FRA)
185 Broschüre über eine neue exklusive Siedlung auf der Karibikinsel St. John. In Braun auf Packpapier gedruckt. (USA)

178, 179 Ces deux titres ont figuré dans le programme de la 2e chaîne de la télévision allemande pour annoncer les émissions dramatiques. (GER)
180–183 Couverture, illustration pleine page et pages doubles du programme du Festival des arts de la Pennsylvanie centrale. Fig. 181, 182: programme des expositions présentées dans le cadre de ce festival; fig. 183: page double avec des poèmes du concours de poésie. Toutes les illustrations sont en noir-blanc. (USA)
184 Six artistes anglais de renom ont réalisé une illustration dans une couleur pour ce portfolio d'un atelier de composition, portfolio dont le tirage était limité à 500 exemplaires. (FRA)
185 Brochure sur un quartier résidentiel exclusif sur l'île caraïbe St. John. Imprimé en brun sur papier d'emballage. (USA)

185

ARTIST / KÜNSTLER / ARTISTE:

186 Joan Walsh
187–189 Guy Billout
190 Russell Drysdale
191 Mark Fisher

DESIGNER / GESTALTER / MAQUETTISTE:

186 Robert J. Warkulwiz
190 Ian Whyte Art Studio
191 Mark Fisher
192 Koos Staal

ART DIRECTOR / DIRECTEUR ARTISTIQUE:

186 Robert J. Warkulwiz
187–189 Ellen Roberts/Cheryl Tortoriello
191 Mark Fisher
192 Koos Staal

AGENCY / AGENTUR / AGENCE – STUDIO:

186 Carlyle & Warkulwiz, Inc.
190 Ian Whyte Art Studio
192 Koos Staal

187

186

190

186 This brochure by the *Citibank* dealing with the theme of money explains to the bank's employees the services it offers which bring in indirect additions to their salaries. The title is in full colour on a blue chequered ground. (USA)

187–189 *By Camel or by Car – a Look at Transportation.* This publication for children on the subject of movement explains in humorous fashion the pictured means of transport. Full-colour illustrations. (USA)

190 Cover of the programme for the Perth Festival. The ground is in red and the swan in black. (AUS)

191 Inside front cover of a small-format self-promotional brochure by the illustrator Mark Fisher. In black and white, address in red. (USA)

192 A combination of typography and photography on the cover of a brochure belonging to an information folder for the Noorder Dierenpark Zoo. This edition is devoted to baboons. (NLD)

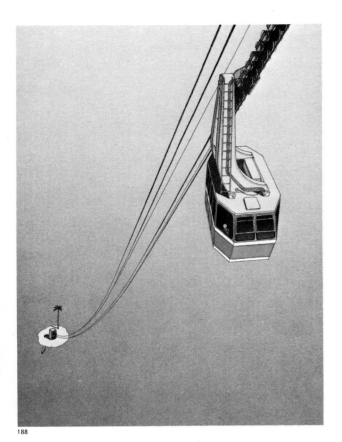

188

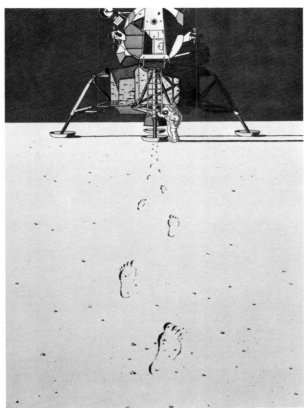

189

191

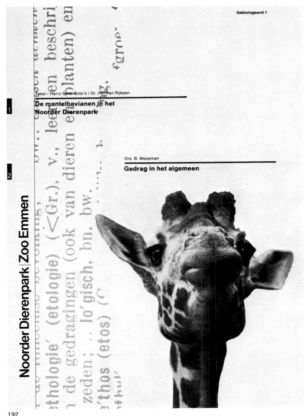

192

186 Mit dieser Broschüre zum Thema «Geld» klärt eine amerikanische Grossbank ihre Angestellten über diejenigen Leistungen auf, die die Bank zusätzlich zu den Lohnzahlungen quasi als indirektes Gehalt erbringt. Mehrfarbiger Titel auf blau kariertem Grund. (USA)
187–189 «Auf dem Kamelrücken oder im Auto.» Diese für Kinder bestimmte Publikation zum Thema «Fortbewegung» gibt auf humorvolle Weise Auskunft über die abgebildeten Transportmittel. Mehrfarbige Illustrationen. (USA)
190 Titelblatt des Programmheftes für das Festival von Perth. Roter Grund, schwarzer Schwan. (AUS)
191 Zweite Umschlagseite einer kleinformatigen Eigenwerbebroschüre des Illustrators Mark Fisher. Schwarzweiss, Adresse in Rot. (USA)
192 Kombination von Typographie und Photographie auf dem Titelblatt einer Broschüre, die zu einer Informationsmappe über einen Tierpark gehört. Diese Ausgabe ist den Mantelpavianen gewidmet. (NLD)

186 C'est par cette brochure au sujet de l'argent qu'une grande banque américaine informe ses employés des prestations complémentaires qu'elle leur accorde comme une sorte de paiement indirect. Titre en couleurs vives sur papier carré en bleu. (USA)
187–189 «Aller à chameau ou en voiture.» Cette publication consacré au sujet du transport est destinée aux enfants et donne, de façon humoristique, des informations sur les divers moyens de transport. (USA)
190 Couverture du programme du Festival de Perth. En polychromie. (AUS)
191 Deuxième page de couverture d'une petite brochure autopromotionnelle distribuée par l'illustrateur Mark Fisher. Illustration en noir et blanc, adresse en rouge. (USA)
192 Couverture d'une brochure (conception typographique combinée avec une photo) qui fait partie d'un portfolio d'information d'un jardin zoologique. Cette édition est consacrée aux babouins. (NLD)

COPY

Put the name of advertiser, date of insertion and size of advertisement on the top of each page.

Number pages in sequence.

Type copy on standard 8½ x 11 white bond paper (do not write copy on layout).

Type on one side only of copy paper.

Double-space all typed copy.

Type all copy to be set: headlines, sub-heads, prices, body copy.

Leave left and right margins… at least 1¾″…in which to write instructions.

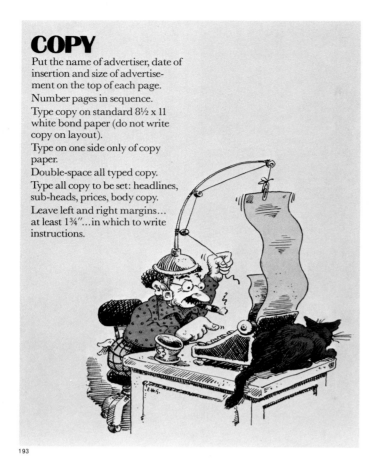

193

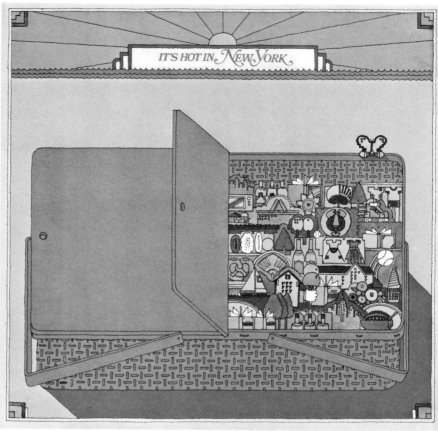

194

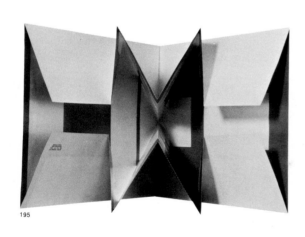

195

196

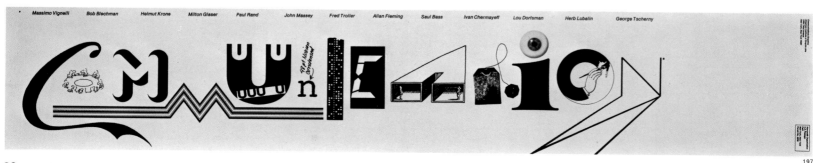

197

193 Guide published by the *New York Times* with information about how advertisers should submit their layouts for advertisements to be published. (USA)
194 Cover of a folder with the advertising deadlines for the Summer-Pleasure issue of the *New York Magazine*. Illustration in full colour. (USA)
195, 196 *The Big Red Book*. Double spread in white and red from an advertising brochure for *Life* magazine, informing the reader that . . . "nothing is bigger than . . . *Life*". The spread is cleverly folded. (See also pages 98 and 99) (USA)
197 Invitation to submit work for an exhibition on communication graphics organized by the American Institute of Graphic Arts. The invitation is in black and white. (USA)
198 Cover illustration from a spiral-bound visitors' book distributed by the *New York Times* to potential advertisers. In actual size. (USA)

193 Dieser von der *New York Times* herausgegebene Leitfaden gibt Auskunft, wie die Inserenten ihre Anzeigenvorlagen einreichen müssen. Diese Seite bezieht sich auf den Text. (USA)
194 Titelblatt eines Faltprospektes, in welchem die Anzeigenschlusstermine für die Sommer-Sondernummer des *New York Magazines* aufgeführt sind. Mehrfarbige Illustration. (USA)
195, 196 Die Texte in dieser Broschüre mit dem Titel «Das grosse rote Buch» – es sind Redewendungen und Abhandlungen zum Wort «gross» – kulminieren in der Aussage «nichts ist grösser als . . . *Life*». Raffiniert gefalzte Doppelseite (weiss auf Rot) aus der Werbebroschüre für die Zeitschrift *Life*. (S. auch S. 98, 99) (USA)
197 Einladung zur Unterbreitung von Arbeiten für die vom American Institute of Graphic Arts organisierte Ausstellung über Kommunikations-Graphik. Illustrationen in Schwarzweiss. (USA)
198 Titelillustration eines ringgehefteten Gästebuches, das die *New York Times* an potentielle Inserenten aus dem Kunst-Business verteilte. In Originalgrösse. (USA)

193 Dans ce manuel, le *New York Times* a réuni les conditions que le client doit observer en ce qui concerne les maquettes des annonces à publier. Cette page-ci se réfère à la préparation du texte. (USA)
194 Couverture d'un dépliant indiquant les dates limites pour la remise des annonces devant paraître dans le numéro spécial d'été du magazine *New York*. Illustration en couleurs. (USA)
195, 196 Les textes – des locutions courantes concernant le mot «grand» – réunis dans cette brochure intitulée «Le grand livre rouge» culminent dans la déclaration que «rien n'est plus grand que . . . *Life*». Page double (blanc sur rouge), pliée de façon ingénieuse, d'une brochure pour le magazine *Life*. (V. aussi les pp. 98, 99) (USA)
197 Invitation à soumettre des travaux pour une exposition sur la communication visuelle organisée par l'American Institute of Graphic Arts. En noir et blanc. (USA)
198 Illustration de couverture d'un livre des hôtes (à reliure spirale): autopromotion du *New York Times* distribuée aux marchands d'objets d'art pour les inciter à placer des annonces. En grandeur originale. (USA)

198

ARTIST / KÜNSTLER / ARTISTE:

193 Elwood Smith
194 Jerome Matejka
198 Randall Enos

DESIGNER / GESTALTER / MAQUETTISTE:

193 Paul Kutil
194 Jerome Matejka
195, 196 Gilbert Lesser
197 Bob Salpeter
198 Andrew Kner

ART DIRECTOR / DIRECTEUR ARTISTIQUE:

193, 198 Andrew Kner
194 Jack Sherin
195, 196 Gilbert Lesser
197 Bob Salpeter

AGENCY / AGENTUR / AGENCE – STUDIO:

194 Sherin & Matejka
197 Bob Salpeter, Inc.

Booklets / Prospekte / Brochures

Adelaide Festival International Arts in Australia   The Friends of the Festival

March 7th–29th   1980

199

Knoll NeoconXI   Dealer Tuesday

200

ARTIST / KÜNSTLER / ARTISTE:

200 Henry Wolf
204, 205 Ivan Chermayeff

DESIGNER / GESTALTER:

199 Ken Cato
200 Arnold Saks
201 Robert Stearns
202, 203 James A. Houff
204, 205 Ivan Chermayeff
206, 207 Douglas Scott

ART DIRECTOR:

199 Ken Cato
200 Arnold Saks
201 Robert Stearns
202, 203 Katherine McCoy
204, 205 Ivan Chermayeff
206, 207 Christopher Pullman

AGENCY / AGENTUR / AGENCE:

199 Cato Hibberd Design Pty Ltd
200 Arnold Saks Inc.
201 Contemporary Arts Center
202, 203 Cranbrook Academy
        Design Dept.
204, 205 Chermayeff & Geismar
        Assoc.
206, 207 WGBH Design

Booklets
Prospekte
Brochures

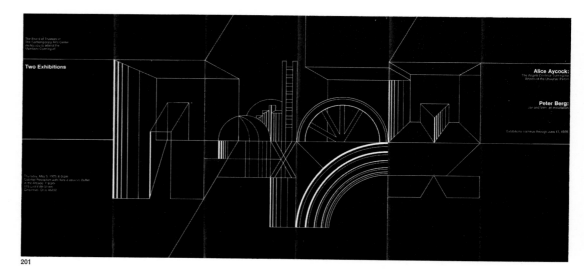

201

199 Example from a uniform series of smallformat brochures for the International Adeleide Arts Festival. This folder is devoted to the promoters of the Festival. (AUS)
200 Recto of an invitation with which *Knoll International* invites its representatives to a cocktail party where new furniture models are to be shown. (USA)
201 Black-and-white invitation (leporello) to the opening of a double exhibition at the Contemporary Arts Center in Cincinnati. (USA)
202, 203 Cover and double spread from the catalogue of the Cranbrook Academy of Art for an exhibition of 21 Detroit artists. Black and white with blue. (USA)
204 Full-colour cover illustration for a press portfolio containing information about a new dramatic television series sponsored by *Mobil*. (USA)
205 Cover of a regular publication printed by the Walker Art Center in Minneapolis. This edition is devoted to the designer Ivan Chermayeff. (USA)
206, 207 Two double spreads from a television company's programme for forthcoming symphonies. (USA)

202

203

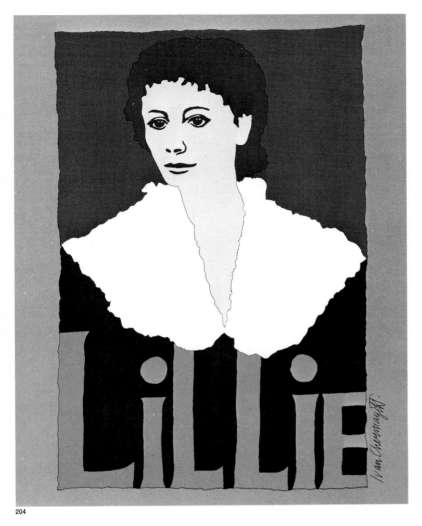

204

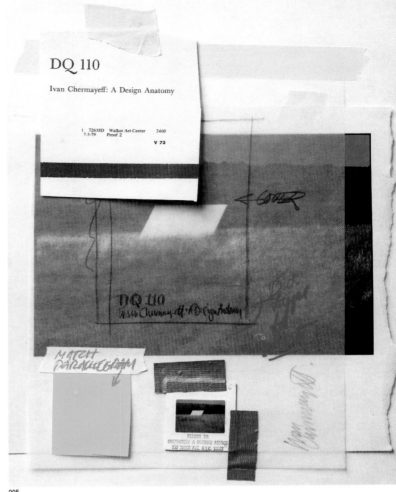

205

206

207

199 Beispiel aus einer einheitlich gestalteten Serie von kleinformatigen Broschüren für das internationale Kunstfestival in Adelaide. Diese Broschüre hier gibt Auskunft über die Förderer dieses Festivals. (AUS)
200 Vorderseite einer Einladung, mit welcher *Knoll International* Vertreter von *Knoll*-Möbeln zu einem Cocktail und einer Vorführung der neuen Modelle einlädt. (USA)
201 Einladung (Leporello) zur Vernissage einer im Contemporary Arts Center in Cincinnati gezeigten Doppelausstellung, die eine mit dem Titel «Die Engel drehen die Räder des Universums weiter», die andere mit dem Titel «Jan and Vern, an installation». Schwarzweiss. (USA)
202, 203 Titelblatt und Doppelseite aus dem Katalog der Cranbrook Academy of Art für eine Ausstellung von 21 Detroiter Künstlern. Handschriftliche Angaben in Blau, die übrigen Texte sind in Schwarz auf hellgrauen Grund gedruckt. (USA)
204 Titelbild einer Pressemappe über eine neue dramatische Fernsehreihe, die durch die finanzielle Unterstützung von *Mobil* ermöglicht wurde. Titel in hellem Lila auf dunkelblauem Grund, braune Haare, grüner Hintergrund. (USA)
205 Titelbild einer vom Walker Art Center in Minneapolis regelmässig herausgegebenen Publikation. Diese Ausgabe ist Ivan Chermayeff gewidmet. (USA)
206, 207 Zwei Doppelseiten aus dem Programmheft über die von einer Fernsehgesellschaft präsentierten Symphonien. Abb. 206: Programmhinweis für ein Trompetenkonzert von Tartini-Thilde und die 4. Symphonie von Tschaikowski, Abb. 207: für das *Schwanensee*-Ballett von Tschaikowski, links mit Aufzeichnungen der Ballettschritte für die Tänzer. (USA)

199 Exemple d'une série de petites brochures de conception uniforme pour le Festival international des arts ayant lieu à Adelaide. La brochure reproduite donne des informations sur les promoteurs de ce festival. (AUS)
200 Recto d'une carte par laquelle *Knoll International* invite ses représentants à participer à un cocktail et à la présentation des nouveaux modèles. (USA)
201 Invitation (en accordéon) au vernissage de l'exposition collective de deux artistes présentés au Contemporary Arts Center de Cincinnati. L'une des expositions est intitulée «Les Anges continuent à tourner les roues de l'Univers», l'autre «Jan and Vern, an installation». En noir et blanc. (USA)
202, 203 Couverture et page double du catalogue d'une exposition collective de 21 artistes de Detroit organisée par la Cranbrook Academy of Art. Mots écrits à la main en bleu, les autres textes sont imprimés sur fond gris. (USA)
204 Couverture d'un portfolio contenant des informations sur une nouvelle série dramatique télévisée qui a été réalisée sous le patronat de *Mobil*. Le titre est en lilas clair sur un fond en bleu foncé, cheveux bruns sur fond vert. (USA)
205 Couverture d'une publication du Walker Art Center de Minneapolis qui paraît régulièrement. Ce numéro est consacré à Ivan Chermayeff. (USA)
206, 207 Deux pages doubles d'un programme sur les concerts symphoniques présentés par une station de TV. Fig. 206: indications concernant un concert de trompette par Tartini-Thilde et la Symphonie no 4 de Tchaïkovski, la fig. 207 concerne *Le Lac des cygnes* de Tchaïkovski, à gauche avec des notations pour les danseurs. (USA)

ARTIST / KÜNSTLER / ARTISTE:

208 Fred Marcellino
209 Tim
210 Jörg Müller
211 Gerhard Lahr
212 Eduard Prüssen

DESIGNER / GESTALTER / MAQUETTISTE:

208 Arnold Kushner
209 Tim
212 Eduard Prüssen

ART DIRECTOR / DIRECTEUR ARTISTIQUE:

208 Andrew Kner

210

209

208 Cover illustration of an information folder from the *New York Times* aimed at potential advertisers for the literary supplement. (USA)
209 New Year's card by the caricaturist TIM who works mainly for the news magazine *L'Express*. Black and white with blue and beige. (FRA)
210 Cover of a catalogue published by the Swiss Union for young people's literature. (SWI)
211 This catalogue by the *Thienemann* publishing company is for children's books. (GER)
212 Double spread from a small-format house organ by the graphic designer Eduard Prüssen, of which 40 copies were printed. It deals here with managers who prefer maternal women. (GER)

208 Titelbild einer Informationsmappe, welche die *New York Times* an potentielle Inserenten für die Literaturbeilage richtete. (USA)
209 Neujahrskarte des Karikaturisten TIM, der vorwiegend für das französische Nachrichtenmagazin *L'Express* arbeitet. Schwarzweiss mit Blau und Beige. (FRA)
210 Titelbild des vom Schweizerischen Bund für Jugendliteratur herausgegebenen Katalogs. (SWI)
211 In diesem Katalog zeigt der *Thienemann*-Verlag seine Kinder- und Jugendbücher an. (GER)
212 Doppelseite aus der in 40 Exemplaren erscheinenden, kleinformatigen Hauszeitschrift des Graphikers Eduard Prüssen. Hier geht es um Manager, die mütterliche Typen bevorzugen. (GER)

208 Couverture d'un portfolio contenant des informations sur le placement d'annonces dans le supplément littéraire du *New York Times*. (USA)
209 Carte du Nouvel An du caricaturiste TIM qui travaille surtout pour le magazine d'information français *L'Express*. Noir-blan avec bleu et beige. (FRA)
210 Couverture du catalogue de la Ligue Suisse pour la littérature de la jeunesse. (SWI)
211 Catalogue consacré aux livres d'enfant et de jeunesse publiés par les Ed. *Thienemann*. (GER)
212 Page double d'un petit journal à tirage limité (40 ex.) de l'artiste graphique Eduard Prüssen. On y parle des managers qui préfèrent des femmes qui les soignent comme des mères. (GER)

Booklets / Prospekte / Brochures

211

212

213

215

214

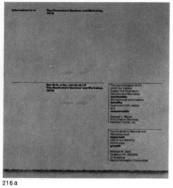

216 a

216

ARTIST / KÜNSTLER / ARTISTE:

213, 214 Brad Holland
215 Mark English
216 Fred Otnes
217, 218 Richard Shaefer/Paul Zalon

DESIGNER / GESTALTER / MAQUETTISTE:

213, 214 Brad Holland
216a John DeCesare
217, 218 Richard Shaefer/Paul Zalon
219 William Longhauser

217

218

213, 214 Illustration in actual size and complete book-mark used for self-promotional purposes by a New York bookshop. The same subject was also printed as a poster. The illustration is in black and white. (USA)
215, 216, 216a Cover in re-cycled paper and two of the six loose-leaf pages with full-colour illustrations by six leading American illustrators who contributed to an illustrators and designers seminar/workshop. (USA)
217, 218 Self-promotion by the company Popshots, Inc. (USA)
219 Cover illustration of a folder for a do-it-yourself centre. Black and white red lettering. (USA)

213, 214 Illustration (in Originalgrösse) und vollständiges Buchzeichen, das eine Newyorker Buchhandlung als Eigenwerbung verteilte. Das gleiche Sujet erschien auch als Plakat. Illustration in Schwarzweiss. (USA)
215, 216, 216a Umschlag aus Umweltpapier und zwei der sechs losen Blätter mit mehrfarbigen Illustrationen von sechs führenden amerikanischen Illustratoren, die für Designer und Illustratoren im Rahmen des Illustrators Seminar and Workshop ein zweiteiliges Programm ausgearbeitet haben. (USA)
217, 218 Eigenwerbung der Firma Popshots, Inc. (USA)
219 Titelbild eines Faltprospektes für ein Do-it-yourself-Center, in welchem vorwiegend Bilderrahmen gemacht werden können, was durch die Werkzeuge und Teile von Rahmen symbolisiert wird. Schwarzweiss, rote Schrift. (USA)

213, 214 Illustration (grandeur originale) et signet, qu'une librairie newyorkaise a distribué comme autopromotion. Le même sujet a paru aussi sous forme d'affiche. Illustration en noir et blanc. (USA)
215, 216, 216a Couverture en papier recyclé et deux des six feuilles volantes avec des illustrations polychromes de six illustrateurs américains de renom. Dans le cadre d'une série de manifestations, ceux-ci ont mis au point un programme pour illustrateurs et designers. (USA)
217, 218 Publicité autopromotionnelle de la maison Popshots, Inc. (USA)
219 Couverture du dépliant d'un centre où chacun peut faire des encadrements de tableaux, ce qui est symbolisé par les outils et les parties en bois. Illustration en noir et blanc, typographie en rouge. (USA)

219

ART DIRECTOR / DIRECTEUR ARTISTIQUE:

213, 214 Brad Holland
215–216a John DeCesare
217, 218 Richard Shaefer/Paul Zalon
219 Howard Coffin

AGENCY / AGENTUR / AGENCE – STUDIO:

215–216a DeCesare Design
219 Fanfare Communications

Happy birthday!

220

221

220 A Swiss illustrator congratulates the United States on its 200th anniversary. Colours of the American flag, reddish yellow sky. (SWI)
221 Invitation to a Christmas party organized by the magazine *Village Voice*. (USA)
222 This artist tried to design a typical Christmas card and then gave it a touch of advertising flair by incorporating a packet of snow-flakes to enhance the festive season. (GBR)
223 Illustration for the *Mississippi Nights* jazz club. (USA)
224 Invitation in black and white to a wedding. (BEL)
225 A card printed by an artist on a manual printing-press with a quote from Shakespeare. Black and brown on olive. (GBR)

220 Ein Schweizer Illustrator gratuliert den Vereinigten Staaten zu ihrem 200. Geburtstag. Freiheitsstatue in den Farben der amerikanischen Flagge, rötlich gelber Himmel. (SWI)
221 Einladung zu der von der Zeitschrift *Village Voice* veranstalteten Weihnachtsparty. (USA)
222 Der Künstler hat versucht, eine typische Weihnachtskarte zu schaffen, gab ihr jedoch noch einen Anstrich von Werbung mit dem Paket Schneeflocken für eine bessere Weihnachtszeit. (GBR)
223 Illustration zum Programm eines Jazzlokals. (USA)
224 Einladungskarte zu einer Hochzeitsfeier. Schwarzweiss. (BEL)
225 Vom Künstler auf einer Handpresse gedruckte Karte mit einem Zitat von Shakespeare. Schwarz und Braun auf Olive. (GBR)

220 Un caricaturiste suisse adresse ses meilleurs vœux aux Etats-Unis à l'occasion du bicentenaire. En polychromie. (SWI)
221 Invitation à une fête que le magazine *Village Voice* organise le jour de Noël. (USA)
222 L'artiste a créé une carte de Noël typique pour ainsi dire, cependant avec une fine allusion à la publicité: un paquet de flocons de neige pour un meilleur temps de Noël. (GBR)
223 Illustration du programme d'une cave de jazz. (USA)
224 Invitation aux fêtes du mariage. Noir-blanc. (BEL)
225 Carte que l'artiste avait imprimée sur sa propre presse à bras avec une citation de Shakespeare. Noir et brun sur olive. (GBR)

222

ARTIST / KÜNSTLER / ARTISTE:

220 René Fehr
221 Mark Alan Stamaty
222 James Marsh
223 Joey Staebell
224 Josse Goffin
225 Paul Peter Piech

DESIGNER / GESTALTER / MAQUETTISTE:

220 René Fehr
222 Brian Morrow

ART DIRECTOR / DIRECTEUR ARTISTIQUE:

220 René Fehr
222 Brian Morrow

223

AGENCY / AGENTUR / AGENCE – STUDIO:

222 TBWA
225 Taurus Press of Willow Dene

Booklets / Prospekte / Brochures

Pour fêter avec eux leur mariage, Dany et Jacques seront heureux de vous compter parmi leurs amis le samedi 11 juin 1977 de 12 à 14 heures.

Amthor - Bredael, rue de Bayarmont 2 à Morsaint Grez-Doiceau   tél. (010) 84 53 28

224

COME WHAT COME MAY. TIME & THE HOURS RUN THROUGH THE ROUGHEST DAY. W. SHAKESPEARE

225

226—228 This small-format brochure entitled *Cultural issues in contemporary psychiatry*, published by the Smith Kline & French Laboratories, is part of a series of brochures dealing with the historical and sociocultural aspects which are important to understand the mental health and mental illness of minority groups in the USA, here Hispanic Americans. (USA)
229 Cover of a programme folder of the Bavarian broadcasting company. Yellow "sun" and a blue sky. (GER)
230 Inside spread in blue and red from the financial and trade magazine *Barron's—The Financial Analyst's Analyst* read by many people in various branches of finance and industry. (USA)
231—234 Cover and double spreads dealing with Mexico from an Itel Corp. brochure. (USA)
235 Brochures dealing with summer meetings at MIT. Red, blue, green on white and black. (USA)

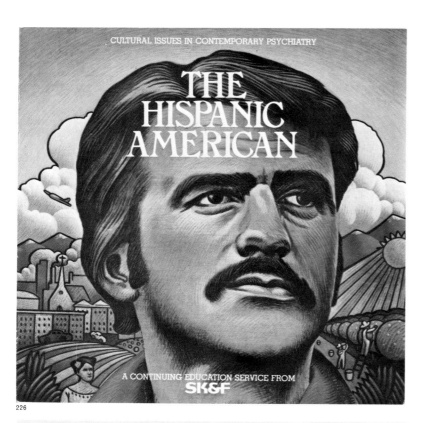

226

227

228

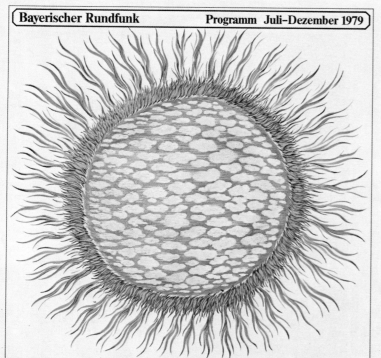

229

230

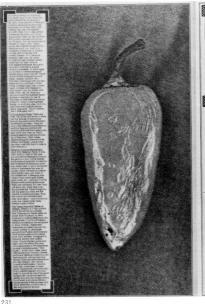

231

Itel Club '78

ARTIST / KÜNSTLER / ARTISTE:

226 John O'Leary
229 Walter Tafelmaier
230 Kevin Harrington
231—234 John Casado
235 Uldis Purins

DESIGNER / GESTALTER / MAQUETTISTE:

226—228 Jonson Pedersen Hinrichs
         Shakery
229 Walter Tafelmaier
230 Kevin Harrington
231—234 John Casado

ART DIRECTOR / DIRECTEUR ARTISTIQUE:

226—228 Alan J. Klawans
229 Walter Tafelmaier
230 Arthur Beckenstein
231—234 John Casado

AGENCY / AGENTUR / AGENCE – STUDIO:

226—228 Smith Kline & French Labs.
230 Dow Jones & Co Inc.
235 Gregory Fossella Assoc.

232

233

MEXICAN FOOD

234

226—228 In dieser, von einer Arzneimittelfabrik herausgegebenen, kleinformatigen Broschüre untersuchen vier Psychiatrie-Professoren die heutige Situation der Hispano-Amerikaner, der zweitgrössten Minderheitengruppe in den Vereinigten Staaten, und diskutieren über die historischen und soziokulturellen Hintergründe, die bei der psychiatrischen Behandlung dieser Patienten unbedingt berücksichtigt werden müssen. Diese Broschüre ist Teil einer Serie über die kulturellen Gesichtspunkte, die in der modernen Psychiatrie eine Rolle spielen. (USA)
229 Programmheft des *Bayerischen Rundfunks*. Gelbe «Sonne», blauer Himmel. (GER)
230 Innenseite des von einer Finanz- und Wirtschaftszeitschrift herausgegebenen Faltprospektes. Der blaue und rote Kasten enthält Prozentzahlen über die Finanzfachleute aus den verschiedensten Wirtschafts- und Industriezweigen, die diese Zeitschrift lesen; auf einem separaten Blatt, das herausgezogen werden kann, finden sich Vergleichszahlen zu andern Wirtschaftsblättern. (USA)
231—234 Umschlag und Doppelseiten aus einer Broschüre der Itel Corp. über Mexiko. (USA)
235 Broschüren über die Sommersitzungen des MIT. Rot, Blau, Grün auf Weiss, resp. Schwarz. (USA)

226—228 Cette petite brochure, publiée par une fabrique de produits chimiques, contient une enquête faite par quatre professeurs de psychiatrie sur la situation actuelle des Hispano-Américains, l'un des groupes minoritaires les plus importants aux Etats-Unis. Sur la base de cette enquête ils discutent aussi les influences historiques et socioculturelles, des facteurs très importants qui devraient être pris en considération dans le traitement psychiatrique de ces patients. Cette brochure fait partie d'une série consacrée à l'histoire de la civilisation de ces minorités qui joue un rôle important dans la psychiatrie moderne. (USA)
229 Couverture du programme de la radiodiffusion bavaroise. «Soleil» jaune, ciel bleu. (GER)
230 Page intérieure d'un dépliant publié par un magazine économique. Les cases bleue et rouge présentent en pour-cent le nombre d'experts financiers des diverses branches économiques et industrielles qui se réfèrent régulièrement à ce magazine; sur une feuille volante à tirer on trouve les chiffres comparatifs se référant aux autres publications économiques. (USA)
231—234 Couverture et pages doubles d'une brochure de l'Itel Corp. sur le Méxique. (USA)
235 Brochures sur les sessions d'été du MIT. En rouge, bleu et vert sur blanc, resp. noir. (USA)

235

236

237

LIFE Direct Mailings
LIFE Direktwerbung
LIFE Publicité directe

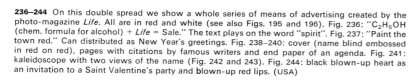

241

236–244 On this double spread we show a whole series of means of advertising created by the photo-magazine *Life*. All are in red and white (see also Figs. 195 and 196). Fig. 236: "C_2H_5OH (chem. formula for alcohol) + *Life* = Sale." The text plays on the word "spirit". Fig. 237: "Paint the town red." Can distributed as New Year's greetings. Fig. 238–240: cover (name blind embossed in red on red), pages with citations by famous writers and end paper of an agenda. Fig. 241: kaleidoscope with two views of the name (Fig. 242 and 243). Fig. 244: black blown-up heart as an invitation to a Saint Valentine's party and blown-up red lips. (USA)

236–244 Auf dieser Doppelseite zeigen wir eine ganze Serie von Werbemitteln für die Photozeitschrift *Life*, alle in Rot und Weiss gehalten (s. auch Abb. 195, 196). Abb. 236: «C_2H_5OH (chem. Formel für Alkohol) + *Life* = Verkauf.» Man spielt hier mit dem Wort «spirit» (geistige Ansprüche der *Life*-Leserschaft und Wein*geist*). Abb. 237: «Streichen Sie die Stadt rot.» Farbbüchse als Neujahrsgruss. Abb. 238–240: Deckel (Name blindgeprägt in Rot auf Rot), Innenseiten mit Zitaten berühmter Schriftsteller für jede Woche und Vorsatzpapier eines Pultkalenders. Abb. 241: Kaleidoskop, in welchem sich in bunter Folge der Name *Life* bildet. Abb. 242, 243: kaleidoskopische Ansichten des Namenszuges. Abb. 244: das schwarze, aufblasbare Herz wurde als Einladung zu einer St.-Valentins-Party verschickt. Aufblasbare rote Lippen, vielleicht als Ermutigung oder Liebesbezeugung für Inserenten gedacht. (USA)

236–244 Sur ces deux pages nous présentons toute une série de moyens de publicité du magazine de l'image *Life*, tous en rouge et blanc (voir aussi les figs. 195, 196). Fig. 236: «C_2H_5OH (symbole chimique pour l'alcool) + *Life* = Ventes.» On joue ici sur le mot «spirit» (esprit et spiritueux). Fig. 237: «Peignez votre ville en rouge.» Vœux de Nouvel An sous forme d'une boîte à peinture. Fig. 238–240: Couverture (nom gaufré en rouge sur fond rouge), pages intérieures avec des citations de grands écrivains et poètes pour chaque semaine et feuille de garde d'un agenda de table. Fig. 241: Kaléidoscope produisant des dessins variés du nom, comme montré sous les figs. 242 et 243. Fig. 244: Ce cœur noir à gonfler a été distribué comme invitation pour une fête du Saint-Valentin. Lèvres rouges à gonfler — est-ce peut-être un encouragement pour les annonceurs éventuels ou une preuve d'amour de la part de *Life*? (USA)

238

239

DESIGNER / GESTALTER / MAQUETTISTE:

236–244 Gilbert Lesser

ART DIRECTOR / DIRECTEUR ARTISTIQUE:

236–244 Gilbert Lesser

240

242

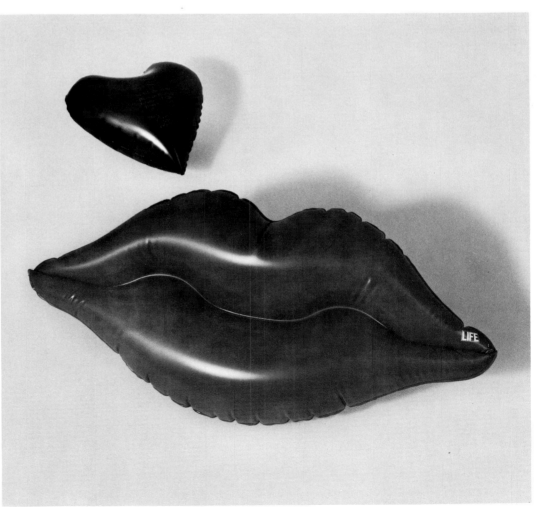

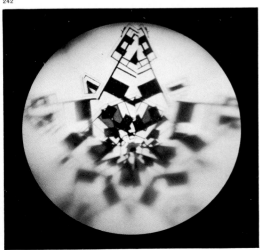

243

244

99

3

Magazine Covers

Magazine Illustrations

Newspaper Illustrations

Trade Magazines

House Organs

Book Covers

Annual Reports

Zeitschriften-Umschläge

Zeitschriften-Illustrationen

Zeitungs-Illustrationen

Fachzeitschriften

Hauszeitschriften

Buchumschläge

Jahresberichte

Couvertures de périodiques

Illustrations de périodiques

Illustrations de journaux

Revues professionnelles

Journaux d'entreprises

Couvertures de livres

Rapports annuels

ARTIST / KÜNSTLER / ARTISTE:

245 Sean McMillan
246 Rich Grote
247 Alex Murawski
248 Fred Marcellino
249 Julius Ciss
250, 251 Carlos Augusto Caldas Sorres

DESIGNER / GESTALTER / MAQUETTISTE:

246, 247 Skip Johnston
248 Fred Marcellino
250, 251 Carlos Augusto Caldas Sorres

ART DIRECTOR / DIRECTEUR ARTISTIQUE:

245 Bob Marchant
246, 247 Skip Johnston
248 Andrew Kner
249 James M. Lawrence

AGENCY / AGENTUR / AGENCE – STUDIO:

245 Aalders & Marchant
250, 251 Assessor Serviços Tecnicos S.A.

PUBLISHER / VERLEGER / EDITEUR:

245 Conferences & Exhibitions
246, 247 21st Century Communications, Ltd.
248 RC Publications
249 Camden House Publishing Ltd.
250, 251 Bolsa de Valores do Rio de Janeiro

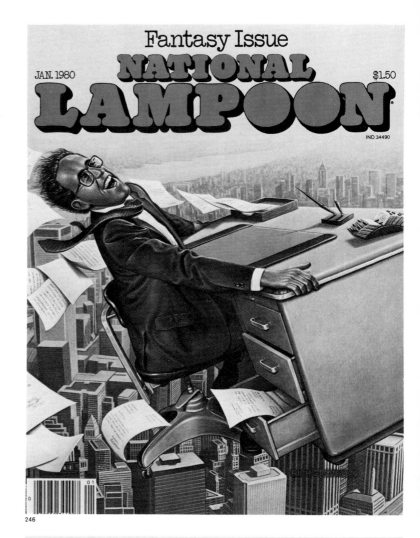

246

245

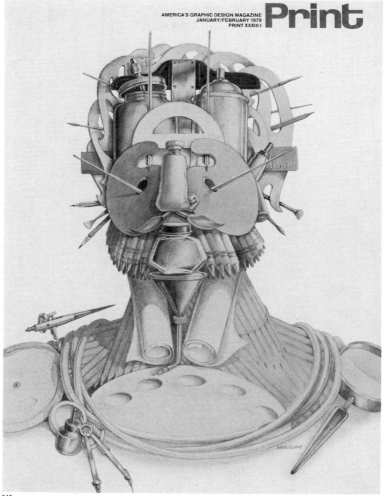

248

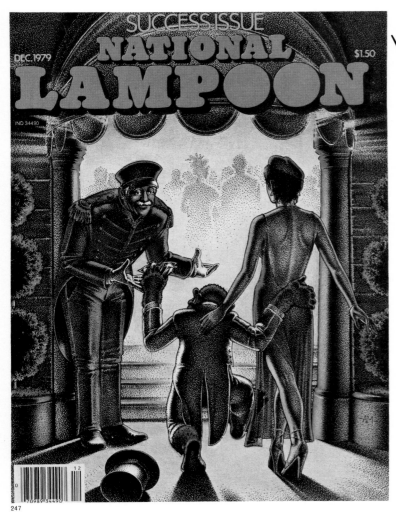

247

249

250

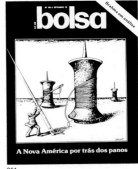

251

245 Cover of the magazine *Conferences & Exhibitions*, illustrating the subject "incentives". (GBR)
246, 247 Covers of two editions of the humorous magazine *National Lampoon*. Full-colour illustrations, name in yellow and olive green. (USA)
248 Cover in mat tones of *Print*, a magazine for graphic design and applied art. (USA)
249 Full-colour cover for a magazine devoted to garden planning, here referring to an article on "Adventures in new horticulture". (CAN)
250, 251 Illustration and complete cover of the magazine *Bolsa*. (BRA)

245 Umschlag der Zeitschrift *Conferences & Exhibitions* mit einer Illustration, die das Thema «Ansporn» symbolisieren soll. (GBR)
246, 247 Titelblätter von zwei Ausgaben der humoristischen Zeitschrift *National Lampoon*, hier für eine Nummer über fantastische Begebenheiten (Abb. 246) und eine über Erfolg. Mehrfarbige Illustrationen, Name in Gelb, resp. Olivegrün. (USA)
248 Titelblatt (in matten Farbtönen) einer Zeitschrift für Graphik und angewandte Kunst. (USA)
249 Mehrfarbiges Titelblatt einer Zeitschrift für Gartenbau, hier zu einem Artikel über Wasserkulturen und neue Versuche in der Hortikultur. (CAN)
250, 251 Illustration und vollständiger Umschlag der Zeitschrift *Bolsa*. (BRA)

245 Couverture du magazine *Conferences & Exhibitions* avec une illustration, symbolisant le sujet «incitations». (GBR)
246, 247 Couvertures de deux éditions du magazine humoristique *National Lampoon*, ici pour des numéros spéciaux consacrés à des événements fantastiques (fig. 246) et au succès (fig. 247). Illustrations polychromes, en-tête en jaune, resp. olive. (USA)
248 Couverture d'un magazine d'arts graphiques et d'arts appliqués. En tons mats. (USA)
249 Couverture (en polychromie) d'un magazine spéciale de jardinage, ici se référant à un article sur l'hydroculture et les expériences faites dans le domaine de l'horticulture. (CAN)
250, 251 Illustration et couverture complète du magazine *Bolsa*. (BRA)

252

254

253

255

252, 253 Two covers from the humorous weekly magazine *Nebelspalter*. Fig. 252 refers to an article about new hairdressing fashions. Full-colour illustrations. (SWI)
254—257 Opened covers and cover illustration in actual size from the magazine *Poland* which appears in various languages. Fig. 254 shows "Cracow"—in brilliant colours with gold; Fig. 255: "The Polish Renaissance"—again in extremely bright colours; Fig. 256, 257: "A strange Look." (POL)

252, 253 Zwei Titelblätter der humoristischen Wochenzeitschrift *Nebelspalter*. Abb. 252 bezieht sich auf einen Artikel über die neue Haarmode. Mehrfarbige Illustrationen. (SWI)
254—257 Geöffnete Umschläge und Umschlagillustration (in Originalgrösse) des in verschiedenen Sprachen erscheinenden polnischen Kulturmagazins *Polen*. Abb. 254: «Krakau» – in bunten Farben mit Gold; Abb. 255: «Polnische Renaissance» – in bunten Farben; Abb. 256, 257: «Ein seltsamer Blick». (POL)

252, 253 Deux couvertures de l'hebdomadaire humoristique *Nebelspalter*. La fig. 252 se réfère à un article sur la nouvelle coiffure. Illustrations polychromes. (SWI)
254—257 Recto et verso de couvertures et illustration (grandeur nature) de *Pologne*, magazine polonais culturel, publié en différentes langues. Fig. 254: «Cracovie» – en couleurs vives avec or; fig. 255: «Renaissance polonaise» – en couleurs vives; fig. 256, 257: «Un regard étrange». (POL)

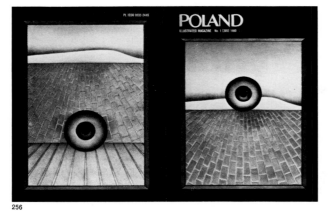

256

ARTIST / KÜNSTLER:

252, 253 Barth
254 Regina Jolanta
     Pawlowska
255 Jerzy Flisak
256, 257 Grzegorz Stanczyk

ART DIRECTOR:

252, 253 Franz Mächler
254–257 Lech Zahorski

PUBLISHER / VERLEGER:

252, 253 Nebelspalter-Verlag
254–257 Polish Interpress
         Agency

257

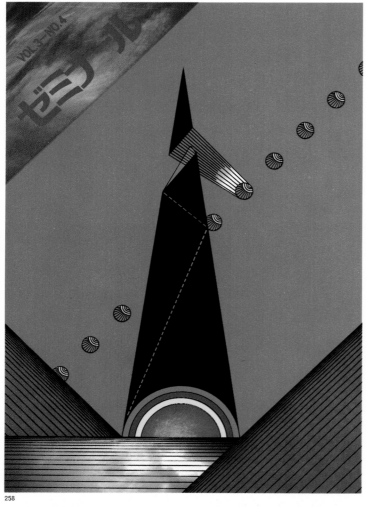

258

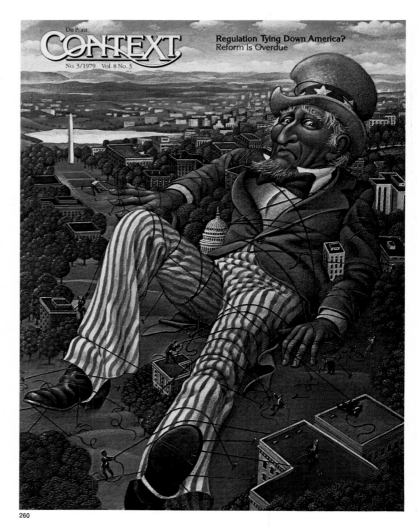

260

259

261

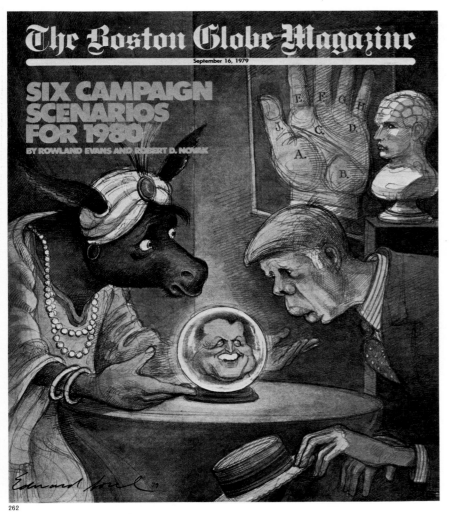

262

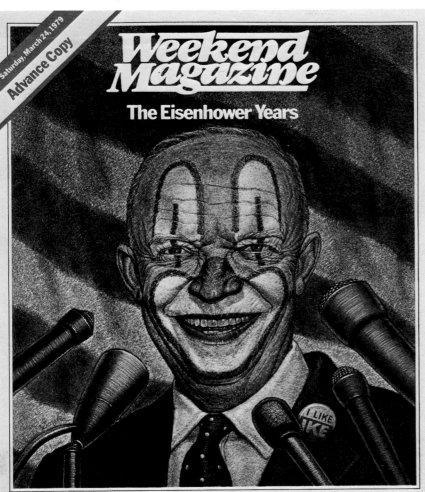

263

Magazine Covers
Zeitschriftenumschläge
Couvertures de périodiques

ARTIST / KÜNSTLER / ARTISTE:

258, 259 Kazumasa Nagai
260 Richard Hess
261 Marvin Rubin
262 Edward Sorel
263 Ed Soyka

DESIGNER / GESTALTER / MAQUETTISTE:

258, 259 Kazumasa Nagai
260 David Franek
262 Ronn Campisi
263 Derek Ungless

ART DIRECTOR / DIRECTEUR ARTISTIQUE:

258, 259 Kazumasa Nagai
260 David Franek
261 Elin Waite
262 Ronn Campisi
263 Robert Priest

AGENCY / AGENTUR / AGENCE – STUDIO:

258, 259 Nippon Design Center
260 Ashton-Worthington, Inc.

PUBLISHER / VERLEGER / EDITEUR:

258, 259 Japan Education Center
260 E.I. DuPont de Nemours & Co.
261 Automobile Club of Southern California
262 Boston Globe Magazine
263 Montreal Standard Publishing Ltd.

258, 259 Covers from a Japanese magazine published by an educational centre. (JPN)
260 Cover from *Context*, the *Du Pont* house organ. The illustration refers to an article about the surfeit of legislation which is stifling America and the much-needed reforms. The illustration is in full colour. (USA)
261 Cover of *Westways*, published by the Californian Automobile Club. This edition is about Irish immigrants. (USA)
262 Cover of the illustrated week-end magazine of the *Boston Globe*. In full colour. (USA)
263 Full-colour cover from *Weekend Magazine* for an article about Eisenhower's presidency. (USA)

258, 259 Titelblätter einer von der japanischen Bildungszentrale herausgegebenen Zeitschrift. (JPN)
260 Titelblatt der von *Du Pont* herausgegebenen Zeitschrift *Context*. Die Illustration bezieht sich auf einen Artikel über die Unmenge von Bestimmungen, die Amerika lahmlegen, und Reformbestrebungen, die überfällig sind. Mehrfarbig. (USA)
261 Umschlag der Zeitschrift *Westways*, die vom kalifornischen Automobilclub herausgegeben wird. Diese Nummer ist den Auswirkungen der irischen Einwanderungswelle in Südkalifornien gewidmet. Die Iren hinterlassen einen grünen Streifen in der sandigen Einöde. (USA)
262 Titelblatt des illustrierten Wochenend-Magazins des *Boston Globe* zu «Sechs Szenenfolgen aus der Präsidentschaftskampagne 1980». Mehrfarbig. (USA)
263 Mehrfarbiges Titelblatt des *Weekend-Magazine* zu einem Artikel über Eisenhowers Präsidentschaft. (USA)

258, 259 Couvertures d'un magazine publié par la centrale japonaise de l'éducation publique. (JPN)
260 Couverture du magazine *Context*, publié régulièrement par *Du Pont*. L'illustration se réfère à un article sur la masse énorme des dispositions qui paralysent les Etats-Unis et les réformes qui sont urgentes. (USA)
261 Couverture du magazine *Westways*, organe officiel du club automobile de Californie. Ce numéro discute les conséquences de l'immigration irlandaise en Californie du Sud. Ces immigrants laissent un trait vert dans la pleine sablonneuse. (USA)
262 Couverture du magazine illustré de fin de semaine du *Boston Globe* se référant à des «Scènes de la campagne électorale présidentielle de 1980». En polychromie. (USA)
263 Couverture polychrome du magazine *Weekend* se rapportant à un article sur la présidence de Eisenhower. (USA)

TV GUIDE
Local Programs Oct. 7-13
35¢

World Series Pitching:
The Perils and Ploys
Page 16

264

TV GUIDE
Local Programs June 24-30

30¢

CAN YOU BELIEVE THE RATINGS?
A new perspective
Page 2

265

TV GUIDE
Local Programs Dec. 23-29
35¢

266

98 Wonderful Cookbooks and How to Read Them
Can John Connally Milk the Electorate? By Joe Klein

ONE DOLLAR   DECEMBER 3, 1979
NEW YORK
Portrait of an Aging Hustler
By Orde Coombs

267

SPECIAL DOUBLE ISSUE

Photography-Contest Winners
Exclusive: Friedkin Talks About 'Cruising'

ONE DOLLAR   AUGUST 13/AUGUST 20, 1979
NEW YORK
THE WOLF IN CENTRAL PARK
AND OTHER TRUE TALES OF NEW YORK

William F. Buckley:
The Criminal Element

Gloria Emerson:
Brief Encounters

David Mamet:
The Animal Kingdom

Truman Capote:
Good Neighbors

Frederic Morton:
Beyond the Fringe

Plus Jessica Mitford,
Gael Greene,
Diana Vreeland,
and More

268

How Russia is Training PLO Terrorists

Special Section: Men's Fall Fashions
New Drug Treatment for Breast Cancer

ONE DOLLAR   SEPTEMBER 24, 1979
NEW YORK
THE TYCOON VANISHES
How Michele Sindona Lost His Fortune in New York, by Nicholas Pileggi

269

ARTIST / KÜNSTLER / ARTISTE:

264 Wilson McLean
265 Jerry Alten/Larry Schafel
266 Ronald Searle
267 Jim McMullan
268 Nina Duran
269 Frank Morris
270 Kiyoshi Awazu

DESIGNER / GESTALTER / MAQUETTISTE:

264—266 Jerry Alten
267—269 Bob Best

ART DIRECTOR / DIRECTEUR ARTISTIQUE:

264—266 Jerry Alten
267—269 Ellen Blissman

PUBLISHER / VERLEGER / EDITEUR:

264—266 Triangle Publications Inc.
267—269 New York Magazine
270 Shokokusha Publishing Co., Inc.

Magazine Covers

264—266 Covers of the television-programme magazine *TV Guide* giving notice of forthcoming programmes: the dangers and tricks employed in baseball, new perspectives in tax assessment, and the Christmas edition. Full-colour illustrations. (USA)
267—269 The cover illustrations from the magazine *New York* refer to the following subjects: a portrait of an ageing swindler, the wolf in Central Park and other genuine stories about New York, and the financial setbacks and ruin suffered by Michele Sindona. The illustrations are in full colour. (USA)
270 Draft for a cover for the magazine *Kenchiku Bunka* painted in poster colours. (JPN)

264—266 Umschläge einer Fernseh-Programmzeitschrift mit Hinweisen auf besprochene Sendungen: Gefahren und Tricks beim Baseballspiel, neue Perspektiven in der Steuereinschätzung und Weihnachtsnummer. Mehrfarbige Illustrationen. (USA)
267—269 Die Titelillustrationen der Zeitschrift *New York* beziehen sich auf folgende Themen: Portrait eines alternden Schwindlers, der Wolf im Central Park und andere wahre Geschichten über New York und der finanzielle Ruin von Michele Sindona. Mehrfarbige Illustrationen. (USA)
270 In Plakatfarben gemalter Umschlagentwurf für die Zeitschrift *Kenchiku Bunka*. (JPN)

264—266 Les illustrations de couverture de ce programme de TV renvoient à des émissions discutées dans les numéros respectifs: dangers et trucs du baseball, nouvelles perspectives concernant l'imposition et numéro de Noël. (USA)
267—269 Couvertures du magazine *New York*. Les illustrations se réfèrent aux sujets suivants: portrait d'un vieux filou, le loup dans le Central Park et d'autres histoires vraies de New York, et la banqueroute de Michele Sindona. Toutes les illustrations sont en couleurs. (USA)
270 Composition de couverture en couleurs affichistes pour le magazine *Kenchiku Bunka*. (JPN)

Magazine Covers
Zeitschriftenumschläge
Couvertures de périodiques

ARTIST / KÜNSTLER / ARTISTE:

271, 274, 275 Mark Hess
272, 273 Béat Brüsch

DESIGNER / GESTALTER / MAQUETTISTE:

272, 273 Béat Brüsch/Robert Zuber
274, 275 Louise Kollenbaum

ART DIRECTOR / DIRECTEUR ARTISTIQUE:

271 Everett Halvorson
272, 273 J.-D. Roullier
274, 275 Louise Kollenbaum

PUBLISHER / VERLEGER / EDITEUR:

271 Forbes Inc.
272, 273 Radio-TV
274, 275 Mother Jones

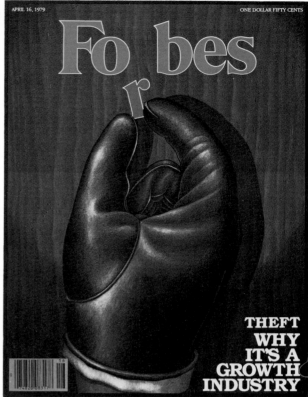

271

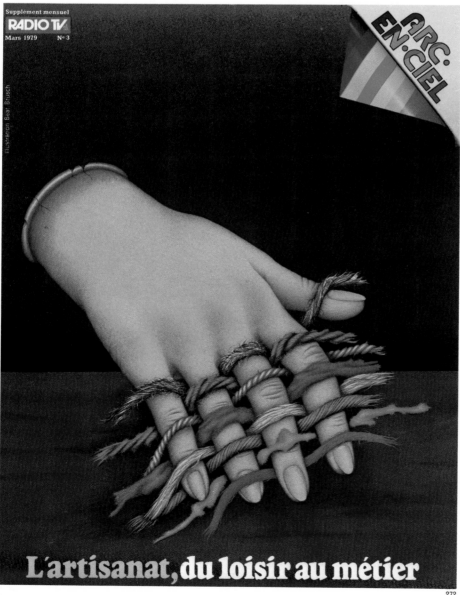

272

273

271 This cover illustration from an edition of *Forbes* magazine refers to a leading article dealing with the question of why stealing has nowadays become a flourishing industry. The glove is in black, the board in brown, and the title in yellow. (USA)
272, 273 Cover from the magazine *Arc-en-ciel* which is included once a month in a television-programme magazine as a supplement. Fig. 272: "How leisure-time craftsmanship can become a profession"; Fig. 273: "Swiss Cheese"—yellow cheese with green Alpine countryside and snow-covered mountains conjuring up the essence of Switzerland. (SWI)
274, 275 The cover of *Mother Jones* shows Connally as an old rooster. (USA)

274

275

271 Dieses Titelbild einer Ausgabe der Zeitschrift *Forbes* bezieht sich auf den Leitartikel, der sich mit der Frage auseinandersetzt, warum Diebstahl heute zu einer «blühenden Industrie» geworden ist. Schwarzer Handschuh, braunes Brett, gelber Titel. (USA)
272, 273 Titelblätter der Zeitschrift *Arc-en-ciel*, die einmal monatlich der Radio- und Fernsehprogrammzeitschrift beigelegt wird. Abb. 272: «Kunsthandwerk, von der Freizeitbeschäftigung zum Beruf»; Abb. 273: «Schweizer Käse» – gelber Käse mit grüner Alplandschaft und Schneebergen. (SWI)
274, 275 Die Umschlagillustration zeigt den alten Hahn Connally, der sich nach einer neuen Brutstätte umschaut. (USA)

271 Cette couverture d'un numéro du magazine *Forbes* se rapporte à l'éditorial qui traite la question du vol qui est devenu aujourd'hui, semble-t-il, une «industrie assez florissante». Gant noir, planche brune, en-tête du magazine en jaune. (USA)
272, 273 Deux couvertures du magazine *Arc-en-ciel*, qui est distribué une fois par mois avec le magazine *Radio-TV «Je vois tout»*. La fig. 272 se réfère à un article qui aborde le problème de l'artisanat qui devient de plus en plus un vrai métier; fig. 273: fromage avec paysage alpestre évoquant la Suisse. (SWI)
274, 275 Cette illustration de couverture montre le vieux coq Connally qui cherche un nouvel endroit de couvaison. (USA)

276, 277, 279 Cover of the French news-magazine *L'Express*: the English electro shock—Prime Minister Margaret Thatcher is taking up office, and the Red Army as a superpower symbolized by the Moscow bear. Fig. 279 is in actual size. (FRA)
278 *Scope*, a magazine by the *Japan Upjohn* chemical company. In shades of blue and green. (JPN)
280, 281 *Saturday Review—The Romance of Ships*. Illustration in actual size. (USA)

276, 277, 279 Titelbilder des französischen Nachrichtenmagazins *L'Express*: Der englische Elektroschock – zum Amtsantritt der Premierministerin Thatcher und Die Rote Armee als Supermacht, symbolisiert durch den Moskauer Bären. Abb. 279 in Originalgrösse. (FRA)
278 Von einer chemischen Fabrik herausgegebene Zeitschrift. In Blau- und Grüntönen. (JPN)
280, 281 «Die Romantik der Hochseedampfer.» Titelillustration (Originalgrösse) auf Grün. (USA)

276, 277, 279 Illustrations de couvertures de *L'Express,* magazine d'information français. Fig. 276, 277: analyse de la situation politique en Angleterre après l'élection de Margaret Thatcher; fig. 279: l'ours moscovite symbolise la superpuissance de l'Armée Rouge. (FRA)
278 Couverture d'un magazine publié par une entreprise de produits chimiques. (JPN)
280, 281 Illustration de Cassandre (en grandeur originale) évoquant les voyages romantiques à bord des grands paquebots. (USA)

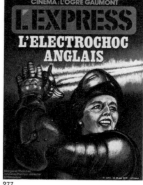

277

276

112

278

ARTIST / KÜNSTLER / ARTISTE:

276, 277 Cyril Arnstam
278 Yoji Kuri
279 Ch. Broutin
280, 281 Cassandre

ART DIRECTOR / DIRECTEUR ARTISTIQUE:

276, 277, 279 Georges Lacroix
280, 281 Bryan Canniff

PUBLISHER / VERLEGER / EDITEUR:

276, 277, 279 Express-Union
278 Nippon Upjohn Ltd.
280, 281 Saturday Review

281

279

280

Magazine Covers
Zeitschriftenumschläge
Couvertures de périodiques

282

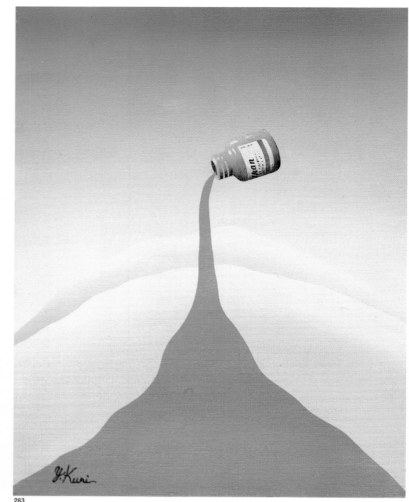

283

284

285

Magazine Covers

ARTIST / KÜNSTLER:

282–287 Yoji Kuri

ART DIRECTOR:

282–285 Sumio Yamashita
286, 287 Yoji Kuri

PUBLISHER / VERLEGER:

282–285 Nippon Upjohn Ltd.
286, 287 Sendai Electronic
College

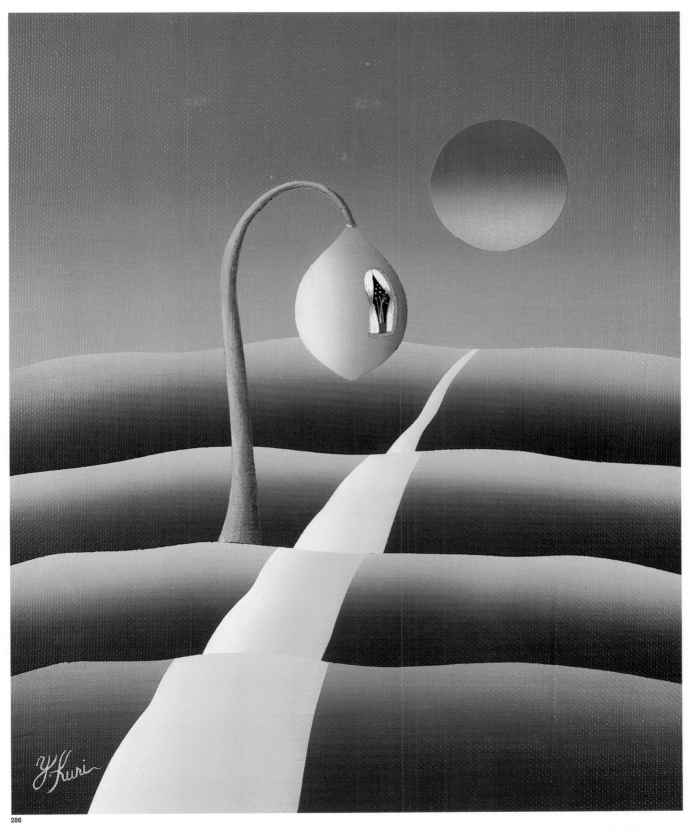

286

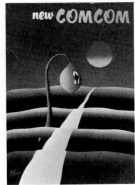

287

282–285 Examples from a series of designs for covers for the magazine *Scope*, published by the *Japan Upjohn* chemical company. (JPN)
286, 287 Illustration in actual size and complete cover of the magazine *New Com Com*, published by the Sendai Electronics College. (JPN)

282–285 Beispiele aus einer Serie von Umschlagentwürfen, für die von der chemischen Fabrik *Japan Upjohn* herausgegebenen Zeitschrift *Scope*. (JPN)
286, 287 Illustration in Originalgrösse und vollständiger Umschlag der Zeitschrift *New Com Com*, die von einer Hochschule für Computerfachleute herausgegeben wird. (JPN)

282–285 Série de compositions de couverture pour le magazine *Scope* publié par *Japan Upjohn*, fabrique de produits chimiques. (JPN)
286, 287 Illustration (en grandeur nature) et couverture complète du magazine *New Com Com*, qu'une école supérieure d'électronique et d'informatique publie. (JPN)

Magazine Covers
Zeitschriftenumschläge
Couvertures de périodiques

ARTIST / KÜNSTLER / ARTISTE:

289 Robert Pryor
290 Morteza Momayez
291 Joan Miró
293 Grzegorz Stanczyk
294, 295 Brad Holland

DESIGNER / GESTALTER / MAQUETTISTE:

288 Ettore Vitale
290 Morteza Momayez

ART DIRECTOR / DIRECTEUR ARTISTIQUE:

288 Ettore Vitale
290 Morteza Momayez
291, 292 Joceleyn Kargère
294, 295 Walter Bernard/Rudolph Hoglund

AGENCY / AGENTUR / AGENCE – STUDIO:

288 Studio Vitale
290 Morteza Momayez

288

289

291

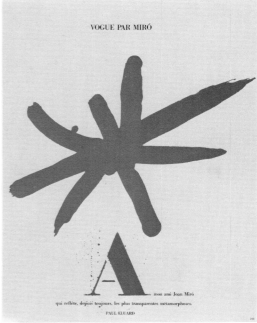

292

PUBLISHER / VERLEGER / EDITEUR:

288 Pace e Guerra
289 The Pennsylvania Gazette
290 Roudaki Magazine
291, 292 Condé Nast S.A.
293 Szpilki
294, 295 Time, Inc.

288 Cover of the first edition of the magazine *Pace e Guerra* (Peace and War). The symbol, which illustrates the opposite meanings of the terms, was printed large here as a sort of introduction, to appear in reduced size next to the title in later editions. Title in red and black. (ITA)

289 *The Pennsylvania Gazette*: the cover illustration of this edition refers to an article about a Supreme Court judge. In black and white with the title in dark red. (USA)

290 Cover illustration in brown and white on ochre from *Roudaki*, a cultural magazine. (IRN)

291, 292 Cover and inside spread from an edition of *Vogue* magazine, with a 32-page report on Mirò. Fig. 292: blue on white with a quotation by Paul Eluard. (FRA)

293 Cover illustration from the satirical magazine *Szpilki*. In various shades of green. (POL)

294, 295 Illustration and complete cover from an issue of *Time* magazine devoted to Ayatullah Khomeini, the man of the year. Illustration in dark shades. (USA)

290

294

293

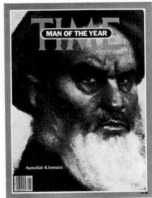

295

288 Titelblatt der ersten Ausgabe der Zeitschrift «Frieden und Krieg». Das Symbol, das die die Gegensätzlichkeit dieser beiden Begriffe aufzeigen soll, wurde hier zur Einführung gross wiedergegeben, wird aber bei spätern Nummern neben dem Titel erscheinen. Titel in Rot und Schwarz. (ITA)
289 Die Umschlagillustration dieser Zeitschrift bezieht sich auf einen Artikel über einen Richter des Obersten Gerichtshofes. Schwarzweiss, Titel in Dunkelrot. (USA)
290 Titelbild (in Braun und Weiss auf Ocker) des Kulturmagazins *Roudaki*. (IRN)
291, 292 Umschlag und Innenseite einer Ausgabe von *Vogue* mit einem 32seitigen Beitrag über Mirò. Abb. 292: Blau auf Weiss, mit einem Zitat von Paul Eluard. (FRA)
293 Titelblatt der satirischen Zeitschrift *Szpilki*. In verschiedenen Grüntönen. (POL)
294, 295 Illustration und vollständiger Umschlag einer Ausgabe des Nachrichtenmagazins *Time* zu einem Artikel über Ayatollah Khomeini. Illustration in dunklen Farbtönen. (USA)

288 Couverture du premier numéro du magazine *Pace e Guerra* (Paix et Guerre) dont le symbole fait évidence de la divergence de ces deux notions. C'était pour introduire ce magazine que le symbole a été reproduit en grand, pour les prochains numéros il sera intégré dans l'en-tête en rouge et noir. (ITA)
289 L'illustration de couverture de ce magazine se réfère à un article qui traite d'un juge de la Cour suprême. En noir-blanc, en-tête en rouge foncé. (USA)
290 Couverture (en brun et blanc sur fond ocre) du magazine culturel *Roudaki*. (IRN)
291, 292 Couverture et page intérieure d'un numéro de *Vogue* contenant un supplément de 32 pages consacré à Mirò. Fig. 292: bleu sur blanc, avec une citation de Paul Eluard. (FRA)
293 Couverture du magazine satirique *Szpilki*. Illustration en divers tons verts. (POL)
294, 295 Illustration et couverture correspondante du magazine d'information *Time* se référant à un article sur l'imam Khomeiny. Illustration en tons foncés. (USA)

FLIGHT OF THE DRAGON

A bold confirmation of bestial evolution

BY PETER DICKINSON

There are three possible views about winged, fire-breathing dragons: (1) They are completely legendary; (2) they are largely legendary but contain elements based on fantasized accounts of real animals; (3) they really existed.

I take the third view.

I don't intend to prove that 27-meter lizards once floated in the skies of Earth and scorched whole villages with plumes of flame, because I don't think that can be proved. And I don't think it possible that fossil remains of a true dragon will ever be found. Moreover, it is unlikely that cave paintings showing tribal heroes of the Stone Age battling this ferocious enemy will ever come to light. But I can present a coherent theory at least as probable as the theory that dragons are completely legendary.

One cannot infer a possible mechanism by which dragons could have breathed fire, another by which they could have flown, and another to account for the supposed magical nature of dragon's blood, without focusing on the principal dynamic of animal evolution: The life form a species

PAINTINGS BY
WAYNE ANDERSON

296

ARTIST / KÜNSTLER / ARTISTE:

296 Wayne Anderson
297, 298 John Schoenherr
299 Wayne McLoughlin

ART DIRECTOR / DIRECTEUR ARTISTIQUE:
296–299 Frank DeVino

PUBLISHER / VERLEGER / EDITEUR:
296–299 Omni International Ltd.

297

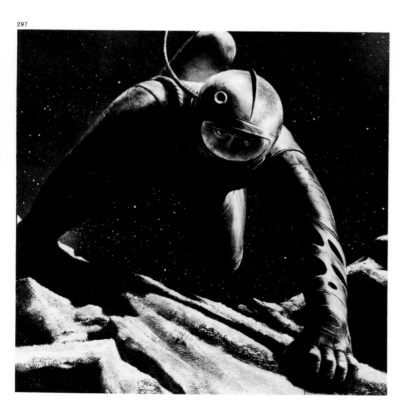

298

296–299 Double spreads and full-page illustration from *Omni*, the magazine of tomorrow. Fig. 296: *Flight of the Dragon*—A bold confirmation of bestial evolution; Figs. 297, 298: illustration from a chapter of the science-fiction novel *Kinsman* in which an astronaut is insulted by officers on board a spaceship; Fig. 299: this illustration introduces an article entitled *Life in Darwin's Universe*. (USA)

296–299 Doppelseiten und ganzseitige Illustrationen aus *Omni*, der Zeitschrift für morgen. Abb. 296: einführende Doppelseite zu einem Artikel mit dem Titel «Der Flug des Drachens», in welchem der Autor beweisen will, dass feuerspeiende Drachen existierten. Abb. 297, 298: Illustration zu einem Auszug aus dem Fiction-Roman *Kinsman*, der von einem Astronauten handelt, der von Offizieren der Raumstation gedemütigt wurde. Abb. 299: diese Illustration leitet einen Artikel über das Leben in Darwins Universum ein. (USA)

296–299 Pages doubles et illustration pleine page du magazine futurologique *Omni*. Fig. 296: première page double d'un article intitulé «Le vol du dragon» – l'auteur cherche à prouver l'existence des dragons crachant du feu; fig. 297, 298: illustration accompagnant un extrait du roman de fiction *Kinsman*, traitant d'un astronaute humilié par les officiers d'un navire spacial; fig. 299: cette illustration introduit un article analysant la vie dans l'univers de Darwin. Toutes les illustrations sont en couleurs. (USA)

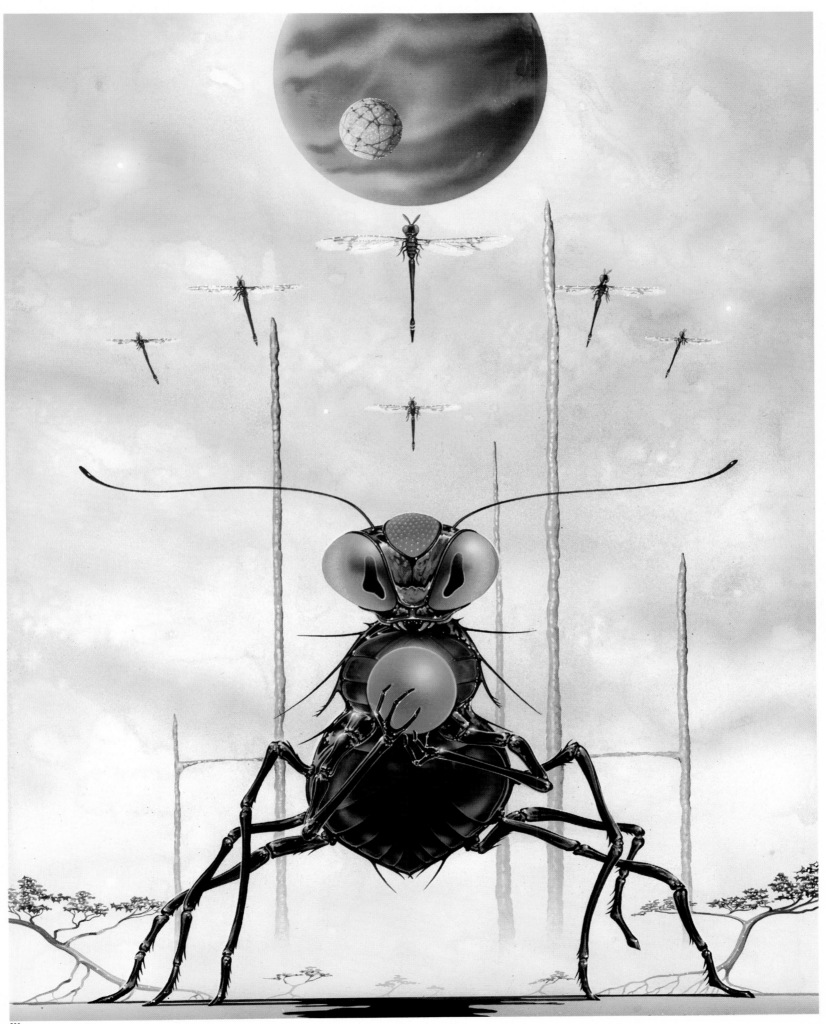

303

MICHAEL FOREMAN'S LONDON CLUBS: 3

The Judge Jeffreys Bar at the Wig and Pen Club, opposite the Law Courts.

29

301

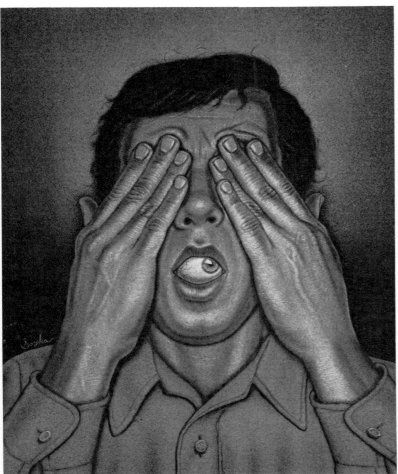

302

ARTIST / KÜNSTLER / ARTISTE:

300, 301 Michael Foreman
302 Ed Soyka
303 Zélio Alves Pinto

DESIGNER / GESTALTER / MAQUETTISTE:

302 Derek Ungless

ART DIRECTOR / DIRECTEUR ARTISTIQUE:

300, 301 Adrianne Leman
302 Robert Priest
303 Cida Junqeira

PUBLISHER / VERLEGER / EDITEUR:

300, 301 The Illustrated London News
302 Montreal Standard Publishing Ltd.
303 Revue Nova

300, 301 Examples from a series about London clubs, published in
The Illustrated London News. (GBR)
302 Full-page illustration in full colour for a short story published
in *Weekend Magazine* about three people who investigated rumours
about UFOs having been sighted in Ontario. (USA)
303 Illustration for an article about men's indiscretions. Mainly in
light blue, pink and yellow. (BRA)

300, 301 Beispiele aus einer in der Zeitschrift *The Illustrated London
News* publizierten Serie über Londoner Clubs, hier den City Golf
Club und die Bar des Richters Jeffrey. (GBR)
302 Ganzseitige illustration zu einer Kurzgeschichte über die Aben-
teuer von drei Personen, die Gerüchten nachspürten, wonach in
Ontario Ufos gesichtet worden waren. Mehrfarbig. (USA)
303 Illustration zu einem Artikel über die Indiskretion der Männer.
Vorwiegend in Hellblau, Rosa und Gelb gehalten. (BRA)

300, 301 Exemples d'une série de peintures de clubs londoniens,
parues dans le magazine *The Illustrated London News*; on voit ici le
City Golf Club et le bar du juge Jeffrey. (GBR)
302 Illustration pleine page accompagnant un récit sur les aventures de trois personnes en quête des soucoupes volantes que des
habitants de l'Ontario auraient aperçues. En polychromie. (USA)
303 Illustration pour un article sur l'indiscretion des hommes. Prédominance de tons bleu clair, roses et jaunes. (BRA)

304

305

306

Magazine Covers
Zeitschriftenumschläge
Couvertures de périodiques

ARTIST / KÜNSTLER / ARTISTE:

304 Taki Ono/Lisa Powers
305 Joe Saffold
306 Ignacio Gomez
307 Sue Coe

DESIGNER / GESTALTER / MAQUETTISTE:

304–306 Michael Brock
307 Derek Ungless

ART DIRECTOR / DIRECTEUR ARTISTIQUE:

304–306 Michael Brock
307 Robert Priest

PUBLISHER / VERLEGER / EDITEUR:

304–306 Playboy Enterprises, Inc.
307 Montreal Standard Publishing Ltd.

304–306 Double spreads from *Oui* magazine. Fig. 304: this article explains how important a kiss is in the relationship between a man and a woman; Fig. 305: here the phenomenon of supernatural psychic power is discussed; Fig. 306: the layman is shown how his money can escape the taxman's clutches—no matter which way the money has been earned. All illustrations are in full colour. (USA)
307 Illustration for an article in *Weekend Magazine* about international terrorism. The illustration shows Carlos in one of his many "hideaway" hotel rooms. (USA)

304–306 Doppelseiten aus der Zeitschrift *Oui*. Abb. 304: dieser Artikel erklärt, wie wichtig der Kuss in der Beziehung zwischen Mann und Frau ist; Abb. 305: hier wird das Phänomen übernatürlicher psychischer Kräfte diskutiert; Abb. 306: der Laie wird darüber aufgeklärt, wie er sein gut-, oder schlechtverdientes Geld dem Zugriff der Steuerbehörden entziehen kann. Alle Illustrationen sind mehrfarbig. (USA)
307 Illustration zu einem in der Zeitschrift *Weekend Magazine* erschienenen Artikel über den internationalen Terrorismus. Sie zeigt Carlos in einem Hotelzimmer. (USA)

304–306 Pages doubles extraites du magazine *Oui*. Fig. 304 explique l'importance du baiser dans les relations entre l'homme et la femme; fig. 305: on discute ici le phénomène du pouvoir surnaturel; fig. 306: on instruit ici les gens mal informés comment ils peuvent éviter la mainmise de l'administration fiscale sur leur argent bien ou mal gagné. Toutes les illustrations sont en polychromie. (USA)
307 Cette illustration, tirée du magazine *Weekend*, accompagne un article sur le terrorisme international. On voit ici le terroriste Carlos dans une chambre d'hôtel. (USA)

Carlos the jackal

Paris: 15 September 1974

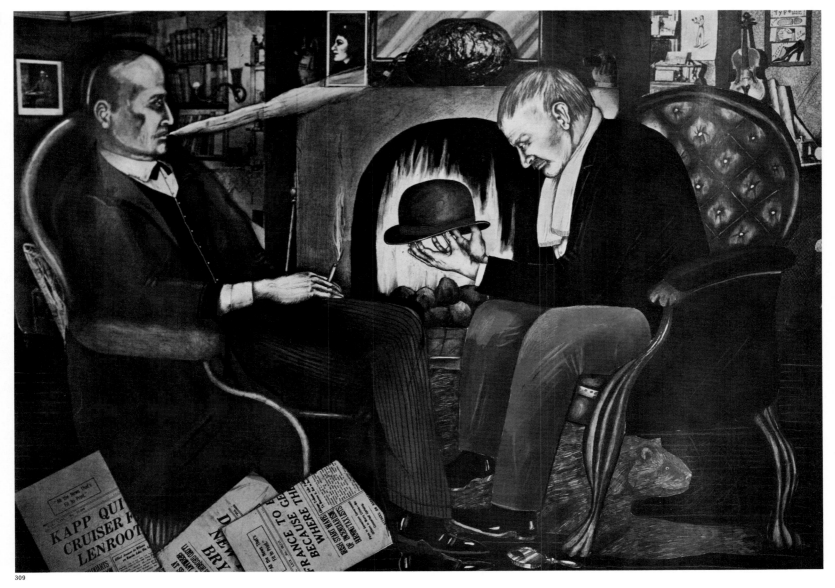

309

308 Full-page illustration in actual size from an article entitled *The Nightmare of Hugh Rivers, Jr.* The illustration and article appeared in *New Times* and tell the story of Hugh Rivers who, in his madness, thought that the President was trying to kill him, but who in reality had almost been ruined by psychiatric treatment. (USA)
309 Unpublished illustration for a Sherlock Holmes story. (USA)
310 Double-spread illustration in black and white from an article about how one can obtain a divorce while still remaining on friendly terms with one's former partner. The article was published in *Marie-Clair* and served as introductory information to a new mutual-agreement divorce law in France. (FRA)

308 Ganzseitige Illustration (in Originalgrösse), die einen Artikel mit dem Titel «Der Alptraum des Hugh Rivers, Jr.» einleitet, der in seinem Wahn glaubte, der Präsident wolle ihn umbringen, in Tat und Wahrheit aber an der psychiatrischen Behandlung beinahe zugrunde ging. Aus *New Times*. (USA)
309 Unveröffentlichte Illustration zu einer Sherlock-Holmes-Geschichte («Der blaue Karfunkel»). (USA)
310 Doppelseitige Illustration (in Schwarzweiss) zu einem Artikel mit dem Titel «Wie man sich auf freundliche Weise scheiden lassen kann». Es geht dabei um die Einführung eines neuen Gesetzes in Frankreich, das die Konventionalscheidung erlaubt. Aus der Zeitschrift *Marie-Clair*. (FRA)

308 Illustration pleine page (en grandeur nature) qui introduit un article intitulé «Le Cauchemar de Hugh Rivers, Jr.». Celui-ci a vécu dans l'illusion que le président aurait l'intention de le tuer, mais en réalité il a failli d'être «tuer» par le traitement psychiatrique qu'il a dû subir. (USA)
309 Illustration inédite qui a été réalisée pour le récit *The Blue Carbuncle* (L'Escarboucle bleue) mettant en scène le fameux Sherlock Holmes. (USA)
310 Illustration sur page double (en noir et blanc) accompagnant un article du magazine *Marie-Clair*, intitulé *Comment réussir un divorce à l'amiable*. Il traite d'une nouvelle loi permettant le divorce par consentement mutuel. (FRA)

ARTIST / KÜNSTLER / ARTISTE:

308, 309 Sue Coe
310 Cyril Arnstam

ART DIRECTOR / DIRECTEUR ARTISTIQUE:

308 Richard Becker
310 Dominique Pennors

PUBLISHER / VERLEGER / EDITEUR:

308 New Times Publishing Co.
310 Marie-Claire

Magazine Illustrations

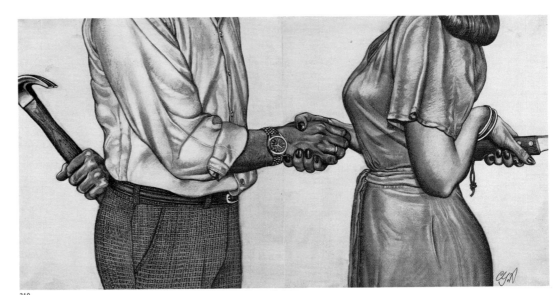

310

311

312

311–315 Double spreads and illustrations from the week-end supplement of the *Boston Globe*. Fig. 311: an introductory black-and-white spread for a short story; Fig. 312: full-colour illustration for a report about men and women in a transitory phase of life; Fig. 313: a red heart in front of a green tiled wall for an article about a contact centre for divorcees; Fig. 314: full-colour illustration for an investigation on brutality in films and Fig. 315 is an illustration in subdued colours for a novel. (USA)
316 Illustration in shades of grey and brown for a grandmother Teresa story published in *Attenzione Magazine*. (USA)
317, 318 "Mirror of my longings, who is the fairest prophet in the kingdom?"—article on the predictions made by sociologists and economists; "The signature"—article on political and other calls signed by Italian intellectuals. (ITA)

311–315 Doppelseiten und Illustrationen aus der Wochenend-Beilage des *Boston Globe*. Abb. 311: einleitende Doppelseite zu einer Kurzgeschichte (Schwarzweiss); Abb. 312: Mehrfarbige Illustration zu einem Bericht über Männer und Frauen in einer Übergangssituation; Abb. 313: rotes Herz vor grüngekachelter Wand zu einem Artikel über ein Begegnungszentrum für Geschiedene; Abb. 314: Farbillustration zu einer Untersuchung über die Brutalität im Film; Abb. 315: Illustration in matten Farben zu einem Fiction-Roman. (USA)
316 Illustration in Grau- und Brauntönen zu einer Geschichte über die Grossmutter Teresa. (USA)
317, 318 «Spiegel meiner Sehnsüchte, wer ist der schönste Prophet im Königreich?» – über die Voraussagen von Soziologen und Wirtschaftswissenschaftern; «Die Unterzeichnung» – über die Aufrufe die von italienischen Intellektuellen unterzeichnet wurden. (ITA)

311–315 Pages doubles et illustrations du magazine de fin de semaine du *Boston Globe*. Fig. 311: page double introduisant un récit (noir-blanc); fig. 312: illustration polychrome accompagnant une analyse sur la période de transition dans laquelle se trouvent les hommes et les femmes; fig. 313: rapport sur un centre de communication pour les divorcés (cœur rouge sur fond vert); fig. 314: enquête sur la brutalité dans les films (en couleurs); fig. 315: illustration accompagnant un roman. (USA)
316 L'illustration présente la grand-mère Teresa dont se souvient l'auteur de cette histoire. En tons bruns et gris. (USA)
317, 318 Sur les prévisions faites par les sociologues et économistes – ils consultent le miroire afin qu'il désigne le plus beau prophète du royaume; «La signature» – article sur les appels signés par les intellectuels italiens. (ITA)

315

316

314

313

ARTIST / KÜNSTLER / ARTISTE:

311, 315 Mel Williges
312 Mark Fisher
313 Charles Waller
314 Renée Klein
316 Nancy Stahl
317, 318 Tullio Pericoli

DESIGNER / GESTALTER / MAQUETTISTE:

311–315 Ronn Campisi
316 Miles Abernethy

ART DIRECTOR / DIRECTEUR ARTISTIQUE:

311–315 Ronn Campisi
316 Paul Hardy

PUBLISHER / VERLEGER / EDITEUR:

311–315 The Boston Globe
316 Attenzione Magazine
317, 318 L'Espresso

317

318

ARTIST / KÜNSTLER / ARTISTE:

319–322 Walter Grieder
323 Blair Drawson
324 Cathy Hull

319

320

DESIGNER / GESTALTER / MAQUETTISTE:

323 Rod Della Vedova
324 Rostislav Eismont

ART DIRECTOR / DIRECTEUR ARTISTIQUE:

319–322 Hans-Peter Platz/Gérard Wirtz
323 George Haroutiun
324 Rostislav Eismont

PUBLISHER / VERLEGER / EDITEUR:

319–322 Basler Zeitung
323 Comac Communications Ltd.
324 Chief Executive Magazine, Inc.

321

Traumlast

Kieve

322

319, 320, 322 From Walter Grieder's sketch-book: full-colour illustrations entitled "The Scream", "Frustrated Woman" and "Dream Burden". From the magazine of the *Basler-Zeitung*. (SWI)
321 "Fear in our Times." From an article about fear in the *Basler-Zeitung* magazine. (SWI)
323 From *Homemaker's Magazine*: children and wisdom. In shades of blue and green. (USA)
324 Double spread from a quarterly magazine for managers and executives called *Chief Executive*. The article is about Keynesian economic theories and their present-day validity. (USA)

319, 320, 322 Aus Walter Grieders Skizzenbuch: Farbillustrationen zu den Themen *Der Schrei*, *Femme frustrée* und *Traumlast*. Aus der Wochenend-Beilage der *Basler-Zeitung*. (SWI)
321 *Die Angst in unserer Zeit.* Zu einem Artikel über die Angst im Magazin der *Basler-Zeitung*. (SWI)
323 Was man den Kindern an Weisheiten mitgeben sollte. In Blau- und Grüntönen. (USA)
324 Doppelseite aus einer vierteljährlich erscheinenden Zeitschrift für Geschäftsleiter. (USA)

319, 320, 322 Illustrations couleur extraites de l'album d'esquisses de Walter Grieder publiée dans le supplément week-end d'un quotidien bâlois. Elles illustrent les sujets suivants: «Le cris», la «Femme frustrée» et le «Poids des rêves». (SWI)
321 Pour un article sur l'angoisse dans le supplément week-end d'un quotidien bâlois. (SWI)
323 Quelles sont les connaissances dont un enfant a besoin pour sa vie? (USA)
324 Page double d'une revue trimestrielle destinée aux chefs d'entreprise. (USA)

323

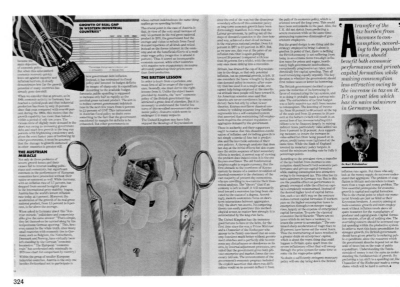

324

Magazine Illustrations
Zeitschriften-Illustrationen
Illustrations de périodiques

ARTIST / KÜNSTLER / ARTISTE:

325, 326 Milton Glaser
327 Michael Foreman
328 Robert Pryor
329 Folon
330, 331 James Marsh

ART DIRECTOR / DIRECTEUR ARTISTIQUE:

325–329 Jerry Alten
330, 331 Roger Gould

PUBLISHER / VERLEGER / EDITEUR:

325–329 Triangle Publications, Inc.
330, 331 Telegraph Sunday Magazine

ARTIST / KÜNSTLER / ARTISTE:

332 Jerzy Flisak
333 Jacqui Morgan
334 Geoffrey Moss
335 Yoji Kuri
336, 337 Etienne Delessert
338 Marguerita

325–329 Double spreads and illustrations from the television-programme magazine *TV Guide*. Figs. 325, 326: adapting Shakespeare's plays for television; Fig. 327: an article about an examination made about television being mainly a medium for the ear; Fig. 328: about the machinations and intrigues in connection with the film *Edward the King*; Fig. 329: the competition within TV management. Full-colour illustrations. (USA)
330, 331 An amusing and thoughtful article in the *Telegraph Sunday Magazine* about first impressions of the female body. (GBR)

325–329 Doppelseiten und Illustrationen aus einer Fernseh-Programm-zeitschrift. Abb. 325, 326: über die Inszenierung von Shakespeare-Stücken fürs Fernsehen; Abb. 327: zu einer Untersuchung über das Fernsehen als vorwiegend fürs Ohr bestimmtes Medium; Abb. 328: über die Machen-schaften im Zusammenhang mit dem Film *Edward the King*; Abb. 329: über den Konkurrenzkampf im TV-Management. In Farbe. (USA)
330, 331 Der Autor beschreibt in diesem Artikel seine ersten Vorstellun-gen über den weiblichen Körper, die er sich anhand von Versandkatalo-gen machte. Aus dem *Telegraph Sunday Magazine*. (GBR)

325–329 Pages doubles et illustrations d'un programme des émissions télévisées. Fig. 325, 326: la mise en scène des drames de Shakespeare pour la TV; fig. 327: enquête sur la télévision étant en premier lieu un médium pour écouter; fig. 328: article sur les machinations pour faire réussir la diffusion du film *Edward the King*; fig. 329: cet article est con-sacré à la concurrence dans le management des stations de TV. Toutes les illustrations sont en couleurs. (USA)
330, 331 L'auteur décrit ici les premières idées qu'il s'est faites du corps féminin en feuilletant des catalogues de maisons de modes. (USA)

325

326

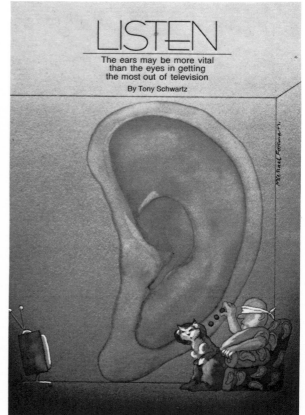

327

330

HOW THE MIGHTY HAVE FALLEN—*FAST*

It's the rare network executive who can remain at the top very long in today's hectic competition

By John Mariani

In Dan Jenkins' and Edwin Shrake's novel "Limo," a fantasy satire on the television industry, a fictional network president bemoans his job, saying, "It's lonely at the top but no one has to stay long." In fact, the stresses and strains on top-level TV management are worse than in most companies. Although some network executives may draw six-figure salaries, command limousines, hobnob with the stars and possess tremendous power to influence what we all watch, it is lonely and they don't often stay in such jobs long enough to enjoy all the glamour. For instance:

☐ In the last four years, CBS Sports has had four different heads, and one of them served in that position twice.

☐ CBS patriarch William Paley overrode his own retirement, fired the man chosen to succeed him (Arthur Taylor), and installed John Backe as chief executive but retained his chairmanship of the board.

☐ In 1976, longtime CBS president Robert Wood resigned, saying he could no longer endure the pressures of the job and vowed, "There is absolutely no way anybody will ever get me back into a network job."

☐ In 1975 at NBC, program chief Larry White resigned and was replaced by Marvin Antonowsky. He was fired nine months later, replaced at first by Paul Klein and Irwin Segelstein and later by Klein alone.

☐ Herb Schlosser, the NBC president who is given credit for such hits as *Tomorrow* and *Saturday Night Live*, signed Gerald Ford and Henry Kissinger to contracts and garnered rights to the 1980 Summer Olympics for his network, was fired last January after NBC hired Fred Silverman, the programming wizard who had previously helped boost CBS and then ABC to hit seasons. (Schlosser has accepted an executive vice presidency of RCA, NBC's parent company.)

☐ At ABC, vice president Barry Diller resigned in 1974 just before the network suffered a disastrous season. Soon after, programmer Marty Starger resigned. A year later Mike Eisner, who developed hits like *Happy Days* and *Roots* for ABC, resigned to become an executive at a movie studio.

☐ When ABC News president Bill Sheehan failed to boost ratings even after hiring Barbara Walters away from NBC, he was demoted to senior vice president of News; and Sports executive Roone Arledge was made News president. →

2

3

332 Caricature from the satirical magazine *Szpilki* from a report about small change. (POL)
333 First page of the entertainment supplement of the *New York Times* with gourmet recipes. (USA)
334 *Pensman*—from an article in the *Washington Post* on the power of the press. (USA)
335 Illustration on the theme "Fields". (JPN)
336, 337 Full-colour interpretations of parts of the Bible: here when Jesus cried at Lazarus' grave (red face, blue sky) and when he healed the blind (Ray Charles, the composer and pianist, who has been blind since seven years of age, shown here in shades of brown). From a regular feature appearing in the youth magazine *Okapi*. (FRA)
338 From *Print Magazine*—Women as advertised—the female image in TV commercials. (USA)

332 Karikatur aus der satirischen Zeitschrift *Szpilki* zu einem Bericht über Kleingeld. (POL)
333 Erste Seite der Unterhaltungs-Beilage der *New York Times*, hier mit Schlemmerrezepten. (USA)
334 «Der Schreiberling.» Zu einem Artikel über die Macht der Presse. (USA)
335 Illustration zum Thema «Felder». (JPN)
336, 337 Mehrfarbige Interpretationen zu Bibelstellen: hier als Jesus am Grab des Lazarus weinte (rotes Gesicht, blauer Himmel) und als er die Blinden wieder sehen machte (hier der Pianist und Komponist Ray Charles, der seit dem 7. Altersjahr blind ist – in Brauntönen). Aus einer regelmässig erscheinenden Rubrik in der Jugendzeitschrift *Okapi*. (FRA)
338 Karikatur zu einem Artikel über die Darstellung der Frau in Fernsehspots. (USA)

332 Caricature du magazine satirique *Szpilki* pour un rapport sur la monnaie. (POL)
333 Première page du supplément «Loisirs» avec des recettes pour les bons vivants. (USA)
334 «L'Homme de la plume.» Cet article traite de la puissance de la presse. (USA)
335 Composition au sujet des «Champs». (JPN)
336, 337 L'artiste interprète ici des extraits de la Bible, ici Jésu qui pleure à la tombe de Lazare (visage rouge, ciel bleu) et lorsqu'il a rendu la vue aux aveugles (le pianiste et compositeur Ray Charles est aveugle depuis l'âge de sept ans – en tons bruns). Extraits d'une rubrique qui paraît régulièrement dans le magazine pour les jeunes *Okapi*. (FRA)
338 Caricature accompagnant un article sur la femme dans les spots télévisés. (USA)

ART DIRECTOR / DIRECTEUR ARTISTIQUE:

333 Jerelle Kraus
334 Geoffrey Moss
338 Andrew Kner

332

335

333

334

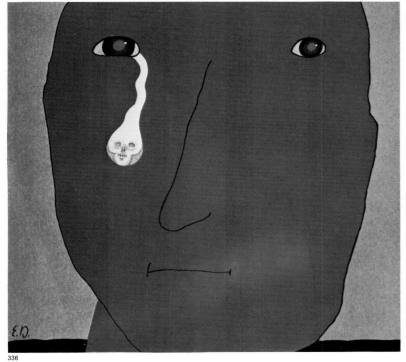

336

337

ARTIST / KÜNSTLER / ARTISTE:

332 Jerzy Flisak
333 Jacqui Morgan
334 Geoffrey Moss
335 Yoji Kuri
336, 337 Etienne Delessert
338 Marguerita

PUBLISHER / VERLEGER / EDITEUR:

332 Szpilki
333 The New York Times
334 Washington Post
335 Nippon Upjohn Ltd.
336, 337 Bayard Presse
338 RC Publications

Magazine Illustrations

338

339

ARTIST / KÜNSTLER / ARTISTE:

339, 342, 343 James Marsh
340, 341 Robert Pryor

ART DIRECTOR / DIRECTEUR ARTISTIQUE:

339 Roger Gould
340, 341 Jerry Alten
342, 343 Geoff Axbey

PUBLISHER / VERLEGER / EDITEUR:

339, 342, 343 Telegraph Sunday Magazine
340, 341 Triangle Publications, Inc.

339 Full-colour illustration from the week-end magazine of the *Sunday Telegraph* referring to an article about smoked fish. (GBR)
340, 341 Illustration and page from *TV Guide*: the former basketball player Bill Russell will discuss various themes on television. (USA)
342, 343 Complete page and full-colour illustration from the *Telegraph Sunday Magazine* from an article about the meaning and origin of certain words. (GBR)

339 Mehrfarbige Illustration aus dem Wochenendmagazin des *Sunday Telegraph* zu einem Artike über geräuchte Fische. (GBR)
340, 341 Illustration und Seite aus einer Fernsehprogrammzeitschrift: der ehemalige Basketball-spieler Bill Russell will nun am Fernsehen die verschiedensten Themen diskutieren. (USA)
342, 343 Vollständige Seite und mehrfarbige Illustration aus dem Magazin des *Sunday Telegraph* zu einem Artikel über die Bedeutung und den Ursprung gewisser Worte. (GBR)

339 Illustration (en polychromie) extraite du magazine de fin de semaine du *Sunday Telegraph*. Elle accompagne un article sur les poissons fumés. (GBR)
340, 341 Illustration et page d'un programme des émissions télévisées: l'ancien joueur de basket-ball, Bill Russell, veut résliser pour la TV des discussions sur n'importe quels sujets. (USA)
342, 343 Page complète et illustration y figurant. Elément du magazine hebdomadaire du *Sunday Telegraph* pour un article sur la signification et l'origine de certains mots. (GBR)

340

341

342

343

344

344–352 Illustrations from various editions of the *New York* magazine. Fig. 344: *House Rules : A guide for the summer grouper*—an article about group holidays; Fig. 345: *Chosen People—King of the Jews,* an article about the decimation wrought by the Nazis; Fig. 346: Paul Bocuse's *La Nouvelle Cuisine : A Skeptic's View*; Fig. 347: *Crude Politics : What America doesn't know about oil*, an article about the USA's naive policies; Fig. 348: nebulous intrigues caused by civil servants: *Who's who in the Hoosegow*; Fig. 349: an article on foot reflexology; Fig. 350 in the "Gazette" column, amusing and serious problems are discussed, here an article about the milk strike in New York; Fig. 351: *Free press and cheap innuendo*: here certain allegations and findings printed in the press are debated upon; Fig. 352: *Jacqueline, Oh!* The French restaurant in New York, *Chez Jacqueline*, is introduced to *New York* readers. (USA)

344–352 Illustrationen aus verschiedenen Ausgaben der Zeitschrift *New York*. Abb. 344: zu einem Artikel über die Schwierigkeiten, die bei Gruppenferien auftreten; Abb. 345: Besprechung eines Romans über die Judenverfolgungen durch das Naziregime; Abb. 346: in diesem Artikel wird die «nouvelle cuisine française» von Paul Bocuse vorgestellt; Abb. 347: dieser Artikel diskutiert die kurzfristigen und kurzsichtigen Massnahmen der USA, um mit der Ölkrise fertigzuwerden; Abb. 348: hier werden undurchsichtige Machenschaften der Stadtbehörden aufgedeckt; Abb. 349: dieser Artikel gibt Aufschluss über die Reflexzonen der Fusssohle; Abb. 350: in der Rubrik «Gazette» werden amüsante und ernsthaftere Probleme diskutiert, hier die Milchknappheit in New York; Abb. 351: hier steht die Pressefreiheit und die Folgen gewisser in der Presse publizierter Unterstellungen zur Diskussion; Abb. 352: hier wird das französische Restaurant *Chez Jacqueline* in New York vorgestellt. (USA)

345

ARTIST / KÜNSTLER:

344, 352 Jacqueline Chwast
345, 347, 348 Randall Enos
346 Gary Thomas
349 Blair Drawson
350, 351 Jo Teodorescu

ART DIRECTOR:

344, 345, 347, 348 Jean-Claude Suarès
346 Tom Bentkowsky
349 Walter Bernard
350–352 Jean-Claude Suarès

PUBLISHER / VERLEGER:

344–352 New York Magazine

Magazine Illustrations

346

347

348

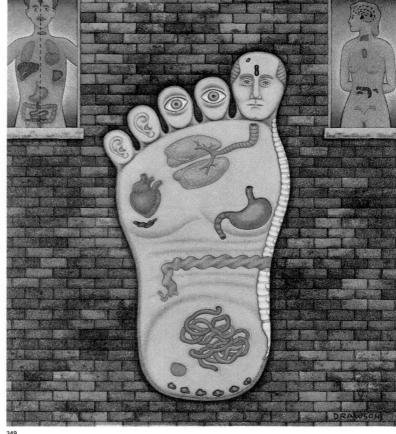

349

350

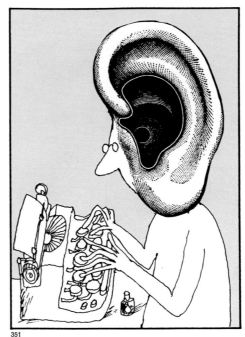

351

344–352 Illustrations tirées de différents numéros du magazine *New York*. Fig. 344: cet article discute les vacances par groupes et les difficultés qui peuvent se présenter; fig. 345: compte rendu d'un roman sur la persécution des Juifs par les Nazis; fig. 346: un auteur assez sceptique présente dans cet article la «nouvelle cuisine française» de Paul Bocuse; fig. 347: on analyse dans cet article les mesures à court terme et irréfléchies que les Etats-Unis ont prises afin de surmonter la crise pétrolière; fig. 348: on dévoile ici les machinations de la municipalité; fig. 349: illustration accompagnant un article sur la réflexologie de la plante des pieds; fig. 350: dans la rubrique «Gazette» on discute des événements amusants et sérieux, ici le manque de lait à New York; fig. 351: on discute ici la liberté de la presse et les conséquences que peuvent avoir les allusions malveillantes y publiées; fig. 352: dans cet article, intitulé *Jacqueline, Oh!*, on présente le restaurant français *Chez Jacqueline* à New York. (USA)

352

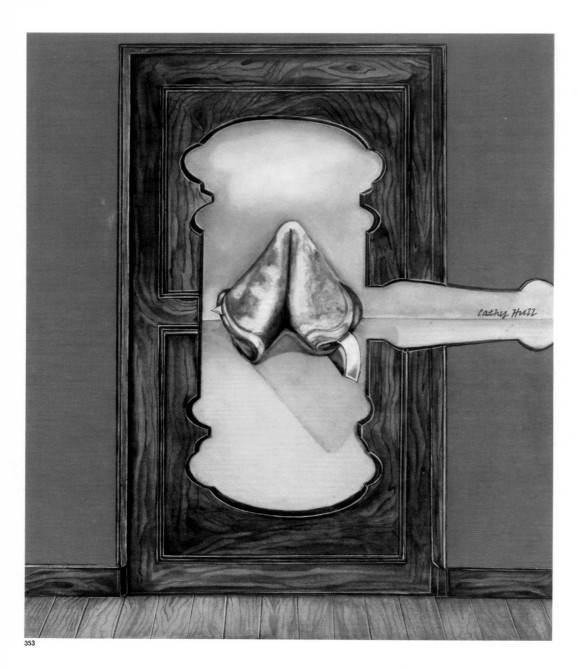

353

355

ARTIST / KÜNSTLER / ARTISTE:

353, 354 Cathy Hull
355, 357 Dickran Palulian
356 Folon
358 Roman Gonzalez Teja
359 Miscellaneous

DESIGNER / GESTALTER / MAQUETTISTE:

353, 354 Bob Clive
355 Frank D. Rothmann
359 Miles Abernethy

ART DIRECTOR / DIRECTEUR ARTISTIQUE:

353, 354 Bob Clive
355 Frank D. Rothmann
356, 357 Jean-Claude Suarès
358 Roman Gonzalez Teja
359 Paul Hardy

PUBLISHER / VERLEGER / EDITEUR:

353, 354 The News
355 Hearst Corp.
356, 357 New York Magazine
358 Lui
359 Attenzione Magazine

353, 354 *Do you know the law?* Illustration and corresponding double spread for a legal quiz for laymen in
the *Sunday News Magazine.* (USA)
355 Introductory double spread from an article in
Science Digest about germ warfare and better ways to
destroy insects. In shades of blue. (USA)
356 Illustration for an article in *New York* magazine
about laziness in the world's busiest city. (USA)
357 *Fowl Play. The great chicken war.* Full-colour illustration on the advertising of chicken farms. (USA)
358 Illustration from the Spanish edition of *Lui* for an
article about Cuban dissidents. (SPA)
359 *Attenzione* magazine: a report about the tremendous success of *Fiorucci*'s Punk fashions. (USA)

353, 354 Diese Illustration (und entsprechende Doppelseite) führt ein juristisches Fragespiel ein, dessen
Antworten den Laien erstaunen. Aus dem Wochenend-
Magazin der Zeitung *The News.* (USA)
355 «Mensch gegen Insekt: taktische Kriegführung.»
Einführende Doppelseite zu einem Artikel, der darauf
hinweist, dass es ausgeklügelter Massnahmen bedarf,
um Insekten auszurotten. In Blautönen. (USA)
356 Illustration zu einem Artikel über die Faulheit in der
geschäftigsten Stadt der Welt. (USA)
357 Über die faulen Tricks und den Werbekrieg, den
Hühnerfarmen führen. Mehrfarbige Illustration. (USA)
358 Illustration aus der spanischen Ausgabe von *Lui*
zu einem Artikel über kubanische Dissidenten. Kopf in
Grautönen vor blauem Himmel. (SPA)
359 «Das *Fiorucci*-Phänomen.» Untersuchung über den
schlagenden Erfolg der Punk-Mode von *Fiorucci*. (USA)

353, 354 Cette illustration (et page double correspondante) introduit un quiz juridique dont les résultats sont
assez surprenants. Eléments du magazine de fin de
semaine du quotidien *The News.* (USA)
355 «L'homme contre l'insecte: la lutte tactique.» Page
double initiale d'un article faisant remarquer qu'il faut
de mesures ingénieuses pour exterminer les insectes.
En tons bleus. (USA)
356 Illustration accompagnant un article sur la paresse
dans la ville la plus active au monde. (USA)
357 Sur les affaires louches et la guerre publicitaire de
quelques éleveurs de poules. En polychromie. (USA)
358 Illustration de l'édition espagnole de *Lui* pour un
article sur les dissidents cubains. Tête en tons gris foncé
et gris clair, ciel bleu. (SPA)
359 «Le phénomène *Fiorucci*.» Enquête sur le succès
fou de la mode Punk lancée par *Fiorucci*. (USA)

New York

Laziness
in the world's busiest city

By Delia Ephron

New York is the easiest city to be lazy in. There is no item that you can't order by telephone and have delivered to your door, no task that someone else won't be happy to do for you, providing the price is right.

But the fact that New York is a catering center is less an accommodation to the lazy life than the working life. People are too exhausted from working to cook for themselves, too overbooked to water their own plants. We are a city of people obsessed with work. What's the first question a person is asked when he is introduced: What do you do?

This interest in always wanting to know first what someone does for a living reflects, as the expression goes, where a New Yorker's head is at, just as the talk in Westchester reveals what's foremost in the suburban mind—real estate. In the suburbs, you are where you live; in New York City, you are what you do. Status and respect are almost entirely

a function of profession. Even the rich who used to be content to give dinner parties and appear in newspaper columns now feel they have to be engagé and to open decorating businesses.

To believe that New Yorkers are work-obsessed, one has only to look at their favorite way to relax: running. Why run? Because it makes a person more alert, less depressed, better able to concentrate. In short, so he will, be in the best possible frame of mind to work.

According to psychology researcher Marilyn Machlowitz, New York City has a very large concentration of workaholics. Machlowitz, an expert on workaholism, came here to interview subjects for her research. She found many of them last summer when the city was blacked out. It was a Thursday morning, 100-degree weather; Mayor Beame had begged people to stay home from work. Machlowitz

26 NEW YORK/AUGUST 14, 1978   Illustration by Folon

356

357

358

HOT NEON:
The Fiorucci Phenomenon

BY SUSAN DUFF

359

Magazine Illustrations
Zeitschriften-Illustrationen
Illustrations de périodiques

139

Newspaper Illustrations
Zeitungs-Illustrationen
Illustrations de journaux

ARTIST / KÜNSTLER / ARTISTE:

360, 361, 366 Sue Coe
362 Terry Allen
363 Mel Williges
364 Patrick Blackwell
365 Steven Guarnaccia
367 Geoffrey Moss

ART DIRECTOR / DIRECTEUR ARTISTIQUE:

360, 361, 366 Pamela Vassil
362–365 Terry Ross Koppel
367 Robert Barkin

PUBLISHER / VERLEGER / EDITEUR:

360, 361, 366 The New York Times
362–365 The Boston Globe
367 Washington Post

360

360 An article from the *New York Times* in which the author speculates about life on other planets. (USA)
361 From the *New York Times*—the dilemma of a woman who is the victim of a knife attack and cannot recognize immediately who the criminal is among the suspects. (USA)
362–365 From the entertainment calendar of the *Boston Globe*: an investigation into the sale of snacks in cinemas; an interview with a singer about the projects she wishes to finance from her record sales; the consequences of the new alcohol law; how one can become a film critic. (USA)
366 This article in the *New York Times* throws light on the discrepancies between the salaries paid to teachers and the high remuneration in profit-oriented companies. (USA)
367 From the *Washington Post Magazine* about how urban pollution is contaminating also backyard plots. (USA)

360 Der Autor untersucht hier die Frage, ob Lebewesen auf anderen Planeten existieren. Aus der *New York Times*. (USA)
361 Das Opfer einer Messerstecherei berichtet über ihr Dilemma, als sie unter mehreren möglichen Tätern den richtigen hätte wiedererkennen sollen. (USA)
362–365 Aus dem Veranstaltungskalender des *Boston Globe*: Untersuchung über den Verkauf von Knabberwaren in Kinos; Interview mit einer Sängerin über die Projekte, die sie aus dem Plattenverkauf realisieren will; Auswirkungen des neuen Alkoholgesetzes; Wie wird man Filmkritiker. (USA)
366 Man diskutiert die Diskrepanz zwischen der schlechten Entlöhnung des Lehrpersonals und den hohen Löhnen, die profitorientierte Unternehmen bezahlen. (USA)
367 Dieser Artikel klärt darüber auf, dass die Luftverschmutzung eine Vergiftung des Kulturlandes bewirkt. (USA)

360 L'auteur examine si des organismes seront viables sur d'autres planètes. Du *New York Times*. (USA)
361 Le victime d'une rixe parle ici de la situation délicate dans laquelle elle se trouvait au moment où elle aurait dû reconnaître le coupable parmi plusieurs autres. (USA)
362–365 Du programme des manifestations du *Boston Globe*: enquête sur les chatteries vendues dans les cinémas; interview avec une chanteuse sur les projets qu'elle veut réaliser; la nouvelle loi restreignant la vente de boissons alcooliques; comment devenir un critique de films. (USA)
366 On discute ici les salaires modérés du personnel enseignant comparés aux salaires très élevés payés par les entreprises industrielles. (USA)
367 Enquête sur la pollution urbaine qui souille l'air aussi bien que le petit jardin derrière la maison. (USA)

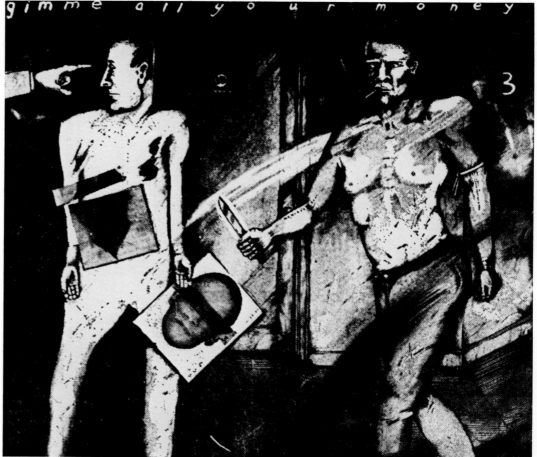

361

MOVIE MUNCHIES
A moviegoer's guide to the tastiest cinema concessions

362

INTERVIEW
BONNIE RAITT
Why the one-time Cambridge singer wants Top 40 success after all these years

363

How to become a
MOVIE CRITIC
Step one: Learn the language

Test your cinema IQ

364

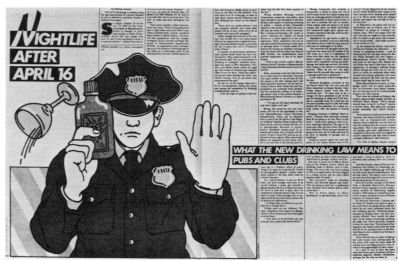

NIGHTLIFE AFTER APRIL 16

WHAT THE NEW DRINKING LAW MEANS TO PUBS AND CLUBS

365

366

G. Morse

367

368

ARTIST / KÜNSTLER / ARTISTE:
368–371 Kent Barton

ART DIRECTOR / DIRECTEUR ARTISTIQUE:
368–371 Kent Barton

PUBLISHER / VERLEGER / EDITEUR:
368–371 The Miami Herald

368, 369 Illustration and corresponding page from *The Miami Herald* in which a professor discusses the political situation in Uganda and tries to forecast the consequences and aftermaths of Idi Amin being ousted. (USA)
370, 371 An article from *The Miami Herald* taken from a report by health authorities in which measures to improve the general health of the public are proposed. (USA)

368, 369 Illustration und entsprechende Seite aus der Zeitung *The Miami Herald*. Ein Professor für politische Wissenschaften untersucht die politische Situation in Uganda und versucht eine Prognose zu stellen für den Fall, dass Idi Amin gestürzt wird. (USA)
370, 371 «Unser todbringender Lebenswandel.» Der Artikel bezieht sich auf einen von der Gesundheitsbehörde veröffentlichten Bericht, in welchem Massnahmen zur Verbesserung der Volksgesundheit diskutiert werden. Aus der Zeitung *The Miami Herald*. (USA)

368, 369 Illustration et page correspondante extraites du quotidien *The Miami Herald*. Un professeur ès sciences politiques analyse la situation actuelle en Ouganda et le développement probable en cas d'un renversement du gouvernement d'Idi Amin. (USA)
370, 371 «Notre train de vie létal.» Cet article se réfère à un rapport publié par l'office de la santé publique qui discute les mesures à prendre afin d'améliorer l'état de santé en générale. Extrait du quotidien *The Miami Herald*. (USA)

369

370

371

ARTIST / KÜNSTLER:

372–374, 376–378 Miran
375 Olaf Gulbransson

ART DIRECTOR:

372–378 Oswaldo Miranda

PUBLISHER / VERLEGER:

372–378 Diário do Paraná

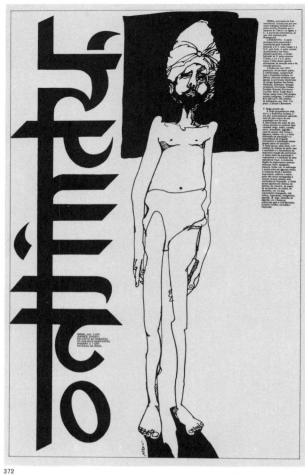

372

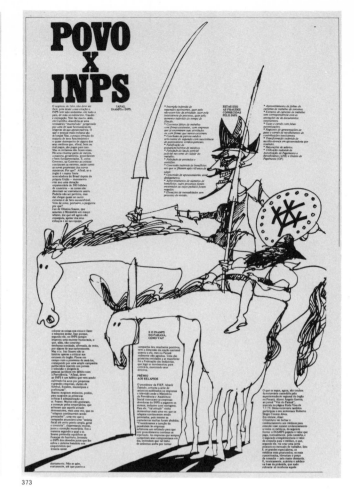

373

375

376

Newspaper
Illustrations

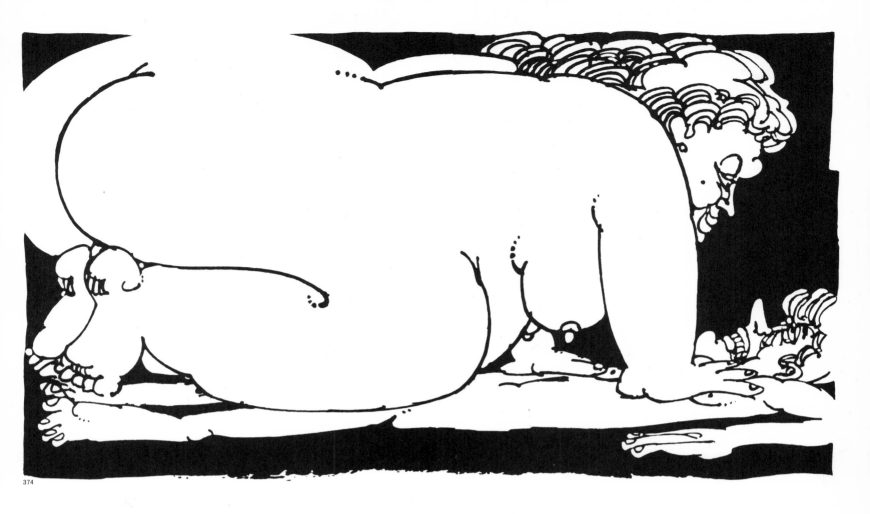

374

337

378

372–378 Pages and illustrations from the daily newspaper *Diario do Paraná*. Fig. 372: first page of the cultural supplement with an article about Hinduism; Fig. 373: Analysis about the battle with social institutions. The emblem on the sign is that of the health service INPS; Fig. 374: humorous story of how an obese woman fooled four lovers; Fig. 375: caricature by Olaf Gulbransson from *Simplizissimus* (1903) from an article about Henrik Ibsen; Fig. 376: from an article about the political and sociocritical films by the Bolivian Rabonet; Figs. 377, 378: "Fragments": illustration and double spread devoted to the author and lyricist Fernando Pessoa. (BRA)

372–378 Seiten und Illustrationen aus der Tageszeitung *Diario do Paraná*. Abb. 372: Titelseite der Kulturbeilage mit einem Artikel über Hinduismus; Abb. 373: Analyse über den Kampf mit den Sozialämtern; das Zeichen auf dem Schild ist dasjenige des Gesundheitsdienstes INPS; Abb. 374: humorvolle Geschichte einer fettleibigen Frau, die vier Liebhaber betörte; Abb. 375: Karikatur Olaf Gulbranssons aus dem *Simplizissimus* (1903) zu einem Artikel über Henrik Ibsen; Abb. 376: zu einem Artikel über die politischen und sozialkritischen Filme des Bolivianers Rabonet; Abb. 377, 378: «Fragmente.» Illustration und Doppelseite, die dem brasilianischen Schriftsteller und Lyriker Fernando Pessoa gewidmet ist. (BRA)

372–378 Pages et illustrations extraites du quotidien *Diario do Paraná*. Fig. 372: page initiale du supplément culturel avec un article sur l'hindouisme; fig. 373: analyse sur la lutte avec les bureaux de l'assistance sociale; le symbole INPS sur le bouclier est celui du service de la santé publique; fig. 374: histoire amusante sur une grosse femme ayant troubler le cœur de quatre amants; fig. 375: caricature d'Olaf Gulbransson extraite de *Simplizissimus* (1903) pour accompagner un article sur Henrik Ibsen; fig. 376: article sur les films politiques et sociaux du Bolivien Rabonet; fig. 377, 378: «Fragments.» Illustration et page double consacrées à l'écrivain et poète brésilien Fernando Pessoa. (BRA)

379 Recto of a newspaper published by a national foundation for the promotion of art. This article explains what goes on behind the scenes when the literature panel meets after someone has applied for a grant from the foundation. (USA)
380 Woodcut reproduced under the title of "The Crisis of Capitalism." In the feuilleton of the newspaper *Folha de Sao Paulo*. (BRA)
381, 382 Both these woodcuts appeared in a publication printed by the Brazilian committee endeavouring for an amnesty for political prisoners; they deal with the subject of those in Brazil who are persecuted for their political beliefs and public statements. (BRA)
383 Woodcut from the *Jornal do Brasil* from an article about bureaucracy which, in general, has a stultifying and blockaging effect. (BRA)

379 Frontseite einer von der nationalen Stiftung für Kunstförderung herausgegebenen Zeitung. Es wird in diesem Artikel gezeigt, was bei der Literatur-Kommission hinter den Kulissen abläuft, wenn sich jemand um einen Förderbeitrag bewirbt. (USA)
380 Im Feuilleton der Zeitung *Folha de Sao Paulo* erschienener Holzschnitt mit dem Titel «Die Krise des Kapitalismus». (BRA)
381, 382 Diese beiden Holzschnitte zum Thema der in Brasilien vermissten politisch Verfolgten erschien in einer Publikation des brasilianischen Komitees, das sich für die Amnestie der politischen Gefangenen einsetzt. (BRA)
383 Holzschnitt aus dem *Jornal do Brasil* zu einem Artikel über die Bürokratie, die sich allgemein als Hemmschuh auswirkt. (BRA)

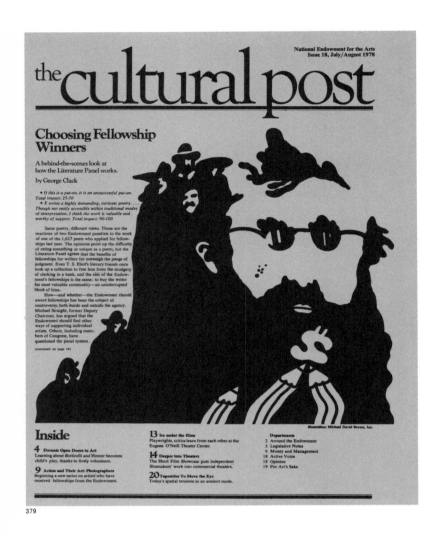

379

380

382

383

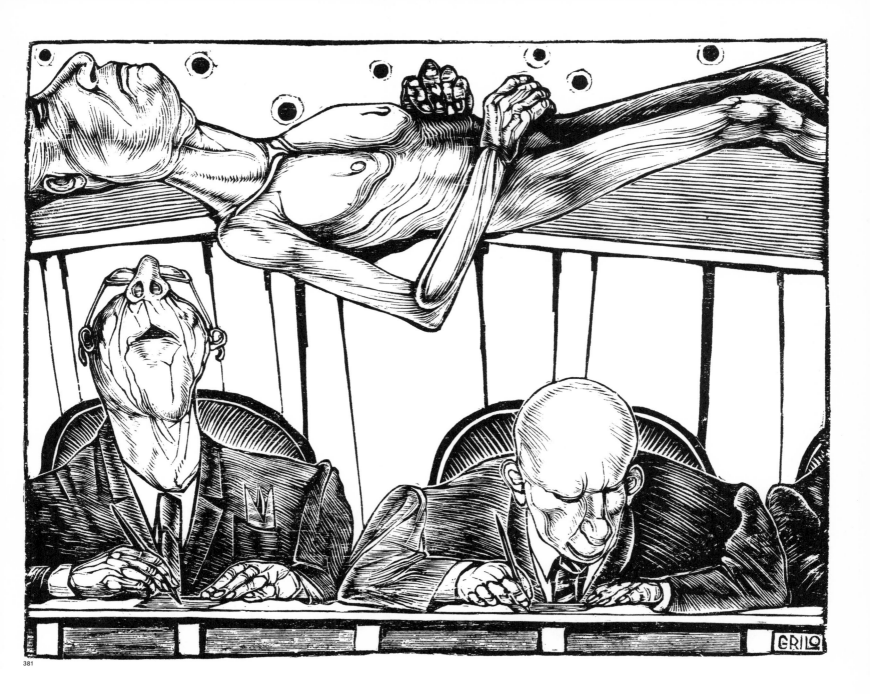

381

ARTIST / KÜNSTLER / ARTISTE:

379 Michael David Brown
380–383 Rubem Campos Grilo

DESIGNER / GESTALTER / MAQUETTISTE:

379 Michael David Brown

ART DIRECTOR / DIRECTEUR ARTISTIQUE:

379 David Hausman

PUBLISHER / VERLEGER / EDITEUR:

379 National Endowment for the Arts
380 Folhetim-Folna de Sao Paulo
381, 382 Comite Brasileiro Pela Anistia
383 Caderno Especial-Jornal do Brasil

379 Frontispice d'un journal publié par la fondation nationale pour la promotion de l'art. Cet article explique la machinerie de la commission littéraire qui se met en marche dans la coulisse dès que quelqu'un demande une bourse. (USA)
380 Gravure sur bois intitulée «La crise du capitalisme». Elle a paru dans le feuilleton du quotidien *Folha de Sao Paulo*. (BRA)
381, 382 Ces deux gravures sur bois illustrant le thème des persécutés politiques portés disparus au Brésil ont parus dans une publication du comité brésilien pour l'amnistie des prisonniers politiques. (BRA)
383 Gravure sur bois extraite du quotidien *Jornal do Brasil*. Elle accompagne un article sur la bureaucratie qui a un effet inhibitif. (BRA)

Newspaper Illustrations
Zeitungs-Illustrationen
Illustrations de journaux

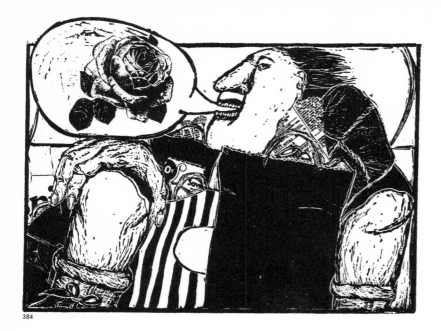

ARTIST / KÜNSTLER / ARTISTE:

384–390 Frances Jetter

ART DIRECTOR / DIRECTEUR ARTISTIQUE:

384 Nancy Kent
385, 388 Pegi Goodman
386 Brian Canniff
387, 389 Victor Navasky
390 Peter Borelli

PUBLISHER / VERLEGER / EDITEUR:

384 The New York Times
385, 388 The American Lawyer
386 Saturday Review
387, 389 The Nation
390 Amicus Magazine

Newspaper Illustrations
Zeitungs-Illustrationen
Illustrations de journaux

388

384 Illustration from a short story in the *New York Times* about a derelict who celebrates Shakespeare's birthday in style somewhere in New York. (USA)
385, 388 These illustrations which appeared in *The American Lawyer* magazine accompany a portrait of a psychiatrist who tries to convince a jury to vote for the death penalty. (USA)
386 Illustration from *Saturday Review* accompanying a review about the novel *Sophie's Choice*. (USA)
387 Report from the magazine *The Nation* about how judges are swayed in their decisions due to a free-market cram course for judges which encourages decisions in favour of Big Business. (USA)
389 Another article from *The Nation* about new technology and the subsequent problems of workers. (USA)
390 An analysis in *Amicus Magazine* on risk and the comprehension of the theory of probabilities. (USA)

384 Illustration zu einer kurzen Geschichte über eine newyorker Schlampe, die sich an Shakespeares Geburtstag zur Feier des Tages fein herausputzte. (USA)
385, 388 Diese in einer juristischen Zeitschrift erschienenen Illustrationen begleiten ein Portrait über einen Psychiater, der die Geschworenen überzeugen will, für die Todesstrafe zu stimmen. (USA)
386 Illustration aus der *Saturday Review* zu einer Besprechung des Buches *Sophie's Choice*. (USA)
387 Bericht aus der Zeitschrift *The Nation* über einen für Bundesrichter organisierten Kurs über freie Marktwirtschaft und die damit zusammenhängende Beeinflussung dieser Richter zugunsten der Industriegiganten. (USA)
389 Artikel über den technischen Fortschritt und die sich daraus ergebenden Konsequenzen für den Arbeiter. (USA)
390 Analyse über die Wahrscheinlichkeitsrechnungen, durch welche sich die Leute in einer falschen Sicherheit wähnen, weil sie eher geneigt sind, eine plötzliche Gefahr auszuschliessen. (USA)

384 Illustration accompagnant une histoire sur une épave newyorkaise qui s'est fait belle pour célébrer l'anniversaire de Shakespeare. (USA)
385, 388 Illustrations d'un périodique juridique figurant dans un article sur un psychiatre qui cherche à convaincre les jurés de voter pour la condamnation à mort. (USA)
386 Illustration pour un compte rendu du livre *Sophie's Choice* (Le choix de Sophie). (USA)
387 Ce rapport du magazine *The Nation* parle d'un cours sur l'économie de libre concurrence organisé pour des juges importants du tribunal fédéral et l'influence de ceux-ci en faveur des géants industriels. (USA)
389 D'un article sur la nouvelle technologie et les conséquences qui en résultent pour les ouvriers. (USA)
390 Cet article analyse les calculs des probabilités en rapport avec des risques éventuels. (USA)

389

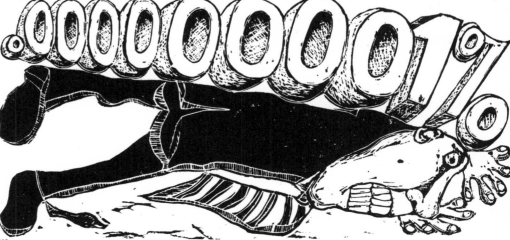

390

391 *The crisis in Afghanistan,* an article from the *Dallas Morning News* with an illustration of the Russian bear's paws reaching out for further domination of states in and around the Gulf of Persia. (USA)
392–394 Cover illustration, cover and inside page of a publication of the Art Directors Club of Boston. The illustrations show what the communication manipulators can do with the consumer. (USA)
395 This illustration was published in a weekly column about things happening in Sweden. From the daily newspaper *Dagens Nyheter.* (SWE)
396 From the *New York Times*: the article entitled *Risk in the long haul* concerns the negotiations between the USA and its NATO partners about the stationing of medium-range missiles in strategic areas in Europe. (USA)
397 A lawn clipping debate in the *New York Times* about how to use cut grass as a natural fertilizer. (USA)
398 *Words and Music under Stalin,* a review in the *New York Times* on Shostakovich's memoirs. (USA)

391 Diese Illustration entstand kurz nach dem sowjetischen Einmarsch in Afghanistan – die russischen Bären, die ihre Tatzen nach weiteren Golfstaaten ausstrecken, symbolisieren die von der Sowjetunion verfolgte Politik, durch Besetzung weiterer Länder an ein warmes Meer zu gelangen. Aus *Dallas Morning News.* (USA)
392–394 Umschlagillustration, Umschlag und Innenseite einer Publikation des Art Directors Clubs von Boston. Die Illustrationen zeigen, was die «Kommunikations-Macher» mit dem Konsumenten alles anstellen. (USA)
395 Aus einer wöchentlich erscheinenden Kolumne über Vorkommnisse in Schweden. (SWE)
396 Zu den Verhandlungen zwischen den USA und seinen NATO-Partnern über die Stationierung von Mittelstreckenraketen in verschiedenen europäischen Staaten. (USA)
397 Dieser Artikel informiert über den Wert des abgeschnittenen Grases als natürliches Düngemittel. (USA)
398 «Worte und Musik unter Stalin.» Besprechung von Schostakowitschs Memoiren. (USA)

391 Cette illustration a été réalisée peu après l'intervention soviétique en Afghanistan – les ours soviétiques qui mettent leurs pattes déjà sur d'autres pays de la région, devraient symboliser la politique de l'URSS qui cherche à s'assurer l'accès libre aux ports non sujetts à geler. (USA)
392–394 Illustration de couverture, couverture et page intérieure d'une publication du Club des directeurs artistiques de Boston. On y montre que le consommateur est manipulé à volonté par les publicitaires. (USA)
395 D'une rubrique hebdomadaire d'un quotidien, consacrée à des événements suédois. (SWE)
396 Illustration se référant aux négociations entre les USA et les Etats membres de l'OTAN sur le stationnement de missiles stratégiques dans plusieurs pays européens. (USA)
397 On discute ici la valeur de l'herbe coupée en tant qu'engrais naturel. (USA)
398 «Mots et musique sous Staline.» Compte rendu des mémoires de Chostakovitch. (USA)

391

392

393

394

395

396

ARTIST / KÜNSTLER / ARTISTE:

391 Paul Kolsti
392–394 Terry Allen/Patrick Blackwell/
Karen Watson/Renée Klein
395 Staffan Schultz
396–398 Eugene Mihaesco

DESIGNER / GESTALTER / MAQUETTISTE:

392–394 Terry Ross Koppel

ART DIRECTOR / DIRECTEUR ARTISTIQUE:

391 Craig Spaulding
392–394 Terry Ross Koppel
395 Britt-Mari Hallbert/Eivor Cederquist
396 Jerelle Kraus
397 Nicki Kalish
398 Steven Heller

PUBLISHER / VERLEGER / EDITEUR:

391 Dallas Morning News
392–394 The Boston Globe
395 Dagens Nyheter
396–398 The New York Times

397

Newspaper Illustrations
Zeitungs-Illustrationen
Illustrations de journaux

398

151

399

ARTIST / KÜNSTLER / ARTISTE:

399—401 Etienne Delessert
402 Paul Perret
403 Pascal Gachet
404 Terry Allen
405 Cathy Hull
406 Robert Pryor

DESIGNER / GESTALTER / MAQUETTISTE:

399—403 Etienne Delessert
404 Terry Ross Koppel

400

401

402

403

ART DIRECTOR / DIRECTEUR ARTISTIQUE:

399—403 Etienne Delessert
404 Terry Ross Koppel
405 Jerelle Kraus

AGENCY / AGENTUR / AGENCE – STUDIO:

399—403 Carabosse

PUBLISHER / VERLEGER / EDITEUR:

399—403 La Suisse
404 The Boston Globe
405 The New York Times
406 Los Angeles Times

406

404

405

399—403 Illustrations on the front page of the week-end supplement of *La Suisse*: Riviera of the dinosaur; Mickey—now 50 years young; a report on the visit of Charles Aznavour and Serge Lama to *La Suisse*; introduction to an article about Charles Trenet, the father of the French chanson. All illustrations are in full colour. (SWI)
404 From the entertainment calendar of the *Boston Globe*. (USA)
405 Putting steel (literally) into America's share of world markets: illustration on the Op-Ed page (opposite the editorial) of the *New York Times* for an article on energy and economic crisis. (USA)
406 Governor Brown of California, a Democrat (= donkey) heading in a conservative direction typical of a Republican (= elephant). Bear and star are symbols of California. *The Los Angeles Times*. (USA)

399—403 Frontseite der Wochenendbeilage von *La Suisse*: Riviera der Dinosaurier; Mickey – ein Junge von 50 Jahren; zu einem Besuch von Charles Aznavour und Serge Lama bei *La Suisse*; zu einem Artikel über Charles Trenet, den Vater des französischen Chansons. Alle Illustrationen sind mehrfarbig. (SWI)
404 Aus dem Veranstaltungskalender des *Boston Globe*. (USA)
405 Illustration auf der Op-Ed-Seite (gegenüber Editorial) der *New York Times*: Analyse über die amerikanische Energie- und Wirtschaftskrise, die durch Exportförderung gedämpft werden kann. (USA)
406 Der kalifornische Gouverneur Brown, ein Demokrat (durch den Esel symbolisiert), verfolgt eine konservative, typisch republikanische Linie (Republikaner als Elephant dargestellt). Bär und Stern sind Symbole Kaliforniens. (USA)

399—403 Illustrations de la première page du supplément week-end du quotidien *La Suisse*, intitulées *La Riviera des Dinosaures, Mickey: un gamin de 50 ans, Aznavour – Lama: la grande java* – sur une visite des deux chansonniers chez *La Suisse*, et *Les adieux du fou chantant* – pour un article sur Charles Trenet, le père de la chanson française. En polychromie. (SWI)
404 Du programme hebdomadaire des manifestations. (USA)
405 Illustration de la page Op-Ed (face à l'éditorial) du *New York Times*: analyse sur la crise pétrolière et économique aux Etats-Unis et son apaisement par l'augmentation des exportations. (USA)
406 Le gouverneur californien Brown, un démocrate (symbolisé par l'âne) suit une politique conservatrice, typique des Républicains (représenté par l'éléphant). L'ours et l'étoile sont des symboles de la Californie. (USA)

Newspaper Illustrations
Zeitungs-Illustrationen
Illustrations de journaux

407 This illustration appeared with an article entitled *Idi Amin: chasing rats for eight years*. The author reports on Amin's reign of terror and the squadrons of death who hunted and cold-bloodedly murdered all those opposed to Amin's regime. This horrifying report and illustration were published in *The Denver Post*. (USA)
408–410 Double spreads from a series which appeared in the cultural supplement of the newspaper *Jornal do Paraná*, a series devoted to great historical personalities—here Napoleon, Edgar Allan Poe and Ludwig van Beethoven. (BRA)
411 This illustration accompanied an article in the *New York Times* about the women's rights movement and the discrimination of women regarding legal matters—although sympathizing in many cases, Justitia is only a powerless observer of women's legal plights. (USA)

407 Diese Illustration erschien zu einem Artikel mit dem Titel «Idi Amin jagte während acht Jahren Ratten». Der Autor berichtet über die Schreckensherrschaft Amins und die Todesschwadronen, die alle jene jagten und kaltblütig ermordeten, die Amin gegen sich wähnte. Aus der Tageszeitung *The Denver Post*. (USA)
408–410 Doppelseiten aus einer in der Kulturbeilage der Zeitung *Jornal do Paraná* erschienenen Serie, die grossen historischen Persönlichkeiten gewidmet ist, hier Napoleon, Edgar Allan Poe und Ludwig van Beethoven. (BRA)
411 Diese Illustration begleitet einen Artikel in der *New York Times* über die Frauenrechtsbewegung und die Diskriminierung der Frau in rechtlicher Hinsicht – diesen Zustand muss auch die Justitia mit einem zwar weinenden Auge machtlos mitansehen. (USA)

407 Cette illustration accompagne un article intitulé «Idi Amin a chassé des rats pendant huit ans». C'est un rapport sur le régime de la terreur en Ouganda et les actes de violence et de meurtre commis par des commandos spéciaux qui chassaient et assassinaient tous ceux qu'Amin croyait être contre lui. Extrait du quotidien *The Denver Post*. (USA)
408–410 Pages doubles faisant partie d'une série consacrée à des personnages importants de l'histoire, ici Napoléon, Edgar Allan Poe et Ludwig van Beethoven. Cette série a paru dans le supplément culturel du quotidien *Jornal do Paraná*. (BRA)
411 Cette illustration est extraite d'un article du *New York Times* sur le mouvement féministe et la discrimination de la femme du point de vue légal – même la Justice est impuissante à l'égard de cette situation. (USA)

408

409

410

407

ARTIST / KÜNSTLER / ARTISTE:

407 Bonnie Timmons
408–410 Miran
411 Cathy Hull

DESIGNER / GESTALTER / MAQUETTISTE:

407 Bonnie Timmons
408–410 Miran

411

ART DIRECTOR / DIRECTEUR ARTISTIQUE:

407 Ray Krolicki
408—410 Oswaldo Miranda
411 John Cayea

PUBLISHER / VERLEGER / EDITEUR:

407 The Denver Post
408—410 Diário do Paraná
411 The New York Times

Newspaper Illustrations
Zeitungs-Illustrationen
Illustrations de journaux

412

ARTIST / KÜNSTLER / ARTISTE:

415

413

414

416

418

412–418 All the illustrations shown on this double spread appeared in the *New York Times*. Fig. 412 was displayed on the Op-Ed page (opposite the leading article); Fig. 413 illustrated an article entitled *A word on behalf of the Mexican tomatoe* (Op-Ed page); Fig. 414 accompanied an analysis on the Russian internal and foreign policies (Op-Ed page); Fig. 415 for an article about composers, in the entertainment supplement; Fig. 416: *Remnants of Watergate*, an article about this legacy in the politics of today; Fig. 417: *The Iron Curtain has rusted, but many restraints persist*, an article about how liberalization is coming slowly to countries such as Czechoslovakia; Fig. 418 is a woodcut that accompanied an article about salmon fishing. (USA)

412–418 Alle auf dieser Doppelseite gezeigten Illustrationen stammen aus der *New York Times*. Abb. 412 erschien auf der Op-Ed-Seite (gegenüber dem Leitartikel); Abb. 413 illustriert einen Artikel über mexikanische Tomaten und die Entwicklung der Marktpreise (Op-Ed-Seite); Abb. 414 begleitet eine Analyse über die russische Innen- und Aussenpolitik (Op-Ed-Seite); Abb. 415: zu einem Artikel über Komponisten, in der Unterhaltungsbeilage erschienen; Abb. 416 «Was von Watergate noch übrigblieb.» Über die Auswirkungen auf die heutige Politik; Abb. 417 «Der Eiserne Vorhang rostet bereits, aber viele Freiheitsbeschränkungen sind geblieben.» Über die Liberalisierung, die kommen muss; Abb. 418: Holzschnitt zu einem Artikel über die Salm-Fischerei. (USA)

412–418 Toutes les illustrations de cette page double ont paru dans le *New York Times*. Fig. 412: illustration de la page Op-Ed (face à l'éditorial); fig. 413 accompagne un article sur les tomates méxicaines et l'évolution des prix du marché (page Op-Ed); fig. 414 illustre une analyse sur la politique intérieure et extérieure de l'URSS (page Op-Ed); fig. 415: pour un article sur des compositeurs, paru dans le supplément «Loisirs»; fig. 416: «Ce qui est resté de Watergate.» Les conséquences concernant la politique actuelle; fig. 417: «Le Rideau de fer se rouille déjà, mais beaucoup de restrictions de la liberté sont restées en vigueur.» Sur la libéralisation qui s'annonce lentement; fig. 418: gravure sur bois sur la pêche du saumon. (USA)

ART DIRECTOR / DIRECTEUR ARTISTIQUE:

412–414, 416 Jerelle Kraus
415 Nicki Kalish
418 Nancy Kent

PUBLISHER / VERLEGER / EDITEUR:

412–418 The New York Times

417

419

420

ARTIST / KÜNSTLER / ARTISTE:

419 Seiji Nakamura
420 Joo Chung
421 Anita Siegel
422–425 Jerry Jeanmard

DESIGNER / GESTALTER / MAQUETTISTE:

422–425 Woody Pirtle/Carol Burke

ART DIRECTOR/ DIRECTEUR ARTISTIQUE:

420–421 Roger Black
422–425 Woody Pirtle/Carol Burke

PUBLISHER / VERLEGER / EDITEUR:

419 Tsukasa Shobu
420, 421 New York Magazine Co., Inc.
422–425 Wick Allison

419 "Good morning." Illustration from *Cinema* magazine published by *Tsukasa Shobu*. (JPN)
420 This full-colour illustration introduced an article in *New West* magazine about the few remaining grizzly bears on the North American continent. (USA)
421 Illustration belonging to an article called *Blood and Money* in which the suspicion is voiced that the great increase in surgical operations in the United States has less to do with medical necessity than with a desire to earn more money. (USA)
422–425 Title page and double spreads from a consumer magazine belonging to an article about the "best" and "worst" to be found in various categories. (USA)

422

423

Magazine Illustrations

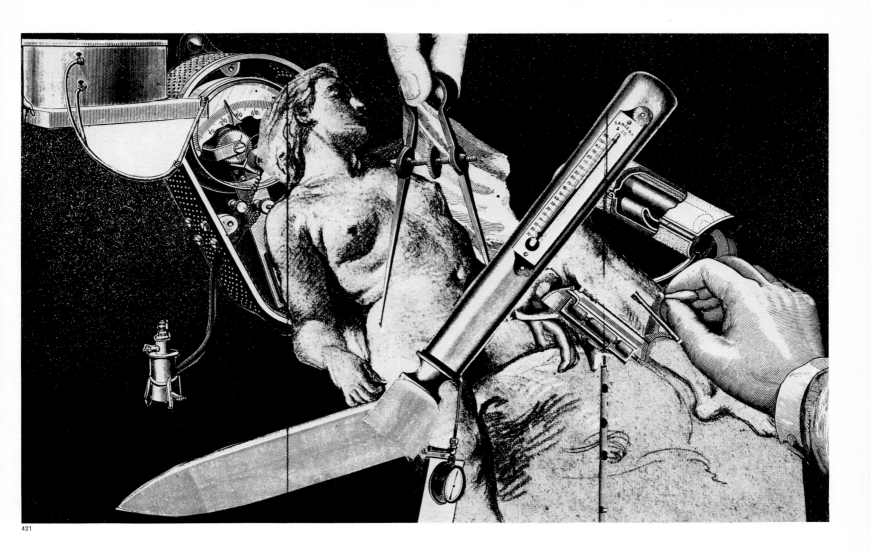

421

419 «Guten Morgen.» Illustration aus der Zeitschrift *Cinema*. (JPN)
420 Diese mehrfarbige Illustration leitet einen Artikel über die letzten, auf dem nordamerikanischen Kontinent noch lebenden Grizzlibären ein. Aus der Zeitschrift *New West*. (USA)
421 Illustration zu einem Bericht mit dem Titel «Blut und Geld», in welchem die Vermutung geäussert wird, dass die ständig steigende Zahl von operativen Eingriffen in den Vereinigten Staaten weniger auf medizinische als vielmehr auf finanzielle Gründe zurückzuführen ist. (USA)
422—425 Titelseite und Doppelseiten aus einer Verbraucherzeitschrift zu einem Artikel über das «Beste» und das «Schlechteste» in verschiedenen Kategorien. (USA)

419 «Bonjour.» Illustration du magazine *Cinema*, publié par *Tsukasa Shobu*. (JPN)
420 Cette illustration (en couleurs) introduit un article sur les derniers grizzlis du continent nord-américain. Elément du magazine *New West*. (USA)
421 Illustration accompagnant un rapport intitulé «Sang et argent». L'auteur présume que le nombre croissant des interventions chirurgicales aux Etats-Unis s'explique plutôt par des raisons financières et non pas par des raisons médicales. (USA)
422—425 Couverture et pages doubles d'un article qu'un magazine a consacré «au meilleur et au pire» de diverses catégories. (USA)

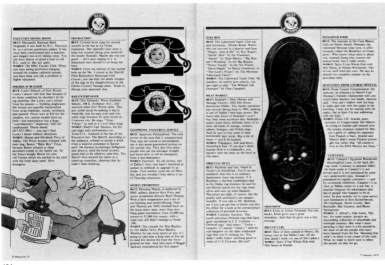

424

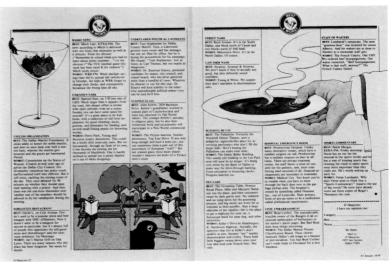

425

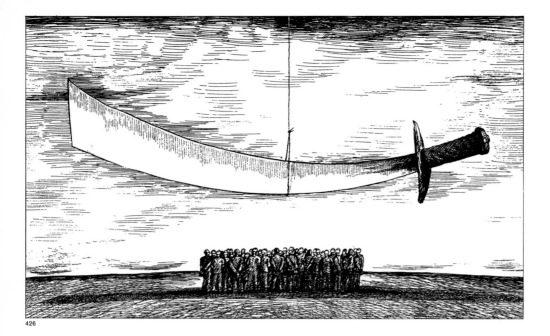

428

ARTIST / KÜNSTLER / ARTISTE:

426 Eugene Mihaesco
427 Shuichi Higurashi
428, 429 Wayne Anderson

DESIGNER / GESTALTER / MAQUETTISTE:

426 Irene Ramp

ART DIRECTOR / DIRECTEUR ARTISTIQUE:

426 Walter Bernard
427 Maurice Coriat
428, 429 Roger Watt

PUBLISHER / VERLEGER / EDITEUR:

426 Time, Inc.
427 Publicness
428, 429 Paul Raymond Publications Ltd.

426 Illustration from *Time* newsmagazine about the Iran problem: Khomeini orders the release of a few hostages, but the crisis continues as well as the test of wills. (USA)
427 Full-page, full-colour illustration from a report in *Zoom* about an exhibition of 130 Japanese illustrators shown in various European cities. (FRA)
428, 429 Double spread and illustration (in actual size) from a short thriller entitled *The Goblin rapist of Dingley Dell* which was published in a men's magazine. (GBR)

426 Illustration aus dem Nachrichtenmagazin *Time* zu einem Artikel über die Iran-Krise und das interne Seilziehen zwischen Khomeini und den Botschaftsbesetzern um die Freilassung der Geiseln. (USA)
427 Ganzseitige Farbillustration aus einem in *Zoom* erschienenen Bericht über eine in verschiedenen europäischen Städten gezeigte Ausstellung von 130 japanischen Illustratoren. (FRA)
428, 429 Doppelseite und Illustration (in Originalgrösse) zu einem Kurzkrimi, der in einem Herrenmagazin publiziert wurde. Es geht dabei um eine Erzieherin, die in einem abgelegenen Haus in Dingley Dell von Kobolden vergewaltigt wurde. (GBR)

426 Illustration du magazine d'information *Time* pour un article sur la crise iranienne et les controverses internes entre l'imam Khomeiny et les étudiants à propos de la libération des ôtages américains. En noir et blanc. (USA)
427 Illustration pleine page (en couleurs) extraite d'un article du magazine de l'image *Zoom* consacré à une exposition itinérante de 130 illustrateurs japonais. (FRA)
428, 429 Page double et illustration (en grandeur nature) d'un roman policier publié dans un magazin pour hommes. Il traite d'une gouvernante qui a été violée par des lutins. (GBR)

426

427

429

430

430 Full-page illustration from the *New York Times* magazine for an article called *New Voices in American poetry*. (USA)
431 Introductory double spread for an article in *Quest Magazine* about loan sharks and their working methods. Dark shades. (USA)
432 Full-colour illustration belonging to a report called *The War of the Razors*—a battle between *Bic* and *Gillette* for supremacy with the daily male shaver. (USA)
433 Illustration in sombre shades from a publication by *Berkley Windhover*. (USA)
434 Introductory double spread from an analysis about nuclear energy's pros and cons. (USA)
435, 436 This report explains how the shock of icy water can kill. Play-on-words title. (USA)

430 Ganzseitige Illustration aus dem Magazin der *New York Times*: der Autor stellt junge amerikanische Schriftsteller vor. (USA)
431 Einleitende Doppelseite zu einem Artikel über Wucherer. In dunklen Farbtönen. (USA)
432 Farbillustration zu einem Bericht über die zwei grössten Hersteller von Rasierklingen und ihr Ringen um die Gunst der Männerwelt. (USA)
433 Illustration in matten Farben zu einer Publikation von *Berkley Windhover*. (USA)
434 Einleitende Doppelseite zu einer Analyse über die Vor- und Nachteile der Atomenergie. (USA)
435, 436 Es wird hier berichtet, dass ein Kentern in zu kaltem Wasser tödliche Folgen hat. (USA)

430 Illustration pleine page extraite du magazine de fin de semaine du *New York Times*: l'auteur y présente des jeunes écrivains américains. (USA)
431 Première page double d'un article consacré aux usuriers. En tons foncés. (USA)
432 Illustration accompagnant un rapport sur les deux fabricants les plus importants de lames de rasoir qui cherche à s'insinuer dans les bonnes grâces des hommes. (USA)
433 Illustration en tons mats figurant dans une publication de *Berkley Windhover*. (USA)
434 Page double introduisant une analyse sur les avantages et les inconvénients de l'énergie nucléaire. (USA)
435, 436 D'un article qui explique pourquoi une chute dans l'eau froide est mortelle. (USA)

431

432

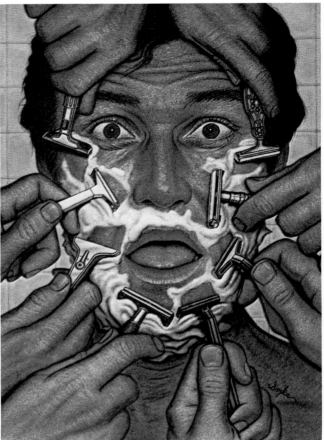

433

ARTIST / KÜNSTLER / ARTISTE:	DESIGNER / GESTALTER / MAQUETTISTE:
430 R.O. Blechman	431 Ursula Kaiser
431 Roger Hill	433 Seymour Chwast
432 Ed Soyka	434–436 Stephen Costello
433 Brad Holland	
434 Martin Springett	
435, 436 Kent Smith	

THE GREAT HIPPY ENERGY CON JOB

AS A RELIGION, SOLAR ENERGY IS FINE. BUT IT WON'T KEEP YOU WARM

By John Dizard

The speeches by the professional anti-nuclear people were over, and the theatricals began. Four lesbian mime players contorted themselves with gestures that showed the boundless evil of atomic energy and the virtue of "natural" power. One of the more clumsy *artistes* sprained herself in a vain attempt to depict a waterwheel-driven factory.

It was a hot day in Boston, and the rest of the troupe seemed in more immediate danger from solar energy than from the invidious atom. But that didn't slow down the itinerant solar advocate in the train of the mime team. "You people in Canada should know better," she said. "I'm going up there next week to lecture on your nuclear program. You're even worse energy junkies than the Americans."

Yes, the sun is coming to Canada. You might have thought it had done so with regularity for the past few billion years; but to hear the sun people talk, the oil conglomerates and the international banks have conspired to keep solar energy out of the hands of the Canadian public. Until now, their pitch has been confined to the odd mimeographed pamphlet and obscure journal; but lately, solar has gone big-time. Recently, the federal government announced a $380-million, five-year solar program, in addition to the pile of grants and civil-service slots that have created an industry with all the growth potential of the youthcult of the '60s.

The Progressive Conservatives were a little miffed by the government's seizing upon the solar issue. "Solar has always been *our* program," sniffs one Tory. "They're just

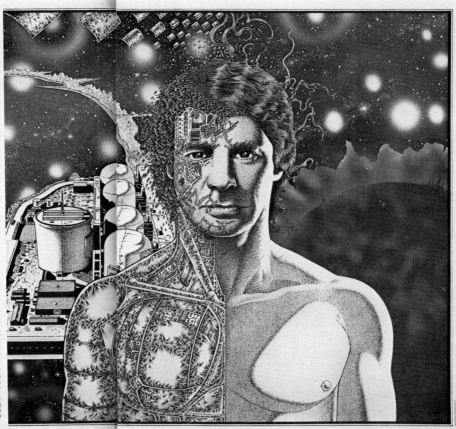

60

434

435

The icy facts on how cold water kills

436

ART DIRECTOR / DIRECTEUR ARTISTIQUE:

431, 434–436 Jon Eby
432 Robert Priest
433 Jean-Claude Suarès

AGENCY / AGENTUR / AGENCE – STUDIO:

433 Push Pin Studios, Inc.

PUBLISHER / VERLEGER / EDITEUR:

430 The New York Times
431, 434–436 Comac Communications
432 Esquire, Inc.
433 Berkley Windhover

437

439

438

440

ARTIST / KÜNSTLER / ARTISTE:

437 Jacqui Morgan
438 Frank Gallo
439 Brad Holland
440, 441 Alain Gauthier

ART DIRECTOR / DIRECTEUR ARTISTIQUE:

437 Rainer Wörtmann
438 Art Paul/Kerig Pope
439 Art Paul/Tom Staebler
440, 441 Régis Pagniez

PUBLISHER / VERLEGER / EDITEUR:

437 Heinrich Bauer Verlag
438, 439 Playboy Enterprises, Inc.
440, 441 Publications Filipacchi

437 Illustration from a novel serialized in the German edition of *Playboy*. (GER)
438 Introductory double spread from a story that appeared in *Playboy*. The illustration was designed by a sculptor. (USA)
439 Title page from *Playboy* magazine for an article about a drug addict. (USA)
440, 441 From the French edition of *Playboy*: bitter experiences at a tender age and an amusing story about love and greed. (FRA)

437 Illustration zu einem in der deutschen Ausgabe von *Playboy* erschienenen Roman. (GER)
438 Einleitende Doppelseite zu einer Erzählung, die in *Playboy* erschien. Die Illustration wurde von einem Bildhauer ausgeführt. (USA)
439 Titelseite eines Artikels über einen Drogensüchtigen. Aus der Zeitschrift *Playboy*. (USA)
440, 441 Aus der französischsprachigen Ausgabe von *Playboy*: bittere Erfahrungen im zarten Alter und eine amüsante Geschichte über Liebe und Geiz. (FRA)

437 Illustration accompagnant un roman publié dans l'édition allemande du *Playboy*. (GER)
438 Page double introduisant une nouvelle qui a paru dans le magazine *Playboy*. L'illustration a été exécutée par un sculpteur. (USA)
439 Première page d'un article sur les drogués. Elément du magazine *Playboy*. (USA)
440, 441 De l'édition française du *Playboy*: *L'âge tendre est parfois sulfureux* et *L'avare*, une histoire d'amour et de radinerie à mourir de rire. (FRA)

442

443

Magazine Illustrations
Zeitschriften-Illustrationen
Illustrations de périodiques

166

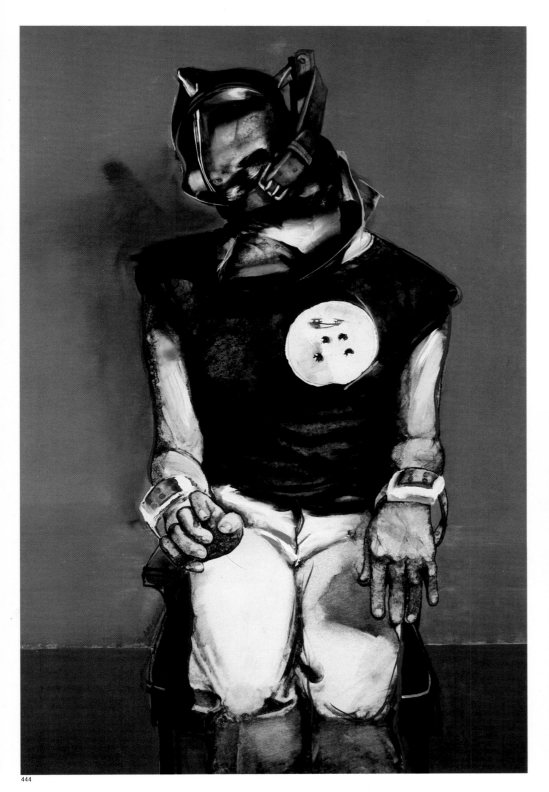

442, 443 Detail of the illustration and introductory double spread from a serialized Mafia novel in *Playboy* called *Blood Sisters*. (USA)
444, 445 Double-spread illustration and page from a preview in *Playboy* of Norman Mailer's book *The Executioner's Song*. (USA)
446 This illustration from *Playboy* in blue and lilac-coloured shades introduces a report called *Fire for Hire*—the flourishing business of the professional arsonist. (USA)

442, 443 Ausschnitt und einleitende Doppelseite aus *Playboy* zu einem Fiction-Roman über ein Mädchen, das sich von seinen Blutsbanden mit der Mafia lösen wollte. (USA)
444, 445 Doppelseitige Illustration und Seite aus einem in Folgen erschienenen Vorabdruck aus einem neuen Buch von Norman Mailer über das Leben von Gary Gilmore. Aus *Playboy*. (USA)
446 Diese Illustration in Blau- und Lilatönen führt einen Bericht ein über bezahlte Brandstifter, deren Geschäft ausgezeichnet floriert. Aus der Zeitschrift *Playboy*. (USA)

442, 443 Détail de l'illustration et première page double de *Playboy*. Ce roman traite d'une jeune fille qui cherche à se dégager des liens du sang l'attachant à la mafia. (USA)
444, 445 Illustration sur page double et page accompagnant un extrait d'un nouveau livre de Norman Mailer consacré à la vie de Gary Gilmore. Elément du magazine *Playboy*. (USA)
446 «Du feu à louer.» Cette illustration (en tons bleus et lilas) introduit un rapport sur les affaires florissantes des incendiaires payés. Du magazine *Playboy*. (USA)

444

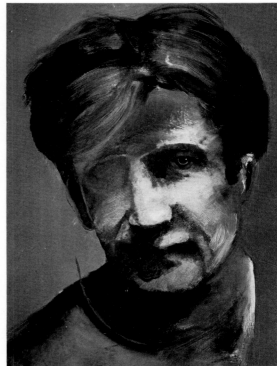

445

ARTIST / KÜNSTLER / ARTISTE:

442, 443 Pater Sato
444, 445 Marshall Arisman
446 Tom Evans

DESIGNER / GESTALTER / MAQUETTISTE:

442, 443 Kerig Pope
444–446 Len Willis

ART DIRECTOR / DIRECTEUR ARTISTIQUE:

442–446 Art Paul/Tom Staebler

PUBLISHER / VERLEGER / EDITEUR:

442–446 Playboy Enterprises, Inc.

446

447

447 Illustration from an article in the French-speaking edition of *Playboy* about the New Romantics in China. (FRA)
448 Introductory double spread from an article about the saxophone and famous saxophone players. This illustration in *Oui* magazine is in shades of yellow. (USA)
449 This article reports on experiments to bring about movements and feelings in people by means of electrodes inserted in the brain. Introductory double spread in *Oui* magazine in subdued colours with a blue operating-table. (USA)
450 Introductory double spread in *Playboy* magazine from a report about a special anti-terror squad trained to resist hijackers. The snakes are in full colour. (USA)
451 *White Lies*. Illustration from a novel in *Playboy* magazine. In full colour. (USA)

447 Illustration zu einem Artikel in der französischsprachigen Ausgabe des *Playboy* über die neuen Romantiker in China. (FRA)
448 Einleitende Doppelseite zu einem Artikel über das Saxophon und berühmte Saxophon-Spieler. Illustration in Gelbtönen. Aus der Zeitschrift *Oui*. (USA)
449 Dieser Artikel berichtet über Versuche, wie man durch im Hirn eingesetzte Elektroden beim Menschen Bewegungen und Gefühle auslösen kann. Einleitende Doppelseite in matten Farben mit blauem Operationstisch, aus der Zeitschrift *Oui*. (USA)
450 Einleitende Doppelseite zu einem Bericht über speziell gegen Flugzeug-Entführer ausgebildete Antiterror-Truppen. Schlangen in bunten Farben. Aus *Playboy*. (USA)
451 Illustration zu einem Fiction-Roman in *Playboy*. Mehrfarbig. (USA)

Magazine Illustrations

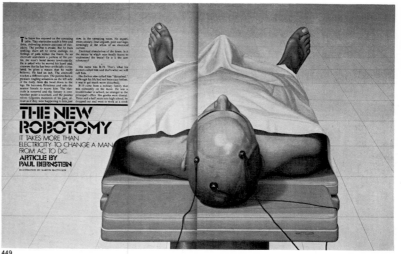

448

449

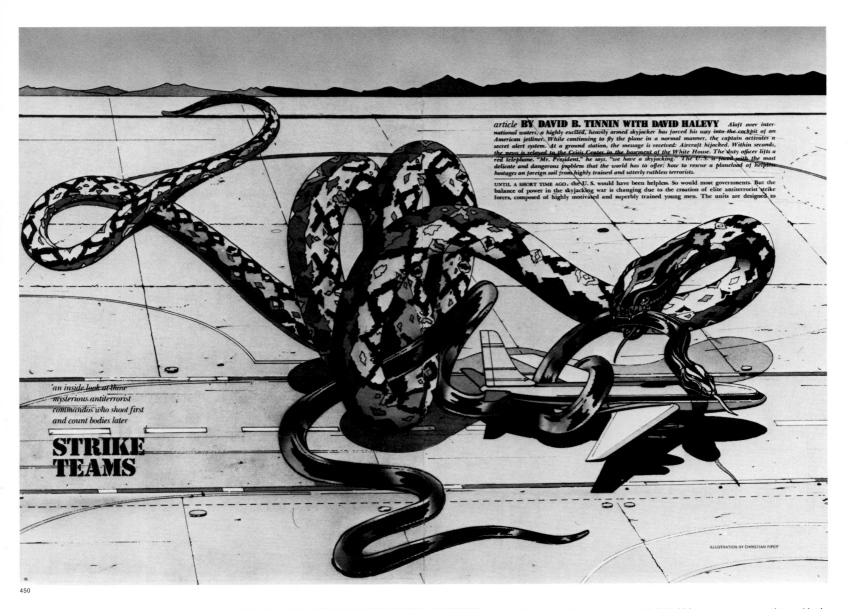

article **BY DAVID B. TINNIN WITH DAVID HALEVY** *Aloft over international waters, a highly excited, heavily armed skyjacker has forced his way into the cockpit of an American jetliner. While continuing to fly the plane in a normal manner, the captain activates a secret alert system. At a ground station, the message is received: Aircraft hijacked. Within seconds, the news is relayed to the Crisis Center in the basement of the White House. The duty officer lifts a red telephone. "Mr. President," he says, "we have a skyjacking. The U.S. is faced with the most delicate and dangerous problem that the world has to offer: how to rescue a planeload of helpless hostages on foreign soil from highly trained and utterly ruthless terrorists.*

UNTIL A SHORT TIME AGO, the U.S. would have been helpless. So would most governments. But the balance of power in the skyjacking war is changing due to the creation of elite antiterrorist strike forces, composed of highly motivated and superbly trained young men. The units are designed to

'an inside look at those mysterious antiterrorist commandos who shoot first and count bodies later

STRIKE TEAMS

ILLUSTRATION BY CHRISTIAN PIPER

450

451

447 Illustration introduisant un article intitulé *Les nouveaux romantiques chinois*, article qui a paru dans l'édition française du *Playboy*. (FRA)
448 Page double initiale d'un article consacré au saxophone et au célèbres saxophonistes. Illustration en tons jaunes extraite du magazine *Oui*. (USA)
449 L'auteur de cet article parle des expériences qu'il avait faites avec des électrodes placées sur le cuir chevelu ou dans l'encéphale afin de provoquer des mouvements et sentiments dont le patient ne se rend pas compte. (USA)
450 Double page initiale d'un article de *Playboy* sur les équipes d'assaut constitués pour lutter contre les pirates de l'air. Serpents en couleurs vives. (USA)
451 Illustration accompagnant un roman publié dans *Playboy*. (USA)

ARTIST / KÜNSTLER / ARTISTE:

447 Cyril Arnstam
448 Joe Saffold
449 Marvin Mattelson
450 Christian Piper
451 Dennis Magnich

DESIGNER / GESTALTER / MAQUETTISTE:

448 Jim Kiehle
449 Michael Brock
450 Bob Post
451 Kerig Pope

ART DIRECTOR / DIRECTEUR ARTISTIQUE:

447 Régis Pagniez
448, 449 Michael Brock
450, 451 Art Paul/Tom Staebler

PUBLISHER / VERLEGER / EDITEUR:

447 Publications Filipacchi
448–450 Playboy Enterprises, Inc.

CHILDREN IN JAIL

THE SPLICE IS RIGHT

SEX AND THE LIBERATED ARAB

ARTIST / KÜNSTLER / ARTISTE:

452 Alex Gnidziejko
453 James Endicott
454 Debbie Kuhn
455 Don Ivan Punchatz
456 Wilson McLean

ART DIRECTOR / DIRECTEUR ARTISTIQUE:

452–456 Joe Brooks

PUBLISHER / VERLEGER / EDITEUR:

452–456 Penthouse International

456

452–456 Introductory double spreads from various articles published in *Penthouse*. Fig. 452: Investigation about youths locked up in American jails without a trial (dark green shades); Fig. 453: discussion about a book in which a film producer writes about his work with Woody Allen and Mel Brooks (brown and green shades); Fig. 454: report about Arabian oil princes who are increasingly satisfying their sexual needs in Europe (in shades of blue); Fig. 455: a report about Par Sondak whose dreams have been recorded by receptors; Fig. 456: a report about the Zebra Murders in San Francisco in which a group of Muslims murdered white people over a period of 179 days. The spotty texture in the illustration is intentional. (USA)

452–456 Premières pages doubles extraites de divers articles parus dans le magazine *Penthouse*. Fig. 452: enquête sur le problème d'un immense nombre de jeunes gens emprisonnés aux Etats-Unis sans avoir été condamnés (en tons verts foncé); fig. 453: compte rendu d'un livre, dans lequel un producteurs de films parle de son travail avec Woody Allen et Mel Brooks (tons bruns et verts); fig. 454: rapport sur les princes arabes des pays producteurs de pétrole, qui viennent de plus en plus chercher leurs amourettes en Europe (tons bleus); fig. 455: rapport sur Par Sondak qui a enregistré ses rêves à l'aide de récepteurs; fig. 456: rapport sur un groupe de musulmans qui ont assassiné des blancs à San Francisco. L'artiste de cette illustration a intentionnellement laissé des taches blanches. (USA)

452–456 Einleitende Doppelseiten zu verschiedenen Artikeln aus *Penthouse*. Abb. 452: Untersuchung über Jugendliche, die in amerikanischen Gefängnissen ohne Prozess einsitzen (dunkle Grüntöne); Abb. 453: Besprechung eines Buches, in welchem ein Filmproduzent über seine Arbeit mit Woody Allen und Mel Brooks schreibt (Braun- und Grüntöne); Abb.454: Bericht über arabische Ölprinzen, die ihre sexuellen Bedürfnisse mehr und mehr in Europa befriedigen (Blautöne); Abb. 455: Bericht über Par Sondak, dessen Träume durch Rezeptoren registriert wurden; Abb. 456: Bericht über eine Gruppe von Muslims, die in San Francisco Weisse niedermetzelten. Die Flecken in der Illustration sind vom Künstler beabsichtigt. (USA)

Magazine Illustrations

Magazine Illustrations
Zeitschriften-Illustrationen
Illustrations de magazine

ARTIST / KÜNSTLER / ARTISTE:

457 Dickran Palulian
458 Bill Greer
459 Dennis Luczak
460 Debbie Kuhn
461, 462 Ralph Steadman

ART DIRECTOR / DIRECTEUR ARTISTIQUE:

457–462 Joe Brooks

PUBLISHER / VERLEGER / EDITEUR:

457–462 Penthouse International

457

458

459   460

172

461

457–462 Illustrations and a double spread from various editions of *Penthouse* magazine. Fig. 457: this illustration introduces an article about *The rat invasion* in big cities—grey rat with the yellow and red Superman symbol on its breast; Fig. 458: *The Agent Orange Time Bomb*, a report about the defoliant produced by the Dow Chemical Co. for use in the Vietnam war—with disastrous and mortal health consequences for soldiers who came into direct contact with the chemical; Fig.460: from a report about industry in the northern states of the USA and their expansion to the south: *The South will fall Again*; Figs. 461, 462: an article dealing with Sigmund Freud's work about the joke and its relation to the subconsciousness. (USA)

457–462 Illustrationen und Doppelseite aus verschiedenen Ausgaben der Zeitschrift *Penthouse*. Abb. 457: diese Illustration leitet einen Artikel über die Ratten-Invasion in Grossstädten ein – graue Ratte mit dem gelb-roten Zeichen des Superman auf der Brust; Abb. 458: zu einem Bericht über die vielen inhaftierten Vietnam-Veteranen – auf getöntem Papier; Abb. 459: zu einem Bericht über das von *Dow* hergestellte und im Vietnam-Krieg verwendete Entlaubungsmittel und den langsamen Tod der Vietnam-Soldaten, die mit diesem Gift in Berührung kamen; Abb. 460: zu einem Bericht über die Industrie des Nordens der USA, die in den Süden expandiert; Abb. 461, 462: zu Sigmund Freuds Werk über den Witz und seine Beziehung zum Unbewussten. (USA)

457–462 Illustrations et page double de différents numéros du magazine *Penthouse*. Fig. 457: cette illustration introduit un article sur l'invasion des rats dans diverses grandes villes – rat gris avec le symbole rouge et jaune de Superman; fig. 458: rapport sur le nombre élevé d'anciens soldats du Viêt-nam emprisonnés encore aujourd'hui, sur papier vergé; fig. 459: rapport sur un produit d'éffeuillage de *Dow* utilisé au Viêt-nam et la mort lente des soldats qui avaient eu à faire avec ce poison pendant la guerre; fig. 460: rapport sur l'expansion de l'industrie du Nord dans le sud des Etats-Unis; fig. 461, 462: un artiste illustre l'ouvrage de Sigmund Freud sur le rire et ses relations avec l'inconscient. (USA)

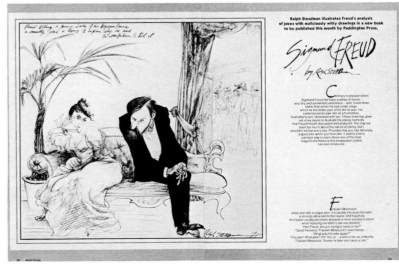

462

464

ARTIST / KÜNSTLER / ARTISTE:

463 Bob Gleason
464, 465 Kip Lott

ART DIRECTOR / DIRECTEUR ARTISTIQUE:

463 Tom Martin
464, 465 Joe Brooks

PUBLISHER / VERLEGER / EDITEUR:

463 Larry Flint Publications
464, 465 Penthouse International

463 This double spread from *Hustler Magazine* is from an article about American military academies and military training centres where also experts and future dictators from abroad get their military training. The double spread is mainly in shades of blue. (USA)
464, 465 Introductory double spread and detail of the illustration in *Penthouse* from a report about the murder of the Chilean dissident Orlando Letelier in Washington. (USA)

463 Diese Doppelseite leitet einen Artikel über amerikanische Militärakademien und militärische Ausbildungszentren ein, an welchen auch zukünftige hohe Militärfachleute und Diktatoren aus dem Ausland ausgebildet werden. Vorwiegend in Blautönen gehalten. (USA)
464, 465 Einleitende Doppelseite und Detail der Illustration zu einem Bericht über die Ermordung des chilenischen Regimekritikers Orlando Letelier in Washington. (USA)

463 Cette page double introduit un article sur les écoles militaires aux Etats-Unis où des experts militaires et des dictateurs futures de pays étrangers sont instruits. Prédominance de tons bleus. Elément extrait de *Hustler Magazine*. (USA)
464, 465 Page double et détail de l'illustration accompagnant un rapport sur l'assassinat à Washington d'Orlando Letelier, critique acerbe du gouvernement. (USA)

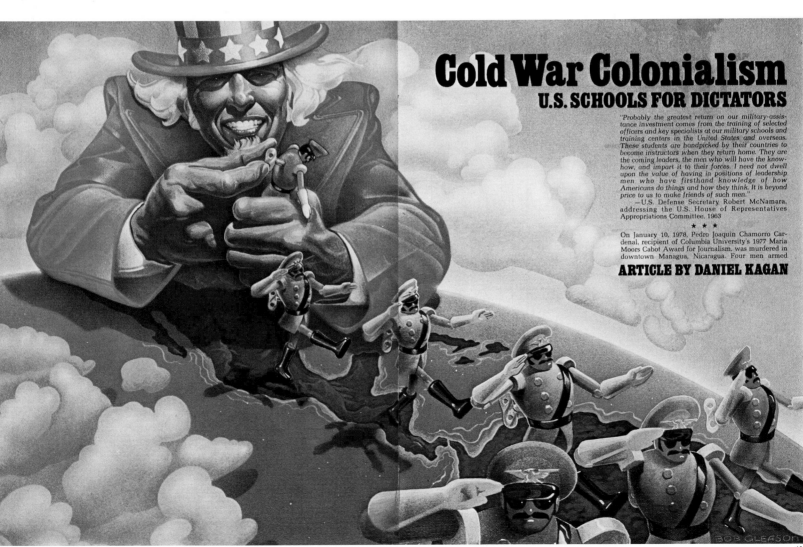

463

467

Magazine Illustrations

468   469

176

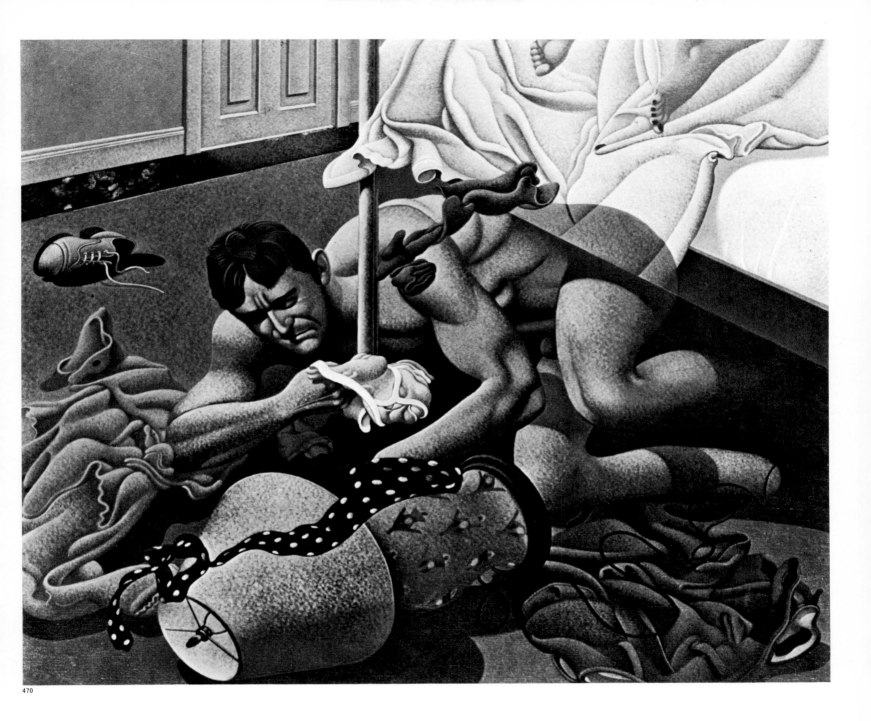

470

471

ART DIRECTOR / DIRECTEUR ARTISTIQUE:
466–471 Joe Brooks

PUBLISHER / VERLEGER / EDITEUR:
466–471 Penthouse International

466, 467 Complete double spread and corresponding illustration in *Penthouse* magazine from a short tale about an ill-fated affair with Inspector Clouseau. (USA)
468 This full-colour illustration introduces an article about attractive Americans. (USA)
469 The daughter of the actress Gloria Joy describes in *Penthouse* her life with Mommy Bitch. (USA)
470 Illustration from a pre-print of a novel entitled *Schultz*. In full colour. (USA)
471 Full-colour illustration from an article about *McDonald's* hamburgers in *Penthouse*. (USA)

466, 467 Vollständige Doppelseite und entsprechende Illustration zu einer in *Penthouse* erschienenen Kurzgeschichte über eine unglückliche Affäre von Inspektor Clouseau. (USA)
468 Diese Farbillustration leitet einen Artikel über den attraktiven Amerikaner ein. (USA)
469 Die Tochter der Schauspielerin Gloria Joy beschreibt das Leben ihrer gehassten Mutter. (USA)
470 Illustration zu einem Vorabdruck aus dem Fiction-Roman *Schultz*. Mehrfarbig. (USA)
471 Mehrfarbige Illustration zu einem Artikel über die berühmten *McDonald's*-Hamburger. (USA)

466, 467 Première page double et illustration d'un récit sur une affaire funeste de l'inspecteur Clouseau. Elément extrait du magazine *Penthouse*. (USA)
468 Illustration couleur sur double page en tête d'un article sur l'Américain séduisant. (USA)
469 La fille de l'actrice Gloria Joy parle de la vie qu'elle passait avec sa mère détestée. (USA)
470 Illustration accompagnant un extrait du roman *Schultz*. En polychromie. (USA)
471 Illustration polychrome d'un article sur la chaîne de restaurants *McDonald's*. (USA)

472

474

473

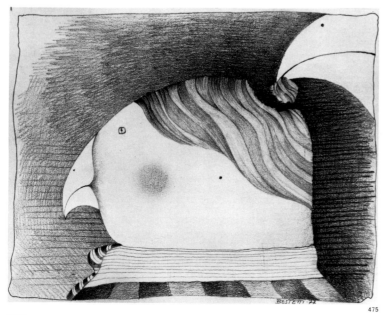

475

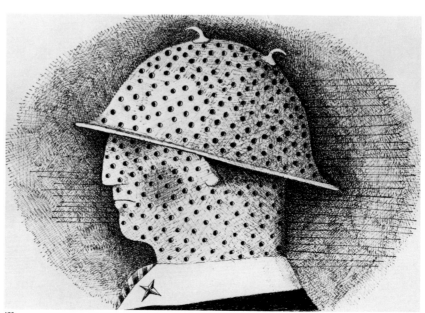

476

477

472, 473 Illustration and introductory double spread from a short story published in *Freundin* magazine about the shock suffered by an Englishman after buying a Sleeping Beauty at a fair. (GER)
474 *The magnificent thinking machine.* Introductory illustration in full colour from *Sky* magazine. (USA)
475, 476 From a series of illustrations that appeared in the cultural supplement of two Italian newspapers, here on the subject of the powerful and on militarism. (ITA)
477, 478 Two full-colour illustrations from an article in *Freundin* magazine in which young female illustrators are introduced. (GER)

472, 473 Illustration und einleitende Doppelseite zu einer Kurzgeschichte in der Zeitschrift *Freundin* über die blauen Wunder, die ein Engländer erlebte, nachdem er sich auf dem Jahrmarkt ein schlafendes Dornröschen gekauft hatte. In matten Farben. (GER)
474 Farbillustration aus der Zeitschrift *Sky,* die einen Artikel mit dem Titel «Die Wunderbare Denkmaschine» einleitet. (USA)
475, 476 Aus einer Serie von Illustrationen, die in der Kulturbeilage von zwei italienischen Tageszeitungen erschienen sind: hier «Die Mächtigen» und «Militarismus». (ITA)
477, 478 Mehrfarbige Illustrationen zu einem Artikel in der Zeitschrift *Freundin,* in welchem junge Illustratorinnen vorgestellt werden. (GER)

472, 473 Illustration et première page double extraites d'une nouvelle publiée dans le magazine *Freundin.* Elle traite d'un Anglais et de ses aventures étonnantes avec la Belle au bois dormant qu'il avait achetée à la foire. En tons mats. (GER)
474 Illustration (en polychromie) introduisant un article du magazine *Sky* intitulé «La magnifique machine à penser». (USA)
475, 476 D'une série d'illustrations qui ont paru dans le supplément culturel de deux quotidiens italiens, se référant ici aux puissants et au militarisme. (ITA)
477, 478 Deux illustrations polychromes d'un article paru dans le magazine *Freundin:* on y présente de jeunes illustratrices. (GER)

478

ARTIST / KÜNSTLER / ARTISTE:

472, 473 Bengt Fosshag
474 Fred Pietsch
475, 476 Pietro Bestetti
477 Arnhild Johne
478 Anne Heseler

ART DIRECTOR / DIRECTEUR ARTISTIQUE:

474 Lynn Lerner
475, 476 Pietro Bestetti

PUBLISHER / VERLEGER / EDITEUR:

472, 473, 477, 478 Burda Verlag GmbH
474 Halsey Publishing Co.
475, 476 Corriere della Sera

479

480

479 Double-spread illustration in full colour that introduced a story published in *Freundin* magazine called "Fear of Marriage." (GER)
480, 482, 483 From a series of full-page illustrations, each one introducing a chapter in the *Life and Health* textbook published by *Random House.* (USA)
481 Black-and-white illustration from a magazine published by *Kisow-Tengai-Sha.* (JPN)

481

482

483

ARTIST / KÜNSTLER / ARTISTE:

479 Kathrin Lindley
480, 482, 483 Dagmar Frinta
481 Tadami Yamada

DESIGNER / GESTALTER / MAQUETTISTE:

480, 482, 483 Dagmar Frinta
481 Keishiro Komatsu

ART DIRECTOR / DIRECTEUR ARTISTIQUE:

480, 482, 483 Dana Kasarsky
481 Kiyomi Kondo

PUBLISHER / VERLEGER / EDITEUR:

479 Burda Verlag GmbH
480, 482, 483 Random House Publishers
481 Kisow-Tengai Sha Co., Ltd.

479 Ganzseitige Farbillustration, die eine in der Zeitschrift *Freundin* publizierte Erzählung mit dem Titel *Angst vor der Ehe* einleitet. (GER)
480, 482, 483 Aus einer Serie von ganzseitigen Illustrationen, die jeweils ein Kapitel in einer Publikation über «Leben und Gesundheit» einführen. (USA)
481 Schwarzweiss-Illustration aus einer Zeitschrift von *Kisow-Tengai-Sha*. (JPN)

479 Illustration pleine page introduisant une nouvelle intitulée «La peur du mariage». Elément extrait du magazine *Freundin*. (GER)
480, 482, 483 Exemples d'une série d'illustrations dont chacune introduit un chapitre dans une publication sur la vie et la santé. (USA)
481 Illustration en noir et blanc tirée d'un magazine des Ed. *Kisow-Tengai-Sha*. (JPN)

484

485

Trade Magazines
Fachzeitschriften
Revues professionnelles

486

ARTIST / KÜNSTLER / ARTISTE:

484, 485 Ute Osterwalder
486 Blair Drawson
487, 488 Ray Condon
489 Ken Cato
490 Ross Goode

DESIGNER / GESTALTER / MAQUETTISTE:

484, 485 Ute Osterwalder
487–490 Ken Cato

ART DIRECTOR / DIRECTEUR ARTISTIQUE:

484, 485 W. Winderlich
486 Neil Shakery
487–490 Ken Cato

AGENCY / AGENTUR / AGENCE – STUDIO:

484, 485 Wolf & Winderlich
487–490 Cato Hibberd Design Pty Ltd

PUBLISHER / VERLEGER / EDITEUR:

484, 485 Axel Springer Verlag
486 Ziff-Davis Publishing
487–490 Lawrence Publishing Co.

487

484, 485 Illustration in actual size and complete cover of the magazine *Ullsteins Gourmet Journal* published by the *Springer* Publishing company. (GER)
486 This illustration published in *Psychology Today* is from an article dealing with the problems of children who grow up in communal homes. (USA)
487—490 Double spread, full-page illustrations (all in black and white) and cover of the magazine *Epicurean*, a magazine for wine lovers and gourmets. Figs. 487, 488: in this second series about New Orleans, a French-speciality restaurant is introduced to the reader; Fig. 489: *Having a Rummy Festive Season*, a play-on-words title for recipes and dishes that require a lot of rum; Fig. 490: full-colour cover illustration on a dark green ground. (AUS)

484, 485 Illustration (in Originalgrösse) und vollständiges Titelbild der vom *Springer Verlag* herausgebrachten Zeitschrift *Ullsteins Gourmet Journal*. (GER)
486 Diese Illustration aus der Zeitschrift *Psychology Today* bezieht sich auf einen Artikel über die Probleme von Kindern, die in Heimen aufwachsen. (USA)
487—490 Doppelseite, ganzseitige Illustrationen (alle in Schwarzweiss) und Umschlag der Zeitschrift *Epicurean*, ein Magazin für Weinkenner und Feinschmecker. Abb. 487, 488: in dieser zweiten Folge über New Orleans wird ein französisches Spezialitäten-Restaurant vorgestellt; Abb. 489: «Für eine ru(h)mvolle Festzeit.» Zu einigen Rezepten für leckere Speisen mit einem Schuss Rum; Abb. 490: mehrfarbige Illustration auf dunkelgrünem Grund. (AUS)

484, 485 Illustration (en grandeur nature) et couverture complète d'un magazine des Ed. *Springer* s'adressant aux gourmets. (GER)
486 Cette illustration extraite du magazine *Psychology Today* se réfère à un article sur les problèmes des enfants qui sont élevés dans un home d'enfants. (USA)
487—490 Page double, illustrations pleines pages (toutes en noir et blanc) et couverture d'un magazine s'adressant au gourmet et au connaisseur de vins. Fig. 487, 488: dans cette deuxième suite sur la Nouvelle Orléans on présente un restaurant de spécialités françaises; fig. 489: «Pour des jours de fête 'au rhum'.» Pour une série de recettes délicieuses préparées avec du rhum; fig. 490: illustration polychrome sur fond vert foncé. (AUS)

488

489

490

491

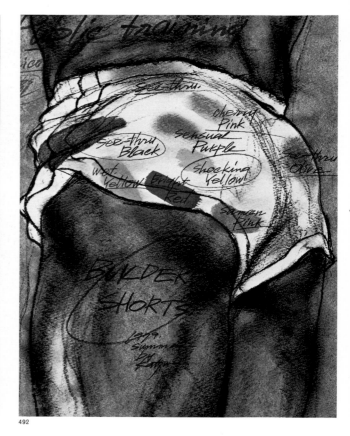

492

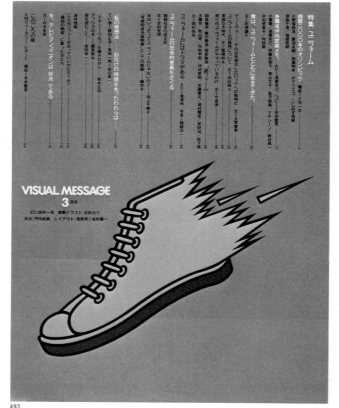

493

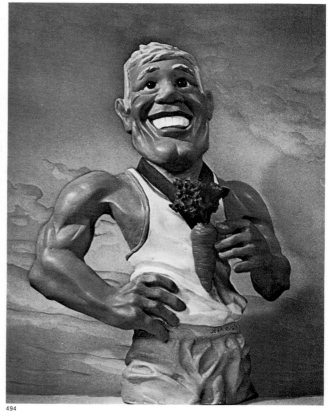

494

ARTIST / KÜNSTLER / ARTISTE

491, 492 Katsu Yoshida
493 Tokiyoshi Tsubouchi
494 Jean Evain
495 Robin Harris
496 Chris Moore
497 Jeff Davis
498 Jack Lefkowitz

DESIGNER / GESTALTER:

495, 496 Keith Ablitt
497, 498 Jack Lefkowitz

491—493 Recto and verso of the cover and inside spread from an edition of the magazine *Visual Message* devoted to the subject of uniforms. Fig. 491: yellow jersey; Fig. 492: white shorts with various full-colour spots; Fig. 493: the table of contents, blue and green, yellow shoe. (JPN)
494 Full-page illustration from an article about the psychological preparation of Olympic competitors which appeared in the magazine *Psychologie*. In full colour on a blue ground. (FRA)
495, 496 Two covers from a magazine devoted to design. Fig. 495 is from an article called *Delving into user tastes—can 'psychographic' research help make better products?*; Fig. 496: *The shape of things to come—just how far can microprocessors take us?* (GBR)
497, 498 Covers from the magazine *Industrial Launderer* from an article about a new energy-saving programme and a preview of the 1980s. The illustrations are in full colour. (USA)

491—493 Vorder- und Rückseite des Umschlages und Innenseite aus einer Ausgabe der Zeitschrift *Visual Message*, die dem Thema «Uniformen» gewidmet ist. Abb. 491: gelbes Leibchen; Abb. 492: weisse Shorts mit verschiedenen Farbflecken; Abb. 493: Inhaltsverzeichnis, Blau und Grün, gelber Schuh. (JPN)
494 Ganzseitige Illustration zu einem Artikel über die psychologische Vorbereitung der Olympia-Teilnehmer, in der Zeitschrift *Psychologie* erschienen. Mehrfarbig, auf blauem Grund. (FRA)
495, 496 Zwei Titelblätter einer Design-Zeitschrift. Abb. 495 bezieht sich auf einen Artikel, in welchem die Frage aufgeworfen wird, ob «psychographische» Forschung zur Herstellung besserer Produkte beiträgt; Abb. 496: zu einem Artikel über Microprozessoren und deren Möglichkeiten. (GBR)
497, 498 Titelblätter der Zeitschrift *Industrial Launderer* zu einem Artikel über ein neues Energiesparprogramm und zu einer Vorausschau auf die 80er Jahre. Mehrfarbige Illustrationen. (USA)

ART DIRECTOR:

491—493 Ikko Tanaka
494 Daniel Sinay
495, 496 Keith Ablitt
497, 498 Jack Lefkowitz

AGENCY / AGENTUR:

494 Idenek
497, 498 Jack Lefkowitz, Inc.

PUBLISHER / VERLEGER:

491—493 Goma Shobo Inc.
494 Psychologie
495, 496 Design Council
497, 498 Institute of Industrial
Launderers

495

497

496

498

491—493 Recto et verso de la couverture et page intérieure d'un numéro du magazine *Visual Message* qui a été consacré au sujet des uniformes. Fig. 491: maillot jaune; fig. 492: short avec des tâches en diverses couleurs; fig. 493: table des matières en bleu et vert, chaussure verte. (JPN)
494 Illustration pleine page extraite d'un article intitulé *Les Jeux olympiques se préparent aussi psychologiquement*. Elément du magazine *Psychologie*. Illustration en polychromie sur fond bleu. (FRA)
495, 496 Deux couvertures d'un magazine d'arts graphiques. Fig. 495 se réfère à un article qui discute les recherches «psychographiques» et leur utilisation éventuelle pour développer de meilleurs produits; fig. 496: pour un article sur les microprocesseurs et leurs possibilités. (GBR)
497, 498 Couvertures d'un périodique professionnel se référant à un article sur un nouveau programme d'économie énergétique et à une prévision sur les années 80. Les illustrations sont en couleurs. (USA)

499

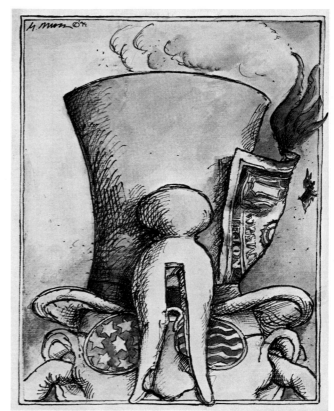

501

500

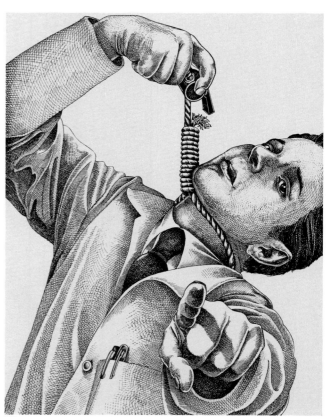

504

499 Cover illustration from *Technology Review*, an MIT magazine, for an article about scientists and human rights. In full colour. (USA)

500 Illustration for the expression "red tape" published in the *Senior Scholastic Magazine*. The expression originated in England where law decrees, were bound in red tape; it is now used to describe bureaucracy in government. (USA)

501 Introductory illustration for an article in the *Anti-nuclear Rally Book* about how more money seems to produce less energy. In full colour. (USA)

502 Article in *Politics Today*. The illustration introduces an analysis about Salt II entitled *The sweet smell of ratification*. (USA)

503 Illustration in orange and pink on blue from an article in *Savings & Loan News* about how outsiders infiltrate into established businesses. (USA)

504 Black-and-white illustration from an interview in *Technology Review* about the danger of atomic power stations. (USA)

505, 506 Cover from an article about the psychological problems involved when leaving a sect (in full colour) and black-and-white illustration for an analysis about the connection between our muscles and our psyche. (FRA)

Trade Magazines

186

502

503

ARTIST / KÜNSTLER:

499–502 Geoffrey Moss
503 Bobbye Cochran
504 Gary Viskupic
505, 506 Gérard Segui

DESIGNER / GESTALTER:

503 Jim Lienhart

ART DIRECTOR:

499, 504 Nancy C. Pokross
500 Audrey Perella
501 Lynn Hollyn
502 Peter Morance
503 Jim Lienhart
505, 506 Daniel Sinay

AGENCY / AGENTUR / AGENCE:

499, 504 MIT Design Services
503 MWD&L
505, 506 Idenek

PUBLISHER / VERLEGER:

499, 504 Massachusetts Institute
of Technology
500 Scholastic Magazines,
501 Musicians United
for Safe Energy
502 Politics Today
503 Savings & Loan News
505, 506 Psychologie

505

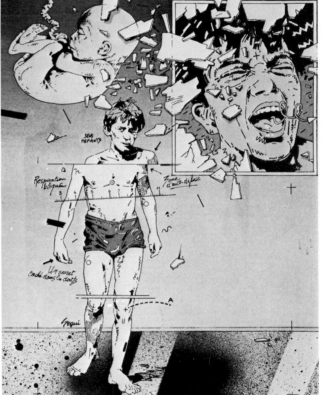

506

499 Umschlagillustration einer Zeitschrift des MIT zu einem Artikel mit dem Titel «Wissenschafter und Menschenrechte». Mehrfarbig. (USA)
500 Illustration zum Ausdruck «red tape» (rotes Band): er stammt ursprünglich aus England, wo Gesetzesbestimmungen mit roten Bändern zusammengebunden wurden, heute steht er für das bürokratische U.S.-Regierungssystem. (USA)
501 Einleitende Illustration zu einem Artikel über die unverhältnismässig hohen Kosten, die für Atomenergie bezahlt werden. Mehrfarbig. (USA)
502 «Der süsse Duft der Ratifikation.» Diese Illustration leitet eine Analyse über das Salt-II-Abkommen ein. (USA)
503 Illustration (Orange, Rosa auf Blau) zu einem Artikel über aussenstehende «Machtprotze», die sich in interne Angelegenheiten der Kleinen mischen. (USA)
504 Schwarzweiss-Illustration zu einem Interview über die Gefahren der Kernkraftwerke. Aus einer Zeitschrift des MIT. (USA)
505, 506 Umschlag zu den psychologischen Problemen beim Austritt aus einer Sekte (mehrfarbig) und Schwarzweiss-Illustration zu einer Analyse über den Zusammenhang zwischen unseren Muskeln und unserer Psyche. (FRA)

499 Illustration de couverture d'un magazine du MIT se référant à un article intitulé «L'homme de science et les droits de l'homme». En couleurs. (USA)
500 Illustration de l'expression «red tape» (bande rouge): d'origine anglaise où les dispositions légales étaient attachées avec une bande rouge, elle signifie aujourd'hui «bureaucratie gouvernementale». (USA)
501 Illustration initiale d'un article discutant les sommes extrêmement élevées qu'on dépense pour l'énergie nucléaire. En polychromie. (USA)
502 «Le parfum suave des ratifications.» Illustration introduisant une analyse sur la ratification de l'accord Salt II. (USA)
503 Illustration (orange, rose sur bleu) pour un article sur les outsiders puissants qui se mêlent des affaires intérieures des petits. (USA)
504 Illustration en noir et blanc accompagnant un interview sur les dangers des centrales nucléaires. D'un magazine du MIT. (USA)
505, 506 Couverture: *Au sortir d'une secte: les problèmes psychologiques*; illustration noir-blanc: article sur une thérapie qui libère les émotions en agissant sur les muscles. Du magazine *Psychologie*. (FRA)

507–511 Introductory double spreads from *Emergency Medicine* for articles about immediate care for patients with heart injuries (black and white), about an inflatable "suit" for patients with internal bleeding that can be reduced due to outside pressure (full colour), on the problem of psychic seizures that are often diagnosed as epileptic attacks, and cover in pink and light blue about warning skin manifestations. (USA)
512 Cover from *Grafiek*, a graphic-design magazine. (NLD)
513 Cover illustration from *Postgraduate Medicine* for the leading article about allergic disease and its diagnosis. (USA)
514 Illustration from *Creative Psychiatry*, a Geigy magazine, here on the subject of basic research. (USA)

Trade Magazines
Fachzeitschriften
Revues professionnelles

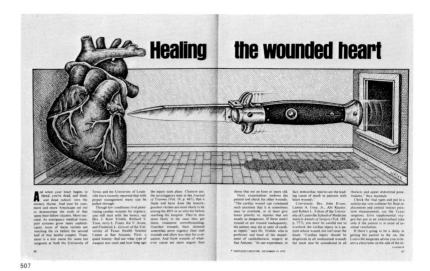

507

509

508

510

ARTIST / KÜNSTLER / ARTISTE:

507 Charles Waller
508 Bob Brown
509, 510 Alan E. Cober
511 Frank Bozzo
512 Paul Ibou
513 John Collier

DESIGNER / GESTALTER / MAQUETTISTE:

507 Louise Petosa
508, 511 Diane Greene
509, 510 Marylee Langman
512 Paul Ibou
513 John deCesare

ART DIRECTOR / DIRECTEUR ARTISTIQUE:

507–511 Tom Lennon
513 Tina Adamek

PUBLISHER / VERLEGER / EDITEUR:

507–511 Fischer Medical Publications
512 Grafiek
513 McGraw-Hill, Inc.
514 Geigy Pharmaceuticals

507–511 Einleitende Doppelseiten aus einer medizinischen Fachzeitschrift zu Artikeln über Sofortmassnahmen bei Patienten mit Herzverletzungen (Schwarzweiss), über einen aufblasbaren «Anzug» für Patienten mit inneren Blutungen, die durch äusseren Druck abgeschwächt werden (mehrfarbig), über psychisch bedingte Zusammenbrüche, die oft als Epilepsie diagnostiziert und behandelt werden und Titelblatt (in Rosa und Hellblau) zu Hautreaktionen als Vorzeichen gewisser Krankheiten. (USA)
512 Titelblatt einer Zeitschrift für Graphik. (NLD)
513 Umschlagillustration einer medizinischen Fachzeitschrift zum Leitartikel über Allergien und deren Diagnosestellung. (USA)
514 Illustration aus einer Publikation, die Geigy an Ärzte verteilt. Diese Ausgabe ist dem Thema der Grundlagenforschung gewidmet. (USA)

507–511 Pages doubles initiales extraites d'un périodique médical. Elles se réfèrent à des articles sur les mesures d'urgance qu'il faut prendre si quelqu'un a une blessure au cœur (noir-blanc), sur un «costume» pneumatique pour des patients souffrant d'hémorragies internes qui peuvent être arrêtées par pression externe, sur les effondrements psychiques qui sont souvent diagnostiqués comme épilepsie et couverture sur les irritations de la peau qui précèdent souvent une maladie. Toutes les illustrations sont en couleurs. (USA)
512 Couverture d'une revue d'arts graphiques. (NLD)
513 Couverture se référant aux allergies et leur diagnostic. (USA)
514 Illustration d'une publication Geigy distribuée au corps médical. Son thème: la recherche de base. (USA)

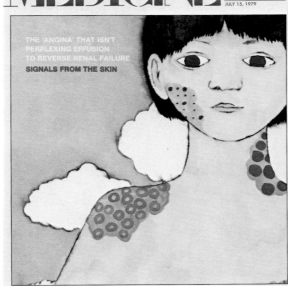

511

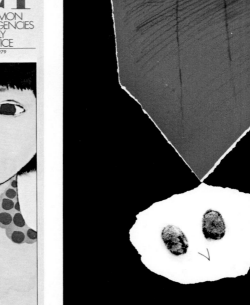

512

513

514

515

House Organs / Hauszeitschriften
Journaux d'entreprise

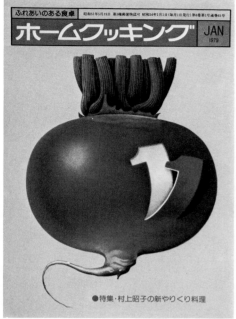

516

517

522

518

519

520

521

515 Illustration in actual size from the *Celanese* company house organ. (USA)
516–521 Covers of a monthly small-format house organ from Kikkoman Shoyu, producer of a large variety of sauces. Here we reproduce the six editions for the first half year what is shown by the numbers integrated in the vegetables. All the illustrations are in full colour. (JPN)
522 Cover in shades of blue for the house organ *Tone*, published by the Armstrong Cork Co., with an article about office interiors and space relationships. (USA)

515 Illustration in Originalgrösse aus der Hauszeitschrift von *Celanese*. (USA)
516–521 Titelblätter einer monatlich erscheinenden, kleinformatigen Hauszeitschrift von *Kikkoman Shoyu*. Wir zeigen hier die sechs Ausgaben des ersten halben Jahres, was durch die in jedem Gemüse integrierte Zahl angezeigt wird. Alle Illustrationen sind mehrfarbig. (JPN)
522 In Blautönen gehaltener Umschlag der Hauszeitschrift *Tone* zu einem Artikel über Büroeinrichtungen und ihre Anpassung an die gegebenen Verhältnisse. (USA)

515 Illustration (en grandeur originale) extraite du journal d'entreprise de *Celanese*. (USA)
516–521 Couvertures du journal d'entreprise à petit format que *Kikkoman Shoyu* publie chaque mois. Nous reproduisons ici les six numéros de la première moitié de l'année. Les chiffres intégrés dans chaque légume indique le mois en question. Toutes les illustrations sont en couleurs. (JPN)
522 Couverture en tons bleus prédominant du journal d'entreprise *Tone*. Elle se réfère à un article sur l'ameublement des bureaux et son adaptation à l'espace donné. (USA)

ARTIST / KÜNSTLER / ARTISTE:

515 Frances Jetter
516–521 Tadashi Ohashi
522 Richard Brown

DESIGNER / GESTALTER / MAQUETTISTE:

515 Frances Jetter
516–521 Tadashi Ohashi
522 Bradley Gast

ART DIRECTOR / DIRECTEUR ARTISTIQUE:

515 Bob Eichinger
516–521 Tadashi Ohashi
522 Bradley Gast

AGENCY / AGENTUR / AGENCE – STUDIO:

515 Eichinger, Inc.

PUBLISHER / VERLEGER / EDITEUR:

515 Celanese Industries
516–521 Kikkoman Shoyu Co., Ltd.
522 Armstrong Cork Company

523 This illustration in poster size was inserted as a supplement in a publication on important events in 1978. In full colour. (SPA)
524 Full-colour illustration on the subject "Motivation" which appeared in the house organ of an advertising agency. (SPA)
525, 526 Illustration and double spread from the *Honeywell Bull* house organ for an article posing the question of whether computerized data in regard to tax administration does not in some way threaten the privacy of the individual. In blue on white. (NLD)
527 Illustration from the house organ *Clinch*, published by an advertising agency. (GER)
528 Illustration in subdued shades of blue, beige and lilac from *Marathon World*, the house organ of a large oil company. The article deals with the various stages of maturity of a human being. (USA)
529 Article from the Scott Paper house organ about the Winter Olympics. Subdued shades. (USA)

523 Diese Illustration wurde als Poster einer Publikation über wichtige Ereignisse des Jahres 1978 beigelegt. Mehrfarbig. (SPA)
524 Mehrfarbige Illustration zum Thema «Motivation», die in der Hauszeitschrift einer Werbeagentur erschienen ist. (SPA)
525, 526 Illustration und Doppelseite aus der Hauszeitschrift von *Honeywell Bull* zu einem Artikel über die Frage, ob die elektronische Datenverarbeitung bei der Steuerverwaltung einen Einbruch in die Privatsphäre des Einzelnen bedeutet. In Blau auf Weiss. (NLD)
527 Illustration aus der Hauszeitschrift *Clinch* der Werbeagentur *Leisten/Bellingradt*. (GER)
528 Illustration in matten Blau-, Beige- und Lilatönen aus der Hauszeitschrift einer Ölgesellschaft. Zu einem Artikel über die verschiedenen Stadien im Reifeprozess eines Menschen. (USA)
529 Zu einem anlässlich der Olympischen Winterspiele erschienenen Artikel. Matte Farbtöne. (USA)

523 Cette illustration sous forme d'affiche a été jointe à une publication sur les événements les plus importants de l'année 1978. En polychromie. (SPA)
524 Illustration (en polychromie) au sujet de la «motivation», publiée dans le journal d'entreprise d'une agence de publicité. (SPA)
525, 526 Illustration et page double extraites du journal d'entreprises de *Honeywell Bull*. On discute dans cet article le traitement électronique d'informations fiscales et les inconvénients éventuels pour le particulier. En bleu sur blanc. (NLD)
527 Illustration du journal d'entreprise *Clinch*, publié par une agence publicitaire. (GER)
528 Illustration du journal d'entreprise d'une compagnie pétrolière accompagnant un article sur les différentes phases de maturité de l'homme. Tons bleus, beiges et lilas. (USA)
529 Article paru à l'occasion des Jeux Olympiques d'hiver. En tons mats. (USA)

ARTIST / KÜNSTLER / ARTISTE:

523, 524 Enric Huguet
525, 526 Louis Visser
527 Wolfgang Bellingradt
528 John Cayea
529 Dakota Design

DESIGNER / GESTALTER / MAQUETTISTE:

523, 524 Enric Huguet
525, 526 Jan Lepair
527 Wolfgang Bellingradt
529 Dakota Design

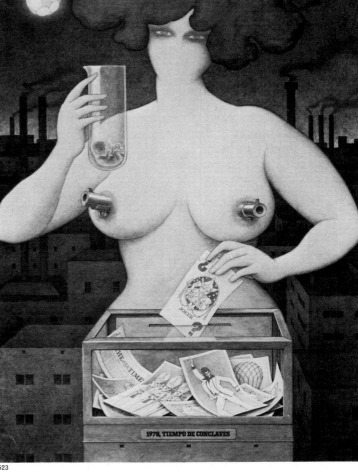

523

524

525

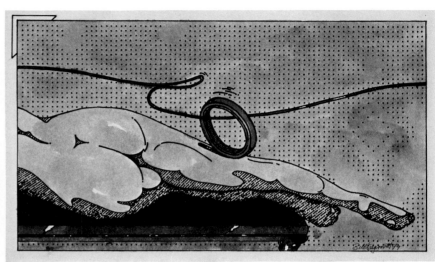

527

526

ART DIRECTOR / DIRECTEUR ARTISTIQUE:

523, 524 Enric Huguet
525, 526 Jan Lepair
527 Vera Schlösser
528 Stan Corfman/Richard Neuman
529 Tom Daniels/Bill Oliver

AGENCY / AGENTUR / AGENCE – STUDIO:

523, 524 Enric Huguet
525, 526 Lepair Design
527 Leisten/Bellingradt
529 Dakota Design Inc.

528

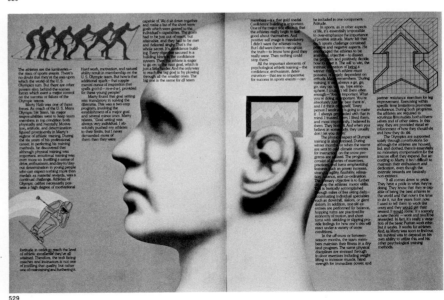

529

PUBLISHER / VERLEGER / EDITEUR:

523 Difusora Internacional, S.A.
524 Arce & Potti, S.A.
525, 526 Honeywell Bull (Nederland) N.V.
527 Leisten/Bellingradt
528 Marathon Oil Company
529 Scott Paper Company

ARTIST / KÜNSTLER / ARTISTE:

531, 532 Wolfgang M. Dehm
533 Milton Glaser

DESIGNER / GESTALTER / MAQUETTISTE:

530 Fred Troller
531, 532 Wolfgang M. Dehm

ART DIRECTOR / DIRECTEUR ARTISTIQUE:

530 Fred Troller
531, 532 Wolfgang M. Dehm

AGENCY / AGENTUR / AGENCE – STUDIO:

530 Fred Troller Associates
531, 532 ACS Art & Concept Studio

PUBLISHER / VERLEGER / EDITEUR:

530 IBM Corporation
531, 532 Emil Daiber
533 IBM Deutschland GmbH

530 Single jigsaw-puzzle pieces in black and silver with full-colour numbers serve as a cover illustration for an IBM magazine about the possibilities of computerized data. (USA)
531, 532 Cover of two editions of a Stuttgart golf club's newspaper with golf balls shown as ice-cream and as an egg. Both illustrations are in full colour. (GER)
533 Illustration in actual size from an IBM newsletter for an article about the technological development of computerized information in the future. (GER)

530 Einzelne Puzzlestücke in Schwarz und Silber mit farbigen Zahlen dienen als Umschlagillustration einer IBM-Zeitschrift über die Anwendungsmöglichkeiten von elektronischen Datenverarbeitungs-Anlagen. (USA)
531, 532 Titelblätter von zwei Ausgaben der Stuttgarter Golf-Nachrichten mit Golfbällen als Glacekugeln und als Ei. Beide Illustrationen sind mehrfarbig. (GER)
533 Illustration in Originalgrösse aus den IBM-Nachrichten, zu einem Artikel mit dem Titel *Die Herausforderung* über die Zukunft der Informationsverarbeitungs-Technologie. (GER)

530 Ces fragments découpés d'un puzzle (en noir et argent avec des chiffres en couleurs) illustrent la couverture d'un magazine de l'IBM sur les possibilités d'application de diverses installations d'informatique. (USA)
531, 532 Couvertures de deux numéros du bulletin du club de golfe de Stuttgart. (GER)
533 Illustration (en grandeur originale) d'un bulletin de l'IBM accompagnant un article sur les perspectives de l'informatique. (GER)

530

House Organs / Hauszeitschriften
Journaux d'entreprise

531

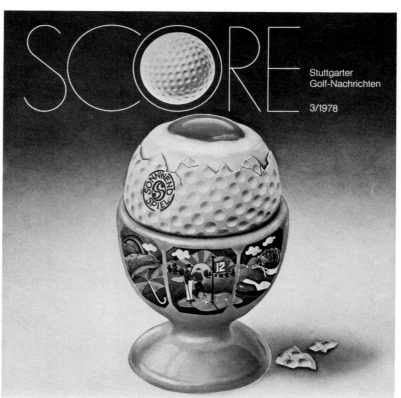

532

534

535

537

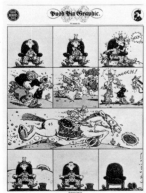

536

ARTIST / KÜNSTLER / ARTISTE:

534, 536 Elwood Smith
535, 537 Emanuel Schongut

DESIGNER / GESTALTER / MAQUETTISTE:

534–537 Richard Mantel

ART DIRECTOR / DIRECTEUR ARTISTIQUE:

534–537 Seymour Chwast

AGENCY / AGENTUR / AGENCE – STUDIO:

534–537 Push Pin Studios, Inc.

PUBLISHER / VERLEGER / EDITEUR:

534–537 Push Pin Graphic, Inc.

534, 536 Cover illustration in actual size and complete cover for a "Great Heroes Issue" of *Push Pin Graphic*, the house organ of the *Push Pin Studios*, published every two months. (USA)
535, 537 Black-and-white illustration and corresponding double spread from a "Grand Illusion Issue" of *Push Pin Graphic*. The illustration accompanies a short story entitled *The Waiting*, a reprint from *The Labyrinth* written by the South American author J. L. Borges. (USA)

534, 536 Umschlagillustration in Originalgrösse und vollständiger Umschlag einer Ausgabe von *Push Pin Graphic*, der von den *Push Pin Studios* alle zwei Monate herausgebrachten Hauszeitschrift. Diese Ausgabe war grossen Helden gewidmet. (USA)
535 Schwarzweiss-Illustration und entsprechende Doppelseite aus einer Ausgabe von *Push Pin Graphic*, die der grossen Illusion gewidmet war. Die Illustration begleitet eine Kurzgeschichte mit dem Titel «Das Warten» aus einem Buch von J. L. Borges *(The Labyrinth)*. (USA)

534, 536 Illustration de couverture (en grandeur originale) et couverture complète d'un numéro de *Push Pin Graphic*, journal d'entreprise des *Push Pin Studios* qui paraît tous les deux mois. Ce numéro-ci a été consacré aux grands héros. (USA)
535, 537 Illustration en noir et blanc et page double correspondante d'un numéro de *Push Pin Graphic*, numéro consacré aux grandes illusions. Cette illustration accompagne une nouvelle intitulée «L'attente» extraite d'un livre de J. L. Borges *(The Labyrinth)*. (USA)

538

ESSO

540

539

39

PEEPING TOM: In 1040 the Lord of Coventry in England agreed to his wife's plea that he reduce oppressive taxes, but only on condition that she in turn ride naked through the city. This she did, and the townspeople so revered her for her action that all averted their eyes. The exception, a tailor named Tom, was struck blind for his impudence. A voyeur was from then on known as a peeping tom. This also applies to Dick & Harry.

GIRL FRIDAY

Robinson Crusoe, by Daniel Defoe, appeared in 1719. In the well-known story, Crusoe, stranded on a desolate island, was lucky enough to be joined by a black man whom he named Friday, that being the day they met. His man, Friday, existed for many years in people's minds as the image of an able and accomplished assistant who could perform any task, no matter how difficult, required of him by R.C. The status of Friday remained quo for many years until a new generation of liberated women proved that they could do what Friday could do, equally as well, or better, any day of the week. And that's when Girl Friday arrived on the scene.

ILLUSTRATIONS BY LIONEL KALISH

542

543

House Organs / Hauszeitschriften
Journaux d'entreprise

538 Full-page illustration of Malcolm X (red on dark brown) from a "Great Heroes Issue" of *Push Pin Graphic*. (USA)
539 Another *Push Pin Graphic* issue devoted to the "Total disaster". The illustration accompanies a story written by Edgar Allan Poe. In dark shades of steely blue. (USA)
540 Cover from the house organ of *Esso France* referring to an article entitled "From the petrol lamp to the *Esso* Oval, 100 years of history in France". The illustration is in subdued colours. (FRA)
541–543 Inside spread and cover from two editions of the quarterly magazine *U&lc* of the International Typeface Corp. Fig. 541: from the chapter Something for Everyone; Figs. 542, 543: these portraits of Pablo Picasso and Leo Castelli have been done in four different weights of type. (USA)

538 Ganzseitige Illustration von Malcolm X (rot auf Dunkelbraun) aus einer Ausgabe von *Push Pin Graphic* über grosse Helden. (USA)
539 Ganzseitige Illustration in dunklen Stahlblautönen zu einer Geschichte von E. A. Poe («Die Maske des roten Todes). Aus einer der «totalen Katastrophe» gewidmeten Ausgabe der Hauszeitschrift *Push Pin Graphic*. (USA)
540 Umschlag der Hauszeitschrift von *Esso France* zum Thema «Von der Petrollampe zum Esso-Oval, 100 Jahre Geschichte in Frankreich». Illustration in matten Farben. (FRA)
541–543 Innenseiten und Titelblatt von zwei Ausgaben der vierteljährlich erscheinenden Zeitschrift *U&lc* der International Typeface Corp. Abb. 541: aus der Rubrik «Für jeden etwas»; Abb. 542, 543: diese beiden in vier verschiedenen Schriftgraden und -stärken gesetzten Portraits zeigen Pablo Picasso und Leo Castelli. (USA)

538 Illustration pleine page de Malcolm X (rouge sur brun foncé) d'un numéro de *Push Pin Graphic* sur les grands héros. (USA)
539 Illustration pleine page (tons bleus acier) accompagnant un récit d'Edgar Allan Poe («Le masque de la mort rouge»). D'un numéro de *Push Pin Graphic* consacré à la «catastrophe totale». (USA)
540 Couverture du journal d'entreprise *Pétrole Progrès* d'*Esso France*: De la lampe à pétrole à l'ovale Esso, cent ans d'histoire en France. Illustration en tons mats. (FRA)
541–543 Pages intérieures et couverture de deux numéros du magazine trimestriel *U&lc*, publié par l'International Typeface Corp. Fig. 541: de la rubrique «Quelque chose pour chacun»; fig. 542, 543: ces deux portraits représentent Pablo Picasso et Leo Castelli ont été composé par divers caractères d'imprimerie. (USA)

ARTIST / KÜNSTLER / ARTISTE:

538, 539 Stanislaw Zagorski
540 André François
541 Lionel Kalish

DESIGNER / GESTALTER / MAQUETTISTE:

538, 539 Richard Mantel
540 Any Dubois
541 Herb Lubalin
542 Paul Siemsen
543 Joseph Amft

ART DIRECTOR / DIRECTEUR ARTISTIQUE:

538, 539 Seymour Chwast
540 Jacques Tribondeau
541–543 Herb Lubalin

AGENCY / AGENTUR / AGENCE – STUDIO:

538, 539 Push Pin Studios, Inc.
541–543 Lubalin, Burns & Co., Inc.

PUBLISHER / VERLEGER / EDITEUR:

538, 539 Push Pin Graphic, Inc.
540 Esso France
541–543 International Typeface Corporation

Book Covers
Buchumschläge
Couvertures de livres

ARTIST / KÜNSTLER / ARTISTE:

544–546 Tadanori Yokoo
547 Kvĕta Pacovská
548 Hans Ulrich Osterwalder
549 Wendell Minor

DESIGNER / GESTALTER / MAQUETTISTE:

544–546 Tadanori Yokoo
549 Wendell Minor
550 Albert Squillace

ART DIRECTOR / DIRECTEUR ARTISTIQUE:

544–546 Tadanori Yokoo
547 Kvĕta Pacovská
548 Dirk Stempel
549 Lidia Ferrara
550 Albert Squillace

545

544

AGENCY / AGENTUR / AGENCE – STUDIO:

549 W. Minor Design

PUBLISHER / VERLEGER / EDITEUR:

544–546 Shinchosha Publishing Co.
547 Grúnd Verlag
548 Deutscher Sparkassenverlag GmbH
549 Alfred A. Knopf
550 The Ridge Press/Playboy Press

544, 545 Complete book cover and front cover in brown-orange and grey on cream-coloured paper. (JPN)
546 Full-colour dust jacket for a book. (JPN)
547 Dust jacket in brilliant colours for the French edition of a Czechoslovakian children's book. (CSR)
548 Dust jacket in blue and green shades of a publication on architecture and life in Württemberg, published on the occasion of the 50th anniversary of the Loan and Building Association of Württemberg. (GER)
549 Full-colour dust jacket of the novel *The Desperadoes*, published by *Knopf*. (USA)
550 Jacket for a publication by *The Ridge Press/Playboy Press* on great inventions. (USA)

544, 545 Vollständiger Buchumschlag und Vorderseite in Braunorange und Grau auf crèmefarbenem Papier. (JPN)
546 Mehrfarbiger Schutzumschlag für ein Buch. (JPN)
547 Schutzumschlag in bunten Farben für die französischsprachige Ausgabe eines tschechischen Kinderbuches. (CSR)
548 In Blau- und Grüntönen gehaltener Schutzumschlag des Werkes *Bauen, Wohnen, Leben in Württemberg*, das von der *Öffentlichen Bausparkasse Württemberg* aus Anlass des 50jährigen Firmenjubiläums herausgegeben wurde. (GER)
549 Mehrfarbiger Schutzumschlag für einen Roman («Die Desperados»). (USA)
550 Schutzumschlag für ein Werk über grosse Erfindungen. (USA)

544, 545 Jaquette dépliée et recto de celle-ci (en brun-orange et gris sur papier vergé) pour un livre. (JPN)
546 Jaquette polychrome pour un livre. (JPN)
547 Couverture de la traduction française d'un livre d'enfant tchèque. Illustration en couleurs vives sur blanc. (CSR)
548 Jaquette d'un ouvrage consacré à l'architecture, l'habitation et la vie au Wurtemberg. Cet ouvrage a été publié d'un crédit foncier du Wurtemberg à l'occasion de ses 50 ans d'existence. Prédominance de tons bleus et verts. (GER)
549 Jaquette polychrome pour un roman («Les risque-tout»). (USA)
550 Couverture d'un ouvrage sur les grandes inventions. (USA)

548

546

宇宙衞生博覽會
筒井康隆

新潮社
Iustust Akatusay

547

Passetou, Siffletou et Miretou

KAREL JAROMÍR ERBEN

Gründ

549

A NOVEL BY RON HANSEN

Desperadoes

550

by Ralph Stein

The Great Inventions

551

552

553

554

ARTIST / KÜNSTLER:

551 Stanislaw Zagorski
552 Béat Brüsch
553 Friso Henstra
554 Georgeta Pusztai
555 Bruno Oldani
556 Heather Cooper
557 Folon

DESIGNER / GESTALTER:

551 Stanislaw Zagorski
553 Friso Henstra
555 Bruno Oldani
556 Jonathan James Books

ART DIRECTOR:

551 Rubin Pfeiffer
552 D. Toutain
553 Wim Mol
554 Viorica Matei
556 Jonathan James Books

AGENCY / AGENTUR / AGENCE:

556 Burns, Cooper, Hynes Ltd.

PUBLISHER / VERLEGER / EDITEUR

551 Harcourt, Brace, Jovanovich
552 Seuil
553 Uitgeverij de Arbeiderspers
554 Editura Meridiane
555 Pax Forlag
556 Jonathan James Books
557 Rikuyo-Sha Publishing, Inc.

Book Covers
Buchumschläge
Couvertures de livres

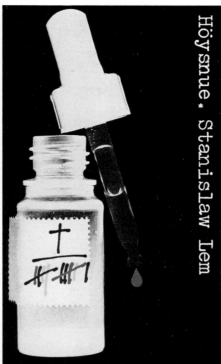

Höysnue * Stanisław Lem

ISBN 82-530-0971-2

日本のパッケージデザイン
ヨーロッパとの対比

A COMPARISON OF PACKAGE DESIGNS IN JAPAN & EUROPE

555

The Illustrated Child

556

551 Dust jacket in sombre shades for a novel. (USA)
552 Dust jacket mainly in shades of green and blue for a novel written by Marie Chaix. (FRA)
553 Cover for the Dutch translation of Herman Hesse's stories, published in a paperback series. (NLD)
554 Cover of a paperback about film history, translated from French. The illustration is in full colour. (RUM)
555 Recto and verso of a paperback cover from a series of criminal stories with social aspects. (NOR)
556 Full-colour dust jacket for a book containing the complete collection of the oil-paintings Heather Cooper painted of her daughter. In full colour. (CAN)
557 Dust jacket of a work comparing package designs in Japan and Europe. Mainly in shades of green, red label. (JPN)

551 Schutzumschlag in düsteren Farben für einen Roman («Griff nach der Ewigkeit»). (USA)
552 Vorwiegend in Grün- und Blautönen gehaltener Schutzumschlag für einen Roman von Marie Chaix. (FRA)
553 Umschlag für die in einer Taschenbuchreihe erschienene holländische Übersetzung von Hermann Hesses Erzählungen. (NLD)
554 Umschlag eines Taschenbuches für eine aus dem Französischen übersetzte Filmgeschichte. Mehrfarbige Illustration. (RUM)
555 Vorder- und Rückseite eines Taschenbuchumschlages aus einer Serie von Kriminalgeschichten mit sozialem Aspekt. (NOR)
556 Mehrfarbiger Schutzumschlag eines Werkes, das die Ölbilder vereinigt, die Heather Cooper von ihrer Tochter malte. (CAN)
557 Schutzumschlag eines Werkes über Packungsgestaltung in Japan und Europa. Vorwiegend in Grautönen gehalten, rotes Schriftband. (JPN)

551 Jaquette pour un roman («Saisir l'éternité»). Tons foncés. (USA)
552 Jaquette pour un roman de Marie Chaix publié par les Ed. *du Seuil*. Prédominance de tons bleus et verts. (FRA)
553 Couverture de la traduction néerlandaise des contes de Hermann Hesse. D'une série de livres de poche. (NLD)
554 Couverture d'un livre de poche: traduction en langue roumaine d'un dictionnaire français des films. Illustration en couleurs. (RUM)
555 Recto et verso de la couverture d'un livre de poche extrait d'une série de romans policiers sociocritiques. (NOR)
556 Jaquette polychrome d'un ouvrage réunissant les peintures à l'huile que Heather Cooper avait faites de sa fille. (CAN)
557 Jaquette d'un ouvrage sur les formes de l'emballage au Japon et en Europe. Prédominance de tons gris, bandes rouges. (JPN)

ARTIST / KÜNSTLER / ARTISTE:

558 Ceste & Torri
559, 560 Ference Pintér
561, 562 Karel Thole
563 Magritte
564 Ute Osterwalder

DESIGNER / GESTALTER / MAQUETTISTE:

558 Claudio Ronchi
564 Ute Osterwalder

ART DIRECTOR / DIRECTEUR ARTISTIQUE:

558 Claudio Bertieri
559, 560 Bruno Binosi

558

559

Book Covers
Buchumschläge
Couvertures de livres

561

562

560

PUBLISHER / VERLEGER / EDITEUR:

558 Iveco
559, 560, 562 Arnoldo Mondadori
561 Editions Marabont
563 Editions Draeger
564 Deutscher Sparkassenverlag GmbH

558 Dust jacket for a publication issued by a company for utility vehicles about the history of the bus from the beginning until the present, including inscriptions on buses, the role of the bus in advertising and on postal stamps. Bus in red, greyish beige and black, brilliant yellow sky. (ITA)
559, 560 Illustration and complete cover for an Agathe Christie novel. (ITA)
561, 562 Cover illustration in full colour from a series of science fiction novels. (ITA)
563 Opened dust jacket for an art volume about Magritte. The curtain is in dark red. (FRA)
564 Cover in dark shades for a collection of tales published in the *Bibliothek S* series. (GER)

558 Schutzumschlag für das von einer Nutzfahrzeugfabrik herausgegebene Werk über die Geschichte des Autobusses: Modelle von den Anfängen bis zur Gegenwart, Busbeschriftungen, der Bus in der Werbung und auf Briefmarken. Bus in Rot, Grau-beige und Schwarz, leuchtend gelber Himmel. (ITA)
559, 560 Illustration und vollständiger Umschlag für einen Kriminalroman von Agathe Christie. (ITA)
561, 562 Umschlagillustrationen aus einer Reihe von Science-Fiction-Romanen. Mehrfarbig. (ITA)
563 Geöffneter Schutzumschlag eines Kunstbandes über Magritte. Dunkelroter Vorhang. (FRA)
564 In dunklen Farbtönen gehaltener Umschlag für einen Erzählband, erschienen in der Reihe *Bibliothek S.* (GER)

558 Jaquette d'un ouvrage sur l'histoire de l'autobus, publié par *Iveco*, une fabrique de transporteurs. On y présente des modèles du début jusqu'à nos jours, la conception graphique de ces véhicules, le bus dans la publicité, sur les timbres-poste etc. Bus en rouge, beige grisâtre et noir, ciel en jaune vif. (ITA)
559, 560 Illustration et couverture complète d'un roman policier d'Agathe Christie. (ITA)
561, 562 Illustrations de couverture extraites d'une série de romans de science-fiction. En couleurs. (ITA)
563 Recto et verso de la jaquette d'un ouvrage des Ed. *Draeger* consacré à Magritte. Rideau en rouge foncé. (FRA)
564 Couverture d'une anthologie publiée dans la série *Bibliothek S*. En tons foncés. (GER)

564

563

Salacrou
Les invités
du bon Dieu

folio

Texte intégral

565

John Steinbeck
Le poney rouge

folio
junior

Texte intégral illustré

566

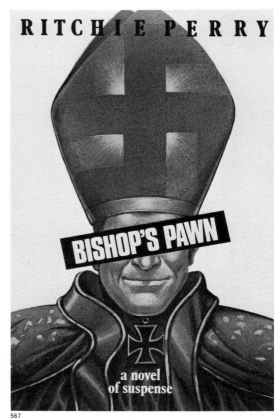

RITCHIE PERRY

BISHOP'S PAWN

a novel
of suspense

567

STUNDE DER
VAMPIRE

Eine Anthologie,
herausgegeben von
Peter Haining

568

COLLECTION 1000 SOLEILS
HANS CHRISTIAN
ANDERSEN/2 CONTES
DE L'AMOUR
NAISSANT
GALLIMARD

569

THE FACE OF
WAR

JEAN LARTEGUY
REFLECTIONS ON MEN AND COMBAT

570

565 Paperback cover for a play entitled "God's Elected Guests".
In full colour with a red curtain. (FRA)
566 A John Steinbeck novel in a paperback series of books for
young people. In full colour. (FRA)
567 Illustration in red shades on the cover of a thriller published
by *Random House.* (USA)
568 Full-colour cover of an anthology of stories published in a
Fischer paperback series. The stories in this collection are about
blood-sucking, horrible ghosts and spirits and appeared under
the title of *Stunde der Vampire* ("Hour of the Vampires"). (GER)
569 Dust jacket of a collection of four volumes of Andersen's
fairy-tales contained in one cassette. Full colour. (FRA)
570 The author of this book published by Bobbs-Merrill Co.
investigates why man wages war. In orange and red. (USA)
571 Dust jacket in dark shades of a work published by Big 0
Publishing about the film *Alien* by H. R. Giger. (GBR)

565 Taschenbuchumschlag für ein Theaterstück («Die Einge-
ladenen des lieben Gottes»). Mehrfarbig, roter Vorhang. (FRA)
566 In einer Taschenbuchreihe für Jugendliche erschienener
Roman *Der rote Pony* von Steinbeck. Mehrfarbig. (FRA)
567 In Rottönen gehaltene Illustration auf dem Umschlag
eines Kriminalromans («Des Bischofs Pfand»). (USA)
568 Mehrfarbiger Umschlag für eine in der *Fischer*-Taschen-
buchreihe erschienene Anthologie von brillianten und schauer-
lichen Geschichten über geisterhafte blutsaugende Un-Tote –
Stunde der Vampire. (GER)
569 Schutzumschlag von einem der vier Bände mit Andersen-
Märchen, die in einer Kassette enthalten sind. Mehrfarbig. (FRA)
570 Der Autor dieses Buches («Das Gesicht des Krieges») untersucht, warum der Mensch Krieg führt. Orange, Rot. (USA)
571 Schutzumschlag (in dunklen Farbtönen) eines Werkes
zum Film *Alien* von H. R. Giger. (GBR)

565 Couverture d'une pièce de théâtre, publiée dans une série de
poche des Ed. *Gallimard.* Polychrome, rideau rouge. (FRA)
566 Pour un roman de Steinbeck, publié dans la série de poche
Folio Junior des Ed. *Gallimard.* En polychromie. (FRA)
567 Illustration de couverture pour un roman policier («Le gage
de l'évêque»). En tons rouges. (USA)
568 Couverture (en polychromie) d'une anthologie d'histoires
brillantes et épouvantables de vampires («L'heure des vampires»).
D'une série de poche. (GER)
569 Couverture de l'un des quatre volumes des Contes d'Andersen
contenus dans une cassette des Ed. *Gallimard.* En couleurs. (FRA)
570 L'auteur de cet ouvrage («Le visage de la guerre») a étudié la
guerre comme phénomène et a cherché les causes qui mènent
l'humanité à faire la guerre. En orange et rouge. (USA)
571 Jaquette d'un ouvrage consacré au film *Alien* de H. R. Giger.
En tons sombres. (GBR)

571

572

574

575

ARTIST / KÜNSTLER / ARTISTE:

572 Tadanori Yokoo
573 Wendell Minor
574, 575 David McKee
577 Walther Götlinger
578 Alfredo Aquino
579 Oskar Weiss
580–582 Henri Galeron

DESIGNER / GESTALTER / MAQUETTISTE:

572 Tadanori Yokoo
573 Wendell Minor
574, 575 David McKee
576 Lüdtke & Franke

ART DIRECTOR / DIRECTEUR ARTISTIQUE:

572 Tadanori Yokoo
573 Lidia Ferrara
574, 575 David McKee
577 Walther Götlinger
578 Alfredo Aquino
579 Oswald Dubacher

AGENCY / AGENTUR / AGENCE – STUDIO:

573 W. Minor Design

PUBLISHER / VERLEGER / EDITEUR:

572 Bungei Shunju Ltd.
573 Alfred A. Knopf
574, 575 Anderson Press
576 Schuler Verlagsgesellschaft
577 Paul Zsolnay
578 Círculo do Livro
579 Ex Libris Verlag
580–582 Gallimard

573

576

577

580

581

578

582

579

Book Covers
Buchumschläge
Couvertures de livres

572 Opened dust jacket of a book. Yellow and red with grey and blue. (JPN)
573 Dust jacket of an advisory work by *Knopf Publishers* about living cheaply in the country. (USA)
574, 575 Small-format volumes about *King Rollo*. Brilliant colours. (GBR/AUS)
576 Dust jacket of an art volume about De Chirico. The reproduction of one of the painter's oils is printed on a light grey ground. (GER)
577 Dust jacket of a man-and-woman novel. The cockerel is in a red-and-white striped jacket. (GER)
578 Cover of a paperback ("In the Course of Time") in olive green and dark green. (BRA)
579 Dust jacked of an investigation about the father's role. Pink hand, brown jacket. (SWI)
580–582 Complete cover and illustration in actual size from two volumes of world literature. (FRA)

572 Geöffneter Schutzumschlag eines Buches. Gelb und Rot, resp. Grau und Blau. (JPN)
573 Schutzumschlag eines Ratgebers, wie man auf dem Lande mit beinahe Nichts genügsam lebt (USA)
574, 575 Kleinformatige Bändchen über die Abenteuer des Königs Rollo. In bunten Farben. (GBR/AUS)
576 Schutzumschlag für einen von *Schuler* herausgegebenen Kunstband über De Chirico. Abbildung des Ölgemäldes *Landschaftsmaler* auf hellgrauem Grund. (GER)
577 Schutzumschlag eines Romans zum Thema Mann und Frau. Rot-weiss gestreifter Kittel. (GER)
578 Umschlag eines Taschenbuches («Im Laufe der Zeit»). In Olivegrün auf Dunkelgrün. (BRA)
579 Schutzumschlag einer Untersuchung über die Vater-Rolle. Rosa Hand, brauner Kittel. (SWI)
580–582 Vollständiger Umschlag und Illustrationen (in Originalgrösse) von zwei Bänden aus einer Taschenbuchreihe für Jugendliche, die Werke aus der Weltliteratur bringt. (FRA)

572 Recto et verso de la jaquette d'un livre. Jaune et rouge, resp. gris et bleu. (JPN)
573 Ce livre donne des conseils comment on peut vivre en campagne avec presque rien. (USA)
574, 575 Couvertures de deux petits livres sur les aventures du roi Rollo. En couleurs vives. (GBR/AUS)
576 Jaquette d'un livre d'art de De Chirico. Représentation de la peinture à l'huile *Le paysagiste*. (GER)
577 Jaquette d'un roman traitant le sujet de l'homme et de la femme. (GER)
578 Couverture d'un livre de poche («Le cours du temps»). En olive sur vert foncé. (BRA)
579 Jaquette d'une enquête sur le rôle que joue le père. Main rose, jaquette brune. (SWI)
580–582 Couvertures et illustrations (en grandeur originale) de deux livres de poche des Ed. *Gallimard*: *Monsieur le Vent et Madame la Pluie* et *Histoire du veritable Gribouille*. (FRA)

583

584

585

ARTIST / KÜNSTLER / ARTISTE:

583, 584 Chris Au/Doug Smaill (Photo)
585, 587 Peter Harrison
586 Folon

DESIGNER / GESTALTER / MAQUETTISTE:

583, 584 Bill Little
585, 587 Randee Rubin

ART DIRECTOR / DIRECTEUR ARTISTIQUE:

585, 587 Peter Harrison
586 Girgio Soavi

AGENCY / AGENTUR / AGENCE – STUDIO:

585, 587 Pentagram Design

583, 584 Full-page illustration in actual size and corresponding double spread from the bi-annual report of the Manitoba Museum of Man and Nature. (CAN)
585, 587 Cover and inside spread with a gatefold from the annual report of Ogden Corp., a diversified industrial company. Fig. 585: red lettering on a yellow ground; Fig. 587 shows a method of converting scrap metal into a valuable raw material for steel mills and foundries. Full colour. (USA)
586 *The Martian Chronicles* by Ray Bradbury — a work sponsored and published by the *Olivetti* company. Double-spread illustration in pink, yellow and lilac-coloured shades. (ITA)

583, 584 Ganzseitige Illustration (in Originalgrösse) und entsprechende Doppelseite aus dem Zweijahres-Bericht des Manitoba Museum of Man and Nature. (CAN)
585, 587 Umschlag und Innenseite mit Ausleger aus dem Jahresbericht eines diversifizierten Industriebetriebes. Abb. 585: rote Schrift auf gelbem Grund; Abb. 587 zeigt die Verarbeitung von Altmetall für die Wiederverwendung in Stahlwerken und Giessereien. Mehrfarbige Darstellung. (USA)
586 Doppelseitige Illustration in Rosa-, Gelb- und Lilatönen aus einem von *Olivetti* herausgegebenen Werk von Ray Bradbury («Die Mars-Chronik»). (ITA)

583, 584 Illustration pleine page (grandeur originale) et page double correspondante d'un rapport que le Manitoba Museum of Man and Nature publie tous les deux ans. (CAN)
585, 587 Couverture et page intérieure avec repli extraites du rapport annuel d'une compagnie industrielle diversifiée. Fig. 585: typo rouge sur fond jaune; fig. 587: installation pour le recyclage de ferraille pour la réutilisation dans les aciéries et les fonderies. Représentation en couleurs. (USA)
586 Illustration sur page double extraite d'un ouvrage de Ray Bradbury («La chronique martienne») publié par *Olivetti*. En tons roses, jaunes et lilas. (ITA)

586

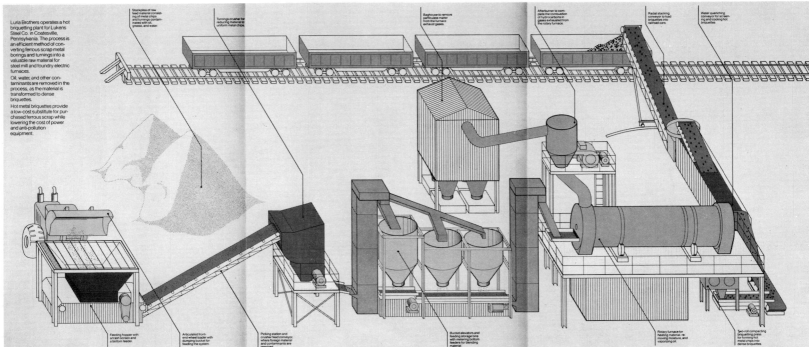

587

588 Diagrams in blue, red, green and yellow from the Seibu Group of Retail Enterprises. (JPN)
589 Double spread from the annual report of Plantronics, Inc. Gradations of brown and blue. (USA)
590 The cover illustration, an abstract conception of the sound-wave, symbolizes the aims of Superscope, Inc. in the field of entertainment electronics. In brown shades. (USA)
591 Cover of the annual report of *Amerada Hess*, an integrated petroleum company. (USA)
592, 593 Cover and illustration in actual size from the report of an optical works. (FRA)
594, 595 Cover and double spread from the annual report of Castle & Cooke, Inc., a company that specializes in foodstuffs. Fig. 594: green leaves. (USA)

588 Diagramme (Blau, Rot, Grün, Gelb) aus dem Bericht eines Detailhandelsunternehmens. (JPN)
589 Aus dem Geschäftsbericht eines Unternehmens der Telekommunikations-Branche. (USA)
590 Die Umschlagillustration, eine abstrakte Darstellung der Schallwelle, soll die Ziele dieser Firma auf dem Gebiet der Unterhaltungs-Elektronik symbolisieren. In Brauntönen. (USA)
591 Jahresbericht einer Ölgesellschaft. Schematische Darstellung geologischer Schichten. (USA)
592, 593 Umschlag und Illustration (Originalgrösse) des Berichts eines optischen Werkes. (FRA)
594, 595 Umschlag und Doppelseite aus dem Jahresbericht eines Unternehmens, das sich auf die Verarbeitung und den Vertrieb von Nahrungsmitteln spezialisiert hat. Abb.594: grüne Blätter. (USA)

588 Diagrammes du rapport annuel d'un groupe de détaillants. En bleu, rouge, vert, jaune. (JPN)
589 Du rapport d'une compagnie spécialisée dans le domaine de la télécommunication. (USA)
590 Cette illustration de couverture – une représentation abstraite d'une onde sonore – devraient symboliser les buts de cette entreprise dans le domaine des installations électroniques pour l'enregistrement et la transmission sonores. En tons bruns. (USA)
591 D'une compagnie pétrolière. Représentation schématique des couches géologiques. (USA)
592, 593 Couverture et illustration (en grandeur originale) du rapport d'*Essilor*. (FRA)
594, 595 D'une société spécialisée dans la transformation et la distribution de denrées. (USA)

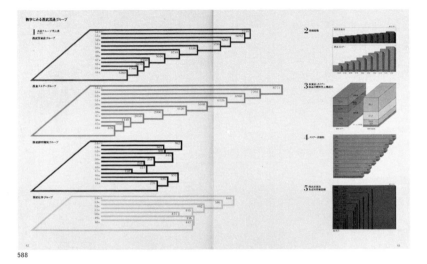

588

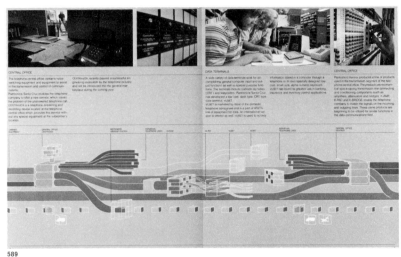

589

590

591

592

ESSILOR
1978

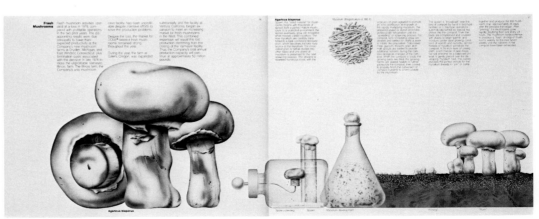

593

Annual Reports
Jahresberichte
Rapports annuels

594

595

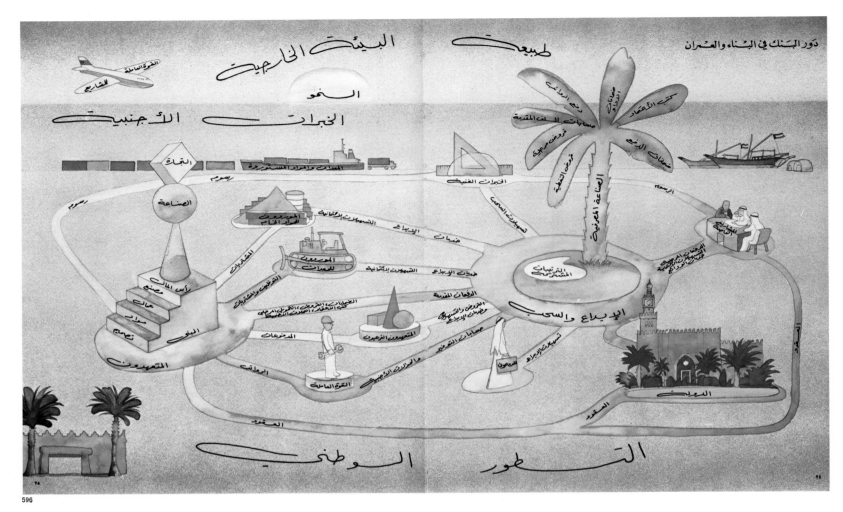

596

596, 597 Double spread and cover of a large-format annual report of the Commercial Bank of Kuwait. The subject of this report was the role of banking within the economy. Various aspects of this connection are made visually clear by the seven illustrations in the report. (KUW)
598 Diagrams in various shades of green and brown from the annual report of a company that plans and constructs hydro-electric plants. (ARG)
599 A leporello quarterly report of Aero-Flow Dynamics, a company that manufactures ventilation and air-conditioning apparatus. Grey with dark blue girders. (USA)
600–602 Double spreads, Fig. 602 with a gatefold, from the annual report of the *Pratt Institute* with a report by the head of the institute (Fig. 600) and reports by the School of Architecture (Fig. 601) and the School of Art and Design (Fig. 602). All the illustrations are in black and white. (USA)

596, 597 Doppelseite und Umschlag eines grossformatigen Jahresberichtes der Commercial Bank of Kuwait. Das Thema dieses Berichtes war die Rolle des Bankwesens in der Wirtschaft; verschiedene Aspekte dieser Verflechtung wurden anhand von sieben Illustrationen beleuchtet. (KUW)
598 Diagramme in verschiedenen Grün- und Brauntönen aus dem Geschäftsbericht einer Firma, die Wasserkraftwerke projektiert und baut. (ARG)
599 Vierteljahres-Bericht (Leporello) eines Unternehmens, das Ventilations- und Wärmeinstallationen herstellt. Grau mit dunkelblauen Balken. (USA)
600–602 Doppelseiten, Abb. 602 mit Ausleger, aus dem Jahresbericht des *Pratt Institutes*, hier zum Bericht des Leiters des Instituts (Abb. 600) und zum Bericht der Architekturabteilung (Abb. 601) und der Abteilung Kunst und Graphik (Abb. 602). Schwarzweiss. (USA)

596, 597 Page double et couverture du rapport annuel à grand format de la Banque Commerciale du Koweit. Ce rapport a été consacré au rôle que jouent les institutions bancaires dans l'économie: divers aspects de cette interpénétration ont été illustrés. (KUW)
598 Diagrammes en divers tons verts et bruns extraits du rapport annuel d'une entreprise qui réalise des projets et des constructions de centrales hydro-électriques. (ARG)
599 Rapport trimestriel (en accordéon) d'une entreprise qui fabrique des installations de ventilation et de chauffage. Gris avec des barres en brun foncé. (USA)
600–602 Pages doubles (fig. 602 avec repli) du rapport annuel du *Pratt Institute*, extraites du rapport du directeur de l'institut (fig. 600), du rapport du département d'architecture (fig. 601) et du département d'arts graphiques (fig. 602). (USA)

ARTIST / KÜNSTLER / ARTISTE:

596, 597 Michael Foreman
600–602 Joseph Ciardiello
         Douglas Wonders (Photo)

DESIGNER / GESTALTER / MAQUETTISTE:

596, 597 Paul Anthony
598 Rubén Fontana/Gustavo Pedroza
599 Eugene J. Grossman/Vern Ford
600–602 J. Michael McGinn

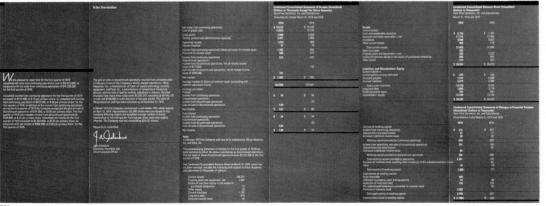

599

597

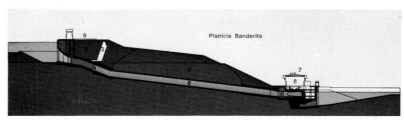

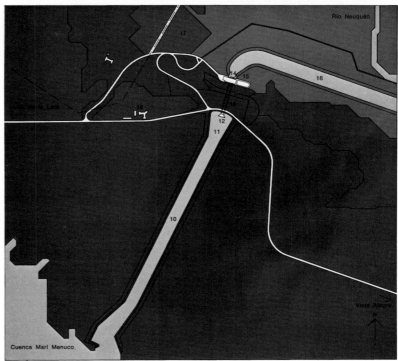

598

600

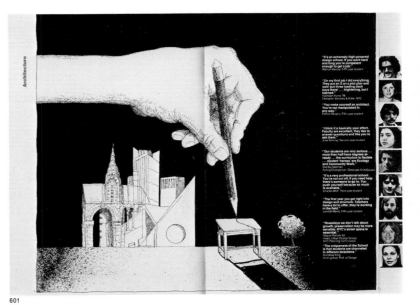

601

602

ART DIRECTOR / DIRECTEUR ARTISTIQUE:

596, 597 Alan Fletcher
599 Eugene J. Grossman
600–602 J. Michael McGinn

AGENCY / AGENTUR / AGENCE – STUDIO:

596, 597 Pentagram Design
598 Fontana/Pedroza
599 Anspach Grossman Portugal Inc.
600–602 J. Michael McGinn

**Annual Reports
Jahresberichte
Rapports annuels**

4

Calendars

Trade marks and symbols

Letterheads

Gramophone Record Covers

Packaging

Kalender

Schutzmarken

Briefköpfe

Schallplatten-Umschläge

Packungen

Calendriers

Marques et emblèmes

En-têtes

Pochettes de disques

Emballages

603

ARTIST / KÜNSTLER / ARTISTE:

603 U. G. Sato
604, 605 Ivan Chermayeff
606, 607 Makoto Komori
608 Akira Yokoyama

DESIGNER / GESTALTER / MAQUETTISTE:

604, 605 Ivan Chermayeff
606—608 Kanichi Ishikawa

603 From a *Design Farm* calendar. Fawn-coloured hand on greenish grey. (JPN)
604, 605 Two sheets from the U.S. Army Calendar entitled *Twelve who left their mark*. Fig. 604: this illustration is of Albert James Myer who conceived the first national weather forecasting service. Blue-and-white and red-and-yellow coloured flags, dark green field, blue sky; Fig. 605 shows Montgomery Cunningham Meigs who, in the middle of the last century, constructed or renovated most of the government buildings in Washington. Buildings in light and dark grey, blue uniform, flag in red and white. (USA)
606—608 Illustrations and complete sheet from the calendar of the Hotel Barmen's Association. Each sheet was designed by a well-known illustrator from Japan or other countries. Fig. 608 is in dark shades. (JPN)

603 Aus einem Kalender für *Design Farm*. Rehbraune Hand auf Grüngrau. (JPN)
604, 605 Zwei Blätter aus einem Kalender der amerikanischen Armee mit dem Titel «Zwölf, die unser Zeitalter mitprägten». Abb. 604: diese Illustration ist Albert James Myer gewidmet, der den ersten, auf nationaler Ebene arbeitenden Wetterdienst einrichtete – blau-weisse und rot-gelbe Flaggen, dunkelgrüne Wiese, blauer Himmel; Abb. 605 zeigt Montgomery Cunningham Meigs, der Mitte des letzten Jahrhunderts einen Grossteil der Regierungsgebäude in Washington konstruierte oder renovierte – Gebäude in Hell- und Dunkelgrau, blaue Uniform, Fahne in Rot-weiss. (USA)
606—608 Illustrationen und ein vollständiges Blatt aus dem Kalender einer Vereinigung für Hotel-Barmänner. Jedes Blatt wurde von einem bekannten Illustrator aus Japan oder anderen Ländern geschaffen. Abb. 608 in dunklen Farbtönen. (JPN)

603 Feuillet d'un calendrier pour *Design Farm*. Main brune sur fond vert grisâtre. (JPN)
604, 605 Feuillets d'un calendrier publié par l'armée américaine sous le titre: «Douze qui avaient laissé leur empreinte». Fig. 604: cette illustration est consacrée à Albert James Myer, qui avait fondé le premier service météorologique travaillant sur un plan national – drapeaux en bleu-blanc et rouge-jaune, pré en vert foncé, ciel bleu; fig. 603: portrait de Montgomery Cunningham Meigs qui avait construit et rénové, au milieu du siècle passé, une grande partie des sièges gouvernementaux à Washington – bâtiments en gris clair et foncé, uniforme bleue, drapeau en rouge et blanc. (USA)
606—608 Illustrations et feuillet complet du calendrier d'une association des barmen. Chaque illustration a été créée par un artiste du Japon ou d'un autre pays. (JPN)

604

605

606

607

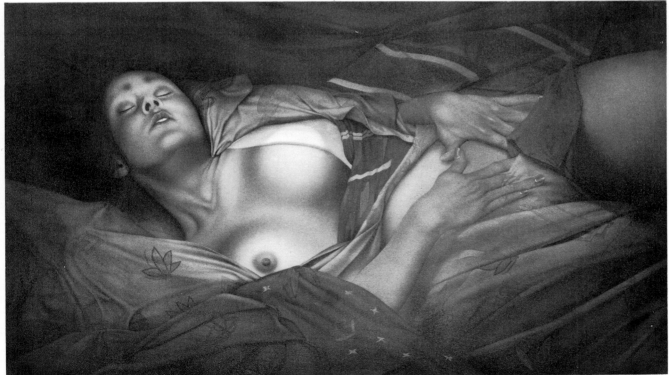

608

ART DIRECTOR:
604, 605 Mickey Tender
606–608 Mitsutoshi Hosaka

AGENCY / AGENTUR:

604, 605 N.W. Ayer Intern.
606–608 Dai Nippon Printing
Creative Design Center

**Calendars
Kalender
Calendriers**

609

609

ARTIST / KÜNSTLER / ARTISTE:

609–611 Heather Cooper

DESIGNER / GESTALTER / MAQUETTISTE:

609–611 Robert Kamnatik
612–615 Keren House/John McConnell

ART DIRECTOR / DIRECTEUR ARTISTIQUE:

612–615 John McConnell

AGENCY / AGENTUR / AGENCE – STUDIO:

609–611 Burns, Cooper, Hynes, Ltd.
612–615 Pentagram Design

609–611 The artist has tried here to explain myths and popular stories in connection with the moon, the basis of our chronology. Fig. 609: Selene or Luna, the moon goddess of the Greeks and Romans, associated with beauty, fertility and creative inspiration; Fig. 610: Thoth, one of the chief gods of ancient Egypt, also associated with the moon. He was the measurer and enumerator of the heavens as well as the scribe of the gods; Fig. 611: the waning of the moon is believed to encourage growth underground which is why bulbs should be planted by the light of the fading crescent. Calendar for *Abitibi Price*. (CAN)

612–615 From the *Face* calendar in which elements in white plus one colour reveal faces on a dark ground. (GBR)

609–611 Die Künstlerin versucht, Mythen und Volksweisheiten im Zusammenhang mit dem Mond (Grundlage unserer Zeitrechnung) zu versinnbildlichen. Abb. 609: Selene oder Luna, Mondgöttin der Griechen und Römer, versinnbildlicht Schönheit, Fruchtbarkeit und Kreativität; Abb. 610: Thot, ägyptischer Gott, auch Mondgott, oft mit einem Ibis-Kopf dargestellt, wurde als Gott der Schreibkunst und Wissenschaft verehrt; Abb. 611: bei abnehmendem Mond sollen Knollengewächse besser gedeihen und deshalb während dieser Mondphase gesetzt werden. (CAN)

612–615 Aus dem Kalender der Schriftsetzerei *Face* (Gesicht). Aus Schriftelementen (weiss plus eine Farbe) werden auf schwarzem Grund Gesichter angedeutet. (GBR)

609–611 L'artiste a cherché d'illustrer divers mythes et légendes en rapport avec la Lune (sur laquelle se fonde notre calendrier). Fig. 609: Selene ou Luna, déesse de la mythologie des anciens Grecs et Romains, symbolise beauté, fécondité et créativité; fig. 610: Thot, dieu de l'ancien Egypte, représenté souvent avec la tête d'Ibis, est le dieu de la calligraphie et des sciences; fig. 611: on dit que les tubercules poussent mieux quand la lune est à son déclin et qu'il faut les planter alors pendant cette période. (CAN)

612–615 D'un calendrier de l'atelier de composition *Face* (visage). Par divers éléments typographiques (blanc avec une couleur) on a tracé des visages sur fond noir. (GBR)

612

613

614

615

610

611

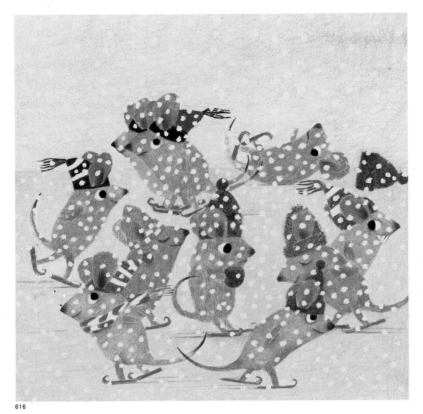

616

617

618

619

616–621 The colourful illustrations by a well-known author and illustrator of children's books show how mice pass their time in the course of the year: in January they are skating in a snow-storm (616), in April they play hide-and-seek (621), in October they pinch grapes (618) and at Christmas they distribute the cheese (619). On the cover illustration (617) we see one mouse for each month. From the *Middelhauve* children's calendar. (GER)

616–621 Die bunten Bilder eines bekannten Kinderbuchautors und -illustrators zeigen, wie sich die Mäuse während des Jahres die Zeit vertreiben: bei Schneetreiben im Januar mit Eislaufen (616), im April mit Versteckenspielen (621), im Oktober mit Trauben klauen (618) und an Weihnachten wird der Käse verteilt (619). Zur Versammlung auf dem Deckblatt (617) trifft je eine Maus der Monatsblätter ein. Aus dem *Middelhauve*-Kinderkalender 1980. (GER)

616–621 Les illustrations en couleurs vives d'un célèbre auteur et illustrateur de livres d'enfants nous montrent comment les souris passent leur temps au courant de l'année: au mois de janvier on patine dans un tourbillon de neige (616), au mois d'avril on joue au cache-cache (621), en octobre on vole des raisins (618) et à Noël on distribue le fromage (619). La feuille de couverture réunit des souris dont chacun représente un mois. (617). (GER)

Calendars
Kalender
Calendriers

620

ARTIST / KÜNSTLER / ARTISTE:

616–621 Leo Lionni

ART DIRECTOR / DIRECTEUR ARTISTIQUE:

616–621 Gertraud Middelhauve

623

T.UNGERER
627

628

T.UNGERER

624

625

629

626

ARTIST / KÜNSTLER / ARTISTE:

623–626 Christine Chagnoux
627, 628 Tomi Ungerer
629 Dick Bruna

ART DIRECTOR / DIRECTEUR ARTISTIQUE:

623–626 Engel Ph. Verkerke
627, 628 Robert Pütz
629 Dick Bruna

AGENCY / AGENTUR / AGENCE – STUDIO:

627, 628 Robert Pütz GmbH & Co.

Calendars
Kalender
Calendriers

623–626 Cover sheet, two illustrations and complete sheet from a Christine Chagnoux calendar called *Christine's Friends*. Shown here are her "friends" in the circus, in the circus in the wood and on the beach. Produced by *Verkerke Reprodukties*. Some of the illustrations are also available as posters and postcards. (NLD)
627, 628 Full-colour illustrations from Tomi Ungerer's work-place calendar designed for *Nixdorf Computer*. Fig. 627: the great step towards productive organization; Fig. 628: organizational strength. (GER)
629 *Dick Bruna's Miffy Calendar* published by Methuen Children's Books. The illustration is in blue, green, white, red and yellow; the calendar in blue with a red border. (GBR)

623–626 Deckblatt, zwei Illustrationen und vollständiges Blatt aus einem Kalender von Christine Chagnoux mit dem Titel «Christines Freunde»: hier im Zirkuszelt, im Zirkus im Wald und am Strand. Der Kalender wurde vom Posterverlag *Verkerke Reprodukties* herausgegeben. Einige Illustrationen sind auch als Poster und Postkarten erschienen. (NLD)
627, 628 Mehrfarbige Illustrationen aus Tomi Ungerers Arbeitsplatz-Kalender, den er für *Nixdorf Computer* herausgab. Abb. 627: Der grosse Schritt zur produktiven Organisation und Abb. 628 Organisationsstärke für Wettbewerbsstärke. (GER)
629 Von einem Kinderbuch-Verlag herausgegebener Kalender über Miffys Abenteuer. Illustration in Blau, Grün, Weiss, Rot und Gelb, Kalendar in Blau mit rotem Rand. (GBR)

623–626 Feuille de couverture, illustrations et feuillet complet d'un calendrier de Christine Chagnoux, intitulé «Les amis de Christine», qu'on voit ici au cirque, au cirque dans le fôret et à la plage. Quelques-unes des illustrations ont paru comme cartes postales ou posters. (NLD)
627, 628 Illustrations en polychromie extraites d'un calendrier de Tomi Ungerer pour les ordinateurs *Nixdorf*. On voit ici le grand pas vers une organisation productive (fig. 627) et l'organisation qui est d'importance vitale pour supporter la concurrence (fig. 628). (GER)
629 D'un calendrier sur les aventures de Miffy. Illustration en bleu, vert, blanc, rouge et jaune. (GBR)

630

632

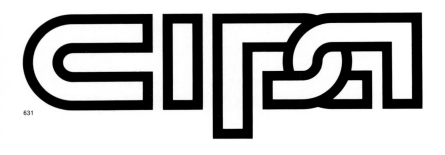

631

633

Trademarks
Schutzmarken
Marques et emblèmes

630 Newly designed typeface for a manufacturer of men's, women's and children's clothes. (AUS)
631 Typeface for a *Fiat* representative garage. (ITA)
632 Symbol on a sign for a natural reserve. Light grey on a dark green ground. (SWI)
633 Trademark of the Edmund Scientific Co., manufacturer and distributor of telescopes and scientific instruments. (USA)
634 For a series of books on architecture published by a state building organization. (CUB)
635 Trademark for Toyo Rayon Co., textile manufacturers. (JPN)
636 Symbol used by *Allergan Pharmaceuticals* for its eye-drops. Blue drop. (USA)
637 Symbol for SUVA, a Swiss accident insurance company. (SWI)
638 Symbol of a research institute for diseases of the blood. (CUB)
639 Trademark for *Suzuki*, the Japanese motorcycle company. (JPN)
640 Symbol of the Washington Mutual Savings Bank. In khaki on white. (USA)
641 Symbol of an aid centre for the mentally retarded. One symbol is in coarse screen. (ARG)
642 Symbol for the Tamarac Medical Center with a combination of the "T" and a cross. (USA)
643 This symbol was designed for a congress on onkology. (CUB)
644 Symbol for the Hennessey Construction Co. (USA)

630 Neugestalteter Schriftzug eines Herstellers von Herren-, Damen- und Kinderkleidern. (AUS)
631 Schriftzug einer Vertragsgarage von *Fiat*. (ITA)
632 Symbol auf Hinweistafeln für Naturschutzgebiete. Hellgrau auf dunkelgrünem Grund. (SWI)
633 Schutzmarke der Edmund Scientific Co., eines Versandhauses und Herstellers von Teleskopen und wissenschaftlichen Geräten. (USA)
634 Für eine von der staatlichen Baubehörde herausgegebene Buchreihe über Architektur. (CUB)
635 Schutzmarke für einen Textilfabrikanten. (JPN)
636 Symbol, das eine Arzneimittelfabrik für ihre Augentropfen verwendet. Blauer Tropfen. (USA)
637 Symbol der Schweizerischen Unfall-Versicherungs-Anstalt SUVA. (SWI)
638 Symbol eines Forschungsinstituts für Blutkrankheiten. (CUB)
639 Schutzmarke des japanischen Motorradfabrikanten *Suzuki*. (JPN)
640 Symbol der Washington Mutual Savings Bank. In Khaki auf Weiss. (USA)
641 Symbol eines Hilfszentrums für geistig Behinderte. Ein Symbol ist grobgerastert. (ARG)
642 Für einen kommunalen Gesundheitsdienst in Tamarac. Man versuchte, das «T» des Ortsnamens mit dem Kreuz zu kombinieren. (USA)
643 Dieses Symbol wurde für einen Kongress über Onkologie geschaffen. (CUB)
644 Symbol für das Bauunternehmen Hennessey Construction Co. (USA)

630 Nouveau logo d'un fabricant de vêtements pour hommes, femmes et enfants. (AUS)
631 Logo d'un concessionnaire de *Fiat*. (ITA)
632 Symbole sur les panneaux signalant une réserve naturelle. Gris sur fond vert foncé. (SWI)
633 Marque de fabrique de la compagnie *Edmund Scientific*, fabricant et distributeur de télescopes et d'appareils scientifiques. (USA)
634 Pour une série de livres d'architecture, publiée par le ministère de l'urbanisme. (CUB)
635 Marque d'une fabrique de matières textiles. (JPN)
636 Symbole qu'une société de produits pharmaceutiques utilise pour ses collyres. (USA)
637 Symbole de la Caisse Nationale Suisse d'Assurance en Cas d'Accidents. (SWI)
638 Symbole d'un institut de recherche dans le domaine de l'hémopathie. (CUB)
639 Marque déposée de *Suzuki*, fabricant japonais de motos. (JPN)
640 Symbole de la Washington Mutual Savings Bank. Kaki sur blanc. (USA)
641 Symbole d'un centre d'assistance aux déficients mentaux. Un symbole à grosse trame. (ARG)
642 Symbole du service de santé communal de Tamarac. On a cherché à combiner le «T» du nom de la ville avec la croix. (USA)
643 Symbole créé pour un congrès d'oncologie. (CUB)
644 Symbole pour la maison de construction Hennessey Construction Co. (USA)

637

641

DESIGNER / GESTALTER / MAQUETTISTE:

630 Gould & Associates, Inc.
631 Carlo Caligaris
632 Georg Almstädt
633 Ronald Manzke
634, 638 Félix Beltrán/Dagoberto Marcelo
635 Takemura Keiko
636, 640 Ken Parkhurst
637 Mark Zeugin
639 Tezeni Masamichi
641 León Chocrón
642 Gordon Tani
643 Félix Beltrán
644 Emil M. Cohen

ART DIRECTOR / DIRECTEUR ARTISTIQUE:

630 Gould & Associates, Inc.
633 Don Ervin
634, 638, 643 Félix Beltrán
635 Isaka Yoshitaro
636, 640 Ken Parkhurst
641 José Luis Ermler
642 Douglas Boyd

AGENCY / AGENTUR / AGENCE – STUDIO:

630 Gould & Associates, Inc.
633 Siegel & Gale
634, 638, 643 Félix Beltrán
636, 640 Ken Parkhurst
641 León Chocrón Publicidad S.A.
642 Douglas Boyd Design & Marketing

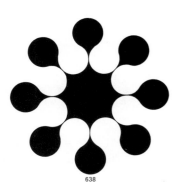

634

635

636

638

639

640

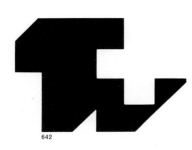

642

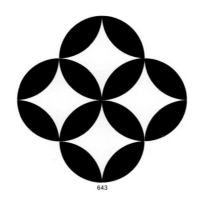

643

644

227

646

645, 646 Symbol, letterhead for Stravinsky Festival Trust. (GBR)
647 Logo in raspberry-red for the *Brin* boutique. (BEL)
648 Symbol for *Pitney Bowes*, a business systems company. (USA)
649 Trademark for *Rodhiatoce*, manufacturers of fibres. (JPN)
650, 651 Symbol and letterhead as examples of the corporate identity programme of Weber spa, manufacturer of car accessories. (ITA)
652 Symbol of the *Cogis* campany. (ITA)
653 Symbol of the *Owl* bar. (CAN)
654 An Indian symbol used here for a financial institution. Used in various shades from yellow to red. (USA)
655, 660 Symbol and letterhead for *Prestel*—the British Post Office viewdata service. (GBR)
656 Symbol for a series of medicaments from *Mediquimica*. (CUB)
657 Geroldswil swimming pool: blue and yellow. (SWI)
658 Symbol of the Transamerica Corporation. (USA)
659 Trademark of the Japanese ammunition association. (JPN)

645, 646 Kombination eines «S» und eines Violinschlüssels für das Stravinsky-Festivalkomitee. Symbol und Briefbogen. (GBR)
647 Schriftzug (in Himbeerrot) der Modeboutique *Brin*. (BEL)
648 Symbol eines Herstellers von Büromaschinen. (USA)
649 Schutzmarke eines Herstellers von Fibern. (JPN)
650, 651 Signet und Briefpapier, als Beispiele aus dem Erscheinungsbild von Weber spa, Hersteller von Autobestandteilen. (ITA)
652 Symbol des Handelsunternehmens *Cogis*. (ITA)
653 Symbol der «Eulen»-Bar. (CAN)
654 Von einem indianischen Zeichen abgeleitetes Symbol für ein Bankinstitut, in Farbabstufungen von Gelb bis Rot verwendet. (USA)
655, 660 Symbol und Briefbogen für den von der britischen PTT zur Verfügung gestellten Datenverarbeitungs-Dienst. (GBR)
656 Symbol für eine Arzneimittelreihe von *Mediquimica*. (CUB)
657 Symbol für das Hallenbad Geroldswil: blau/gelb. Es wurde auch für T-Shirts und Badetaschen verwendet. (SWI)
658 Symbol der Transamerica Corporation. (USA)
659 Schutzmarke der japanischen Vereinigung der Sportwaffen- und Munitionsfabrikanten. (JPN)

645, 646 Combinaison d'un «S» et d'un clef de sol pour le comité du Festival Stravinsky. Symbole et en-tête. (GBR)
647 Logo (rose fraise) de la boutique de mode *Brin*. (BEL)
648 Symbole d'un fabricant de machines de bureau. (USA)
649 Marque déposée d'un fabricant de fibres. (JPN)
650, 651 D'un programme d'identité globale de marque pour Weber spa, fabricant de carburateurs et d'accessoires d'autos. (ITA)
652 Symbole de l'entreprise commerciale *Cogis*. (ITA)
653 Symbole d'un bar s'appelant Hibou. (CAN)
654 Ce symbole pour une banque a été dérivé d'un signe Indien. Il est appliqué en divers tons jaunes et rouges. (USA)
655, 660 Symbole et lettre du service d'informatique mis à disposition par les P & T anglaises. (GBR)
656 Symbole pour une gamme de produits pharmaceutiques. (CUB)
657 Piscine Geroldswil: bleu/jaune. Sur T-shirts et sacs. (SWI)
658 Symbole de la Transamerica Corporation. (USA)
659 Marque déposée pour l'association japonaise des armuriers spécialisés dans la fabrication d'armes de sport et de chasse. (JPN)

647

648

652

653

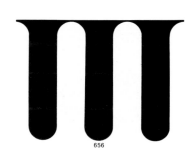

656

657

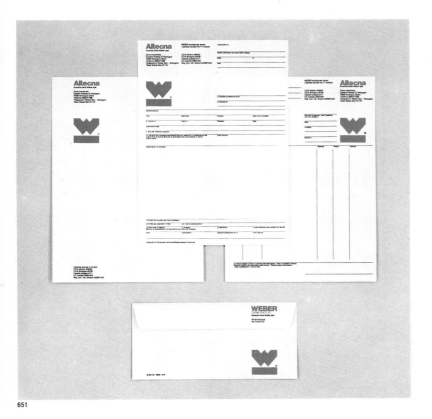

651

DESIGNER / GESTALTER / MAQUETTISTE:

645, 646 Alan Fletcher
647 Alain Constant
648, 658 Don Ervin
650, 651 Walter Ballmer
653 Ernst Roch
654 Ken Parkhurst
655, 660 Mervyn Kurlansky/Laura Starling
656 Félix Beltrán/Dagoberto Marcelo
657 Rosmarie Tissi
659 Takenobu Igarashi

ART DIRECTOR / DIRECTEUR ARTISTIQUE:

648, 658 Don Ervin
653 Ernst Roch
654 Ken Parkhurst
655, 660 Mervyn Kurlansky
656 Félix Beltrán
657 Rosmarie Tissi
659 Takenobu Igarashi

AGENCY / AGENTUR / AGENCE – STUDIO:

645, 646, 655, 660 Pentagram Design
648, 658 Siegel & Gale
649, 652 Unimark International
653 Design Collaborative
654 Ken Parkhurst
656 Félix Beltrán
657 Odermatt & Tissi
659 Takenobu Igarashi Design

649

650

654

655

658

659

660

661

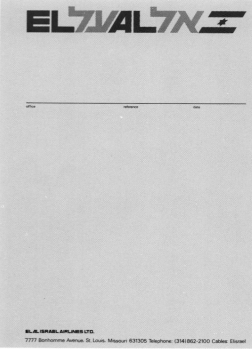

662

665

666

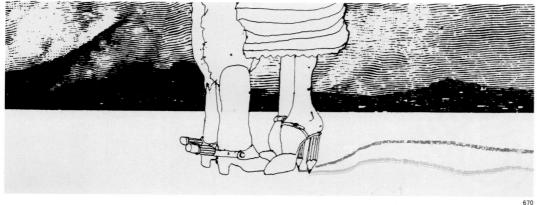

670

671

663

664

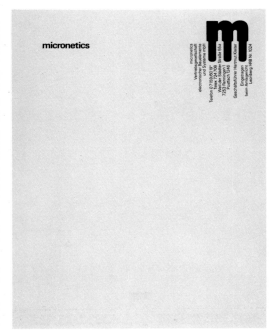

667

668

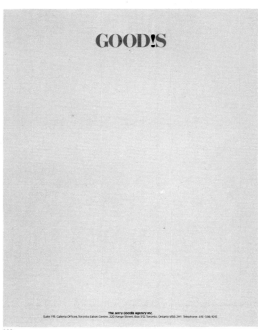

669

661 Stationery and enveloppe as examples from an advertising studio's corporate identity programme. On grey paper. (FRA)
662 Stationery of the Israelian airline EL AL. The letterhead is in blue and grey. (ISR)
663 Stationery with blind embossed letterhead of a wholesaler for natural stone pavements. (GER)
664 Example from the corporate identity programme of the architectural company *4B*. Name in red, address in black. (NOR)
665, 666 Stationery, envelope and note-paper for short answers from Kindred Design Associates. Thick lines in red under the name and black under the address. (USA)
667 Stationery in red and white for *Micronetics*, a trading company for electronic building elements and systems. The trademark has also been integrated into the letterhead. (GER)
668 For a magazine published by a television company. Letterhead in red, name on the stationery in grey. (USA)
669 Stationery of an advertising agency. Letterhead in grey with a blind embossed exclamation mark in silver. (CAN)
670, 671 Stationery and letterhead of the graphic designer Lanny Sommese. The full-colour lines have been done by hand. (USA)

661 Briefbogen und Umschlag als Beispiele aus dem Erscheinungsbild eines Werbestudios. Auf grauem Papier. (FRA)
662 Briefbogen der israelischen Fluggesellschaft EL AL. Briefkopf in Blau und Grau. (ISR)
663 Briefbogen mit blindgeprägtem Briefkopf für ein Grosshandelsunternehmen für Natursteinpflaster. (GER)
664 Beispiel aus dem gesamten Erscheinungsbild des Architekturbüros *4B*. Name in Rot, übriger Text in Schwarz. (NOR)
665, 666 Briefbogen, Umschlag und Bogen für Kurzantworten von Kindred Design Associates. Balken unter dem Namen in Rot, unter der Adresse in Schwarz. (USA)
667 Briefbogen in Rot auf Weiss für *Micronetics*, einer Vertriebsgesellschaft für elektronische Bauelemente und Systeme. Im Briefkopf wurde auch die Schutzmarke integriert. (GER)
668 Für die von einer Fernsehgesellschaft herausgegebene Zeitschrift. Briefkopf rot, Name auf dem Briefbogen grau. (USA)
669 Briefbogen einer Werbeagentur. Briefkopf in Grau mit geprägtem Ausrufungszeichen in Silber. (CAN)
670, 671 Briefbogen und Briefkopf des Graphikers Lanny Sommese. Farbige Linien werden von Hand hinzugefügt. (USA)

661 En-tête et enveloppe faisant partie du programme d'identité globale d'une agence publicitaire. Sur papier gris. (FRA)
662 En-tête de la compagnie aérienne israélienne EL AL. Caractères hébraïques en bleu, les autres en gris. (ISR)
663 Lettre avec en-tête gaufrée à sec pour une entreprise qui vend des pierres naturelles. (GER)
664 Exemple du programme d'identité globale du bureau d'architecture *4B*. Nom en rouge, texte en noir. (NOR)
665, 666 En-tête, enveloppe et bulletin de réponse de Kindred Design Associates. Les barres sous le nom sont en rouges, celles sous l'adresse en noir. (USA)
667 En-tête en rouge sur blanc de *Micronetics*, une société de vente de systèmes et d'éléments de construction électroniques. La marque déposée a été intégrée dans l'en-tête. (GER)
668 Pour un magazine publié par une station de TV. En-tête en rouge, nom du magazine en gris. (USA)
669 En-tête d'une agence de publicité. En-tête en gris avec point d'exclamation gaufré en argent. (CAN)
670, 671 En-tête personnel de Lanny Sommese. Les lignes de couleur sont à chaque fois ajoutées à la main. (USA)

672

673

674

675

676

677

678

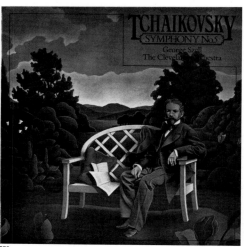

679

Record Covers
Schallplattenhüllen
Pochettes de disques

ARTIST / KÜNSTLER / ARTISTE:

672 Dieter Ziegenfeuter
673 Mark Hess
674 Brad Holland
675 Jim McMullan
676 Robert Van Nutt
677, 681 Bruno Oldani
678 Tadanori Yokoo
679 Neil Breeden
680 Andrzej Dudzinski
682 Josse Goffin

DESIGNER / ART DIRECTOR:

672 Marietta Frommberger
673 Mark Hess/Lynn Breslin
674 Katherine Smith
675 Paula Scher
676 Henrietta Condak
677, 681 Bruno Oldani
678 Tadanori Yokoo
679 Roslav Szaybo
680 Ron Kellum
682 Josse Goffin

AGENCY / PUBLISHER:

672 Frommberger/Ziegenfeuter/Global Records
673 Atlantic Recording Corp.
674 Album Graphics/Verve Records
675, 676, 679 CBS Inc.
677 Bruno Oldani/RCA Records
678 CBS/Sony
680 A. Dudzinski/Arista Records
681 Bruno Oldani/NorDisc/Polydor
682 Josse Goffin/INELCO

672 For a record by the Tightrope group. Blue butterflies. (GER)
673 For recordings on *Atlantic* of a band put together by wellknown jazz musicians. Cover illustration in various brown shades. (USA)
674 Cover of a jazz record in greenish brown shades. (USA)
675 Full-colour cover for a country and folk music record. (USA)
676 For Prokofiev's 5th Symphony. Blue, green-grey and red. (USA)
677 For Dixieland jazz, self composition. Full-colour title. (NOR)
678 Full-colour cover for a single called *Shonan Elegy*. (JPN)
679 Cover in sombre shades for Tchaikovsky's 5th Symphony. (GBR)
680 Illustration for recordings by the saxophonist Hawkins. (USA)
681 Recording by two guitarists. In green and lilac. (NOR)
682 Full-colour cover for a Belgian singer's latest record. (BEL)

672 Platte der Gruppe Tightrope. Blaue Schmetterlinge. (GER)
673 Für Aufnahmen einer aus bekannten Jazzmusikern zusammengestellten Band. Illustration in verschiedenen Brauntönen. (USA)
674 In Grünbrauntönen gehaltene Hülle einer Jazzplatte. (USA)
675 Farbige Hülle für eine Platte mit Folk- und Countrymusik. (USA)
676 Für Prokofievs 5. Symphonie. Blau, grüngrau und Rot. (USA)
677 Für Dixiland-Jazz. Farbiger Titel («selbstkomponiert»). (NOR)
678 Hülle einer Single mit dem Titel *Shonan Elegy*. (JPN)
679 Hülle in düsteren Farben für Tschaikowskis 5. Symphonie. (GBR)
680 Zu Aufnahmen des Jazz-Saxophonisten Hawkins. (USA)
681 Aufnahmen von zwei Gitarristen. Instrumente grün u. lila. (NOR)
682 Für eine neue Platte eines belgischen Chansonniers. Farbig. (BEL)

672 Pour un disque du groupe Tightrope. Papillons bleus. (GER)
673 Pour l'enregistrement d'un groupe constitué de divers musiciens de jazz de renom. En divers tons bruns. (USA)
674 Pochette pour un disque de jazz. En tons verts brunâtre. (USA)
675 Pochette polychrome pour un disque de musique folk. (USA)
676 Pour la Symphonie no 5 de Prokofiev. Bleu, gris et rouge. (USA)
677 Pour un disque de jazz Dixiland. Titre en couleurs vives. (NOR)
678 Pochette polychrome d'un disque intitulé *Shonan Elegy*. (JPN)
679 Pour la Symphonie no 5 de Tchaïkovski. Tons sombres. (GBR)
680 Pour un enregistrement du saxophoniste Hawkins. (USA)
681 Enregistrement de deux guitaristes. En vert et lilas. (NOR)
682 Pour le nouveau disque d'un chansonnier belge. (BEL)

680

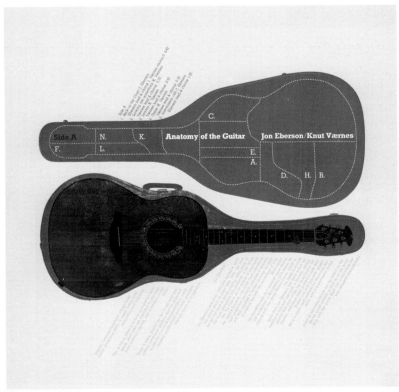

681

682

683

684

685

686

683 Cover of a record of 16 piano studies played by John Cage for The Tomato Music Co. Map of the southern hemisphere's stars at night; Cage indicated those seen from Australia and then transcribed them on to the musical score. (USA)
684 Record cover in dark brown and brilliant colours for disco music. (USA)
686 *S.Q.N. Records'* cover in dark shades for a recording of Stravinsky's *Histoire du Soldat* and a violin concert by Paul Hoffert. (CAN)
686 The cover of this CBS record for recordings by Tommy McLain illustrates the title of the record. In full colour. (USA)
687, 688 Cover and illustration for recordings by Margot Thomas. (USA)

683 Hülle für 16 Etuden für Klavier von John Cage. Karte des südlichen Sternenhimmels in hellen Grüntönen, auf welcher Cage von Australien aus zu sehende Sterne einzeichnete und diese dann auf Notenlinien übertrug. (USA)
684 Schallplattenhülle in Dunkelbraun und bunten Farben für Disco-Musik. (USA)
684 Schallplattenhülle in Dunkelbraun und bunten Farben für Disco-Musik. (USA)
Histoire du Soldat und ein Violinkonzert von Paul Hoffert. (CAN)
686 Der Umschlag dieser Plattenhülle für Aufnahmen von Tommy McLain illustriert den Titel «Abenteuer an einem Gewässer im Urwald». Mehrfarbig. (USA)
687, 688 Hülle und Illustration für Aufnahmen von Margot Thomas. (USA)

683 Pochette pour 16 études pour piano de John Cage. Carte céleste de l'hémisphère austral en tons verts clair. Sur une feuille transparente, Cage indiquait les étoiles qu'il voyait de l'Australie et en tirant les lignes, ces points lui servaient de notes. (USA)
684 Pochette pour un disque de music Disco. Brun et couleurs vives. (USA)
685 Pochette en tons sombres pour un enregistrement de l'*Histoire du soldat* de Stravinski et un concerto pour violon de Paul Hoffert. (CAN)
686 L'illustration de cette pochette pour un enregistrement de Tommy McLain fait allusion au titre «Les aventures au bord d'un étang dans le forêt vierge». (USA)
687, 688 Pochette et illustration pour un enregistrement de Margot Thomas. (USA)

Record Covers
Schallplattenhüllen
Pochettes de disques

ARTIST / KÜNSTLER / ARTISTE:

683 Matthew Klein
684, 687, 688 Milton Glaser
685 Heather Cooper
686 Mark Hess

DESIGNER / GESTALTER / MAQUETTISTE:

683 Milton Glaser/David Freedman
684, 687, 688 David Freedman
685 Heather Cooper/Robert Burns

ART DIRECTOR / DIRECTEUR ARTISTIQUE:

683, 684, 687, 688 Milton Glaser
685 Heather Cooper
686 Paula Scher

PUBLISHER / VERLEGER / EDITEUR:

683, 684, 687, 688 The Tomato Music Co.
685 SQN Records Ltd.
686 CBS Inc.

687

689

ARTIST / KÜNSTLER / ARTISTE:

689 Heather Cooper
690 Olaf Leu
693 Garry Emery/Ken Stanley

691

690

DESIGNER / GESTALTER / MAQUETTISTE:

689 Heather Cooper/Carmen Dunjko
690 Olaf Leu
691, 692 David Stuart
693 Garry Emery/Ken Stanley
694 Cliff Barrow
695 Katsu Kimura

689 Two tins of bath cosmetics by *Yardley*. The tins are in a wood-like texture with brown designs. The top is in black. (CAN)
690 Packaging for cigarettes of the *Reemtsma* continental blend. The text was printed in German and Russian language. (GER)
691, 692 Label in actual size with the can and bottle design for *Watneys* brown ale. (GBR)
693 This packaging contains a sample of a dermatological product distributed by *Glaxo Australia* at the annual Australasian dermatologists' meeting. Red point, year in steely blue. (AUS)
694 Packaging for *Skol* export beer in a sixpack, and bottle design. Label in yellow and white, lettering in grey and dark red. (NLD)
695 Gift packaging for Japanese pastries of the Nakamuraya Co. Box in olive green, the Japanese symbols are in yellow and white. (JPN)

689 Zwei Dosen für Badekosmetik von *Yardley*. Dosen mit Holzstruktur in Braun bedruckt, Deckel in Schwarz. (CAN)
690 Automaten-Packung für Zigaretten nach Kontinentaler Art von *Reemtsma*. Der Text wurde in Deutsch und Russisch gedruckt. (GER)
691, 692 Etikett in Originalgrösse und Dosen- und Flaschengestaltung für dunkles Bier. (GBR)
693 Die Packung enthält ein Muster eines dermatologischen Produktes. Sie wurde anlässlich eines Dermatologen-Kongresses 1979 verteilt. Roter Punkt, Jahrzahl in Graublau. (AUS)
694 Packung für sechs Flaschen und Flaschengestaltung für ein holländisches, für den Export bestimmtes Bier. Etikett in Gelb und Weiss, Schrift in Grau und Dunkelrot. (NLD)
695 Geschenkschachtel für japanische Kuchen. Schachtel in Olivegrün, japanische Schriftzeichen in Gelb und Weiss. (JPN)

689 Deux boîtes pour des produits cosmétiques pour le bain de *Yardley*. Boîtes en bois, imprimées en brun, resp. en noir sur le couvercle. (CAN)
690 Paquet de cigarettes *Reemtsma* «Continental». Le texte est écrit en langue allemande et en langue russe. (GER)
691, 692 Etiquette (grandeur originale) et conception de boîtes et de bouteilles pour *Watneys*, une bière brune. (GBR)
693 Ce paquet contient un échantillon d'un produit dermatologique. Il a été distribué à l'occasion d'un congrès de dermatologues. Point rouge, année en bleu grisâtre. (AUS)
694 Carton contenant six bouteilles et conception de la bouteille pour une bière hollandaise d'exportation. Etiquette en jaune et blanc, typo en gris et rouge foncé. (NLD)
695 Boîte de cadeau pour des gâteaux japonais. Boîte en vert olive, caractères japonais en jaune et blanc. (JPN)

692

693

ART DIRECTOR / DIRECTEUR ARTISTIQUE:

689 Heather Cooper
690 Olaf Leu
691, 692 John McConnell
693 Garry Emery
694 Cliff Barrow
695 Katsu Kimura

AGENCY / AGENTUR / AGENCE – STUDIO:

689 Burns, Cooper, Hynes Ltd.
690 Olaf Leu Design + Partner
691, 692 Pentagram Design
693 Interact Communications
694 J. Walter Thompson Design
695 Katsu Kimura & Packaging Direction Co. Ltd.

694

695

696

ARTIST / KÜNSTLER / ARTISTE:

699 Elwood Smith

DESIGNER / GESTALTER / MAQUETTISTE:

696, 697 Katsu Kimura
698 Robert P. Gersin/Candice Cain
700, 701 John Nowland

ART DIRECTOR / DIRECTEUR ARTISTIQUE:

696, 697 Katsu Kimura
698 Robert P. Gersin
700, 701 John Nowland

AGENCY / AGENTUR / AGENCE – STUDIO:

696, 697 Katsu Kimura & Packaging
        Direction Co. Ltd.
698 Robert P. Gersin Associates, Inc.
699 Push Pin Studios, Inc.
700, 701 John Nowland Design

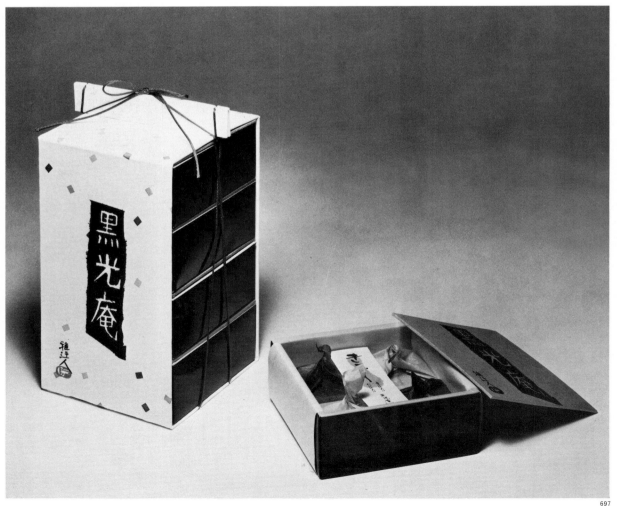

697

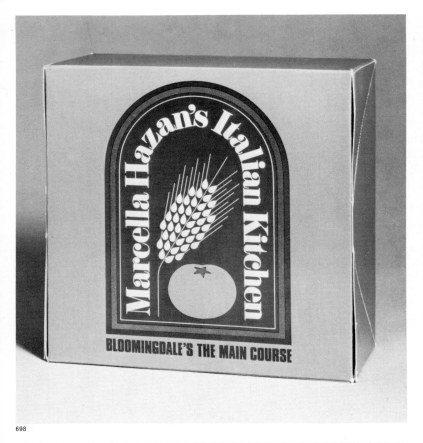

698

699

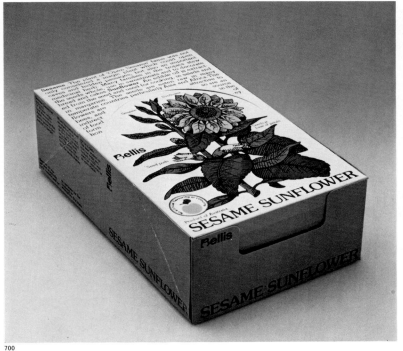

700

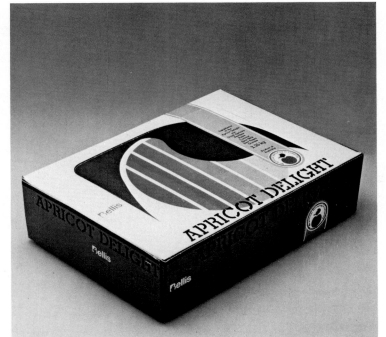

701

696 Carrier bag and wrapping paper for traditional Japanese cakes by the Nakamuraya Co. Bag in light beige, paper in white and grey with a yellow strip of lettering. (JPN)
697 Boxes for various Japanese cakes by the Nakamuraya Co. Opened box with a mustard-yellow top, cakes wrapped in mustard-yellow and dark bluish paper. (JPN)
698 Box for Italian noodles sold by *Bloomingdale's*. Red ground with magenta and green, red tomato, beige corn. (USA)
699 Full-colour folding box in the shape of a small basket for *McDonald's* hamburgers. All four sides of the box have been printed with children's games. (USA)
700, 701 From a packaging series for *Bellis Fruit Bars*. Fig. 700: yellow flower, green leaves, border in dark yellow; Fig. 701: design in green and orange, orange border. (AUS)

Packaging
Packungen
Emballages

696 Tragtasche und Einwickelpapier für traditionelle japanische Kuchen. Tragtasche in hellem Beige, Einwickelpapier in Weiss und Grau mit gelbem Schriftband. (JPN)
697 Schachteln für verschiedene japanische Kuchen. Geöffnete Schachtel mit senfgelbem Deckel, Kuchen in senfgelbes und dunkelblau-graues Papier eingeschlagen. (USA)
698 Schachtel für italienische Teigwaren, die von einer Warenhauskette verkauft werden. Roter Grund mit Magenta und Grün, rote Tomate, beige Ähre. (USA)
699 Farbiger Faltkarton in Form eines kleinen Tragkorbes für Hamburger von *McDonald's*. Auf allen vier Seiten sind Kinderspiele aufgedruckt. (USA)
700, 701 Aus einer Packungsreihe für Fruchtbonbons. Abb. 700: gelbe Blume, grüne Blätter, Rand der Schachtel in dunklem Gelb; Abb. 701: Design in Grün und Orange, Rand in Orange. (AUS)

696 Sac en papier et papier d'emballage pour des gâteaux japonais. Sac en beige, papier d'emballage en blanc et gris avec bande jaune. (JPN)
697 Boîtes pour un assortiment de gâteaux japonais. Boîte ouverte avec couvercle en jaune moutarde, gâteaux emballés en jaune moutarde ou bleu grisâtre. (JPN)
698 Boîtes pour des pâtes alimentaires italiennes, vendues par une chaîne de grands magasins. Fond rouge avec magenta et vert, tomate rouge, épis jaune. (USA)
699 Carton pliant sous forme d'un petit panier pour les hamburger *McDonald's*. Imprimé en polychromie et illustré de jeux d'enfants sur les côtés. (USA)
700, 701 Exemples d'une gamme d'emballages pour des barres aux fruits. Fig. 700: fleur jaune, feuilles vertes, bord en jaune foncé; fig. 701: vert et orange, bord en orange. (AUS)

Packaging / Packungen / Emballages

702 Examples from a packaging series for *Cacharel* cosmetics. Flowers in dull shades of yellow and pink on a light green and light bluish grey ground. (FRA)
703 Examples from a range of gift packaging for *Yardley* cosmetics. Light grey boxes imprinted in white and dark ruby-red. (AUS)
704 Box for an eau de toilette and bottle design for a body lotion. In olive green with the flower pattern in brilliant colours. (GER)
705 Examples of a packaging series for *Gilchrist & Soames* bathing cosmetics with cubes of six different herbs, a foam bath—plastic bottle with a cork—and a small pot for an aromatic candle. The illustrations are in full colour. (GBR)
706 Packaging for four bars of *Yardley* soap. Wooden box with brown print. (CAN)
707 Promotional packaging for a packaging firm. Fox and packaging in red-white stripes. (MEX)

703

704

705

702 Beispiele aus einer Packungsreihe für kosmetische Produkte von *Cacharel*. Blumen in matten Gelb- und Rosatönen auf hellgrünem, resp. hellblaugrauem Grund. (FRA)
703 Geschenkpackungen für kosmetische Produkte von *Yardley*. Hellgraue Faltschachteln in Weiss und dunklem Weinrot bedruckt. (AUS)
704 Faltschachtel für ein Eau de Toilette und Flaschengestaltung für eine Körperlotion. In Olive-grün, Blumenmotif in bunten Farben. (GER)
705 Beispiele aus einer Packungsreihe für Badekosmetika, hier Würfel für Badezusätze aus sechs verschiedenen Kräutern, ein Schaumbad – Plastikflasche mit Korkdeckel – und eine kleine Dose für eine Duftkerze. Mehrfarbige Illustrationen. (GBR)
706 Packung für vier Stück Handseife von *Yardley*. Holzkistchen in Braun bedruckt. (CAN)
707 Werbegeschenk einer Verpackungsfirma. Fuchs und Packung in Rot-Weiss gestreift. (MEX)

702 Exemples d'une gamme de produits cosmétiques lancés par *Cacharel*. Fleurs en tons jaunes et roses atténué sur fond vert et bleu pâle. (FRA)
703 Emballage de cadeau pour les produits cosmétiques de *Yardley*. Boîtes pliantes en gris clair, imprimées en blanc et rouge foncé. (AUS)
704 Boîte pliante pour une eau de toilette et conception du flacon pour une lotion pour les soins du corps. En olive, fleurs en couleurs vives. (GER)
705 Exemples d'une gamme de produits pour le bain, ici pour six cubes aux herbes, un bain de mousse – flacon en matière plastique avec couvercle en liège – et une petite boîte contenant une bougie odoriférante. Illustrations en couleurs. (GBR)
706 Emballage pour quatre briques de savon *Yardley*. Boîte en bois, imprimée en brun. (CAN)
707 Cadeau publicitaire d'une entreprise de conditionnements. En rouge et blanc. (MEX)

706

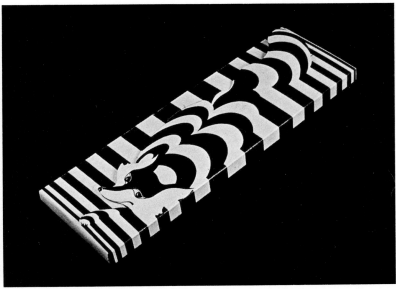

707

708

709

708 Bottle and label design for an Australian Riesling and a Cabernet. Labels in white on a dark green and dark red ground. From the Lindemans Wines company. (AUS)
709 The numbered labels for a Californian Cabernet Sauvignon show motifs of almost extinct American animals from a collection of graphics by John J. Audubon. The whole series was sold by *Windsor Vineyards*, a mailorder company, the proceeds used for the protection of these animals. The illustrations are in full colour. (USA)
710 Paper bag (in brown on wrapping paper) for a health food shop. (USA)
711 These numbered labels for the *Windsor Vineyards* show motifs of pictures by Frédéric Remington from his *Western Frontier* collection. The labels were on bottles of Californian Cabernet Sauvignon sold by mail order. (USA)
712, 713 From a series of promotional packaging of a packaging company. (MEX)

708 Flaschen- und Etikettgestaltung für einen australischen Riesling und einen Cabernet. Etikett auf dunkelgrünem, resp. dunkelrotem Grund. (AUS)
709 Die numerierten Etiketten für einen kalifornischen Cabernet Sauvignon zeigen Motive von selten gewordenen amerikanischen Tierarten aus einer Sammlung von graphischen Blättern von John J. Audubon. Der Wein wurde von einem Versandhaus zum Schutze dieser Tiere verkauft. Mehrfarbige Illustrationen. (USA)
710 Tüten (in Braun auf Packpapier) für ein Reformhaus. (USA)
711 Diese numerierten Etiketten zeigen Motive von Bildern von Frédéric Remington aus seiner *Western Frontier*-Sammlung. Für einen von einem Versandhaus vertriebenen kalifornischen Cabernet Sauvignon. (USA)
712, 713 Aus einer Serie von Werbegeschenkpackungen einer Verpackungsfirma. Abb. 712 in Abstufungen von Dunkelbraun über Rot und Gelb. (MEX)

708 Conception de bouteilles et d'étiquettes pour un Riesling et un Cabernet Sauvignon australien. Etiquettes en blanc sur fond foncé, resp. sur rouge foncé. (AUS)
709 Ces étiquettes numérotées pour un Cabernet Sauvignon californien présentent différents animaux devenus rares aux Etats-Unis. Les motifs sont extraits d'une collection de feuilles graphiques de John J. Audubon. Toute la gamme a été vendue par une maison pour la protection de ces animaux. En polychromie. (USA)
710 Sacs (brun sur papier d'emballage) d'un magasin de produits diététiques. (USA)
711 Ces étiquettes numérotées présentent des motifs de la collection de peintures que Frédéric Remington avait réalisée sous le titre *Western Frontier*. Pour un Cabernet Sauvignon californien. (USA)
712, 713 Exemples d'une gamme d'emballages pour des cadeaux publicitaires destinés aux clients d'une entreprise de conditionnements. Fig. 712: en brun, passant au rouge et jaune. (MEX)

711

710

Packaging
Packungen
Emballages

ARTIST / KÜNSTLER / ARTISTE:

709 John T. Audubon
711 Frederic Remington
712, 713 Diana Garcia

DESIGNER / GESTALTER / MAQUETTISTE:

708 Ken Cato
709, 711 David Broom
710 Douglas Hoppe Stone
712, 713 Diana Garcia

ART DIRECTOR / DIRECTEUR ARTISTIQUE:

708 Ken Cato
709, 711 David Broom
710 Douglas Hoppe Stone
712, 713 Diana Garcia

AGENCY / AGENTUR / AGENCE – STUDIO:

708 Cato Hibberd Design Pty Ltd
709, 711 Broom & Broom
710 Douglas Stone & Associates
712, 713 Laboratorio de Diseño y Análisis de
Mercado/Cartón y Papel de México SA

712

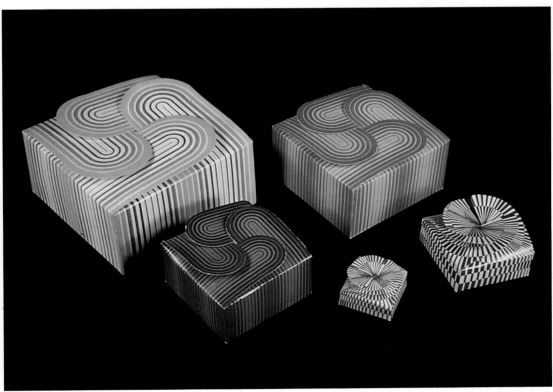

713

ARTIST / KÜNSTLER / ARTISTE:

715 Peter Kramer
718 Randall Swatek/David Romanoff

DESIGNER / GESTALTER / MAQUETTISTE:

714 Frank Vigliotti
715 Peter Kramer
716 Olaf Leu
717 Derek Spaull
718 Randall Swatek/David Romanoff
719 Alfred Lutz

ART DIRECTOR / DIRECTEUR ARTISTIQUE:

714 Markus J. Löw
715 Jack Goldstein/Peter Kramer
716 Olaf Leu
717 Derek Spaull
718 Randall Swatek/David Romanoff
719 Alfred Lutz

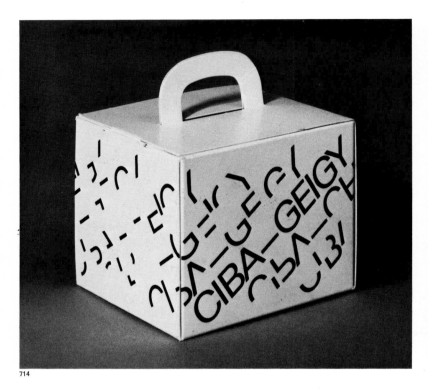

714

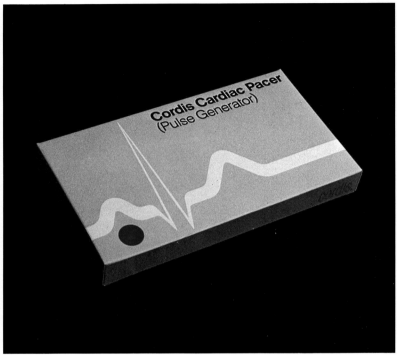

715

AGENCY / AGENTUR / AGENCE – STUDIO:

714 Ciba-Geigy
715 Cordis/Graphics Dept.
716 Olaf Leu Design & Partner
717 Derek Spaull Graphics
718 Swatek Romanoff Design

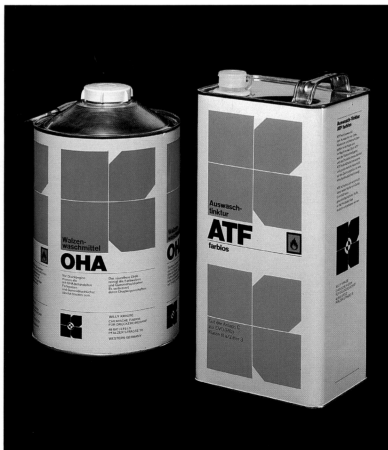

716

714 This white and blue package contains a ceramic receptacle that *Ciba-Geigy* sent to customers as a promotional gift. (USA)
715 Folding box for a *Cordis* cardiac pacemaker. Grey and white with a red point. (USA)
716 Metal container for a liquid cleaning agent used by printers. (GER)
717 From a series of uniformly designed packaging manufactured in various colours for pharmaceuticals made by the *Parke Davis* company. (USA)
718 This plexiglass box contains two red balls and "jacks" used in a game by the same name. It was sent as a promotional gift by Swater Romanoff Design. White and black on silver. (USA)
719 For six glasses. The compositions (black, grey and one colour) are available as posters. (GER)

714 Diese weiss und blaue Packung enthielt ein Keramik-Gefäss, das *Ciba-Geigy* als Werbegeschenk an Kunden verschickte. (USA)
715 Faltschachtel für einen Herzschrittmacher. Grau und weiss mit rotem Punkt. (USA)
716 Metallbehälter für ein flüssiges Reinigungsmittel, das in Druckereien verwendet wird. (GER)
717 Aus einer Serie von einheitlich gestalteten Packungen in verschiedenen Farben für Arzneimittel von *Parke Davis*. (USA)
718 Diese Plexiglasschachtel enthält zwei rote Bälle und «jacks» für das Spiel «Jacks». (USA)
719 Beispiele aus einer Packungsreihe für je 6 Gläser der *Wiesenthalhütte*. Das organische Farbenspiel (Grau, Schwarz und eine Farbe, hier Gelb und Orange) bildet die Basis dieser Kompositionen, die als Poster erhältlich sind. (GER)

714 Cette boîte pliante en blanc et bleu contient un bol en céramique, que *Ciba-Geigy* avait envoyé à ses clients comme cadeau publicitaire. (USA)
715 Boîte pliante pour un pacemaker. Gris et blanc avec point rouge. (USA)
716 Conditionnement de détergents liquides destinés à l'industrie graphique. (GER)
717 Exemples d'une gamme de boîtes de conception uniforme en différentes couleurs pour les produits pharmaceutiques de *Parke Davis*. (USA)
718 Cette boîte en plexiglas contient deux balles rouges et des «jacks» pour jouer un jeu qui s'appelle «Jacks». Cadeau publicitaire d'un studio de design. Noir et blanc sur argent. (USA)
719 D'une série de boîtes pour six verres. Toutes les compositions en noir et gris avec une autre couleur (ici en jaune et orange) ont été publiées sous forme d'affiche. (GER)

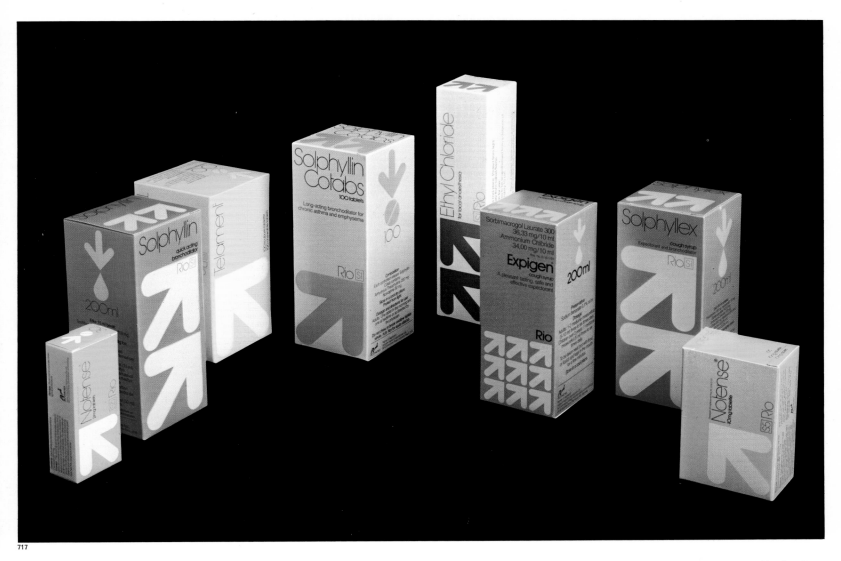

717

718

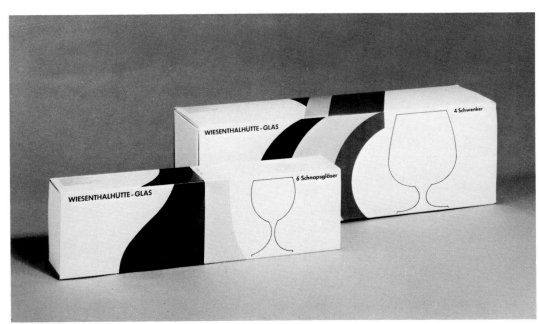

719

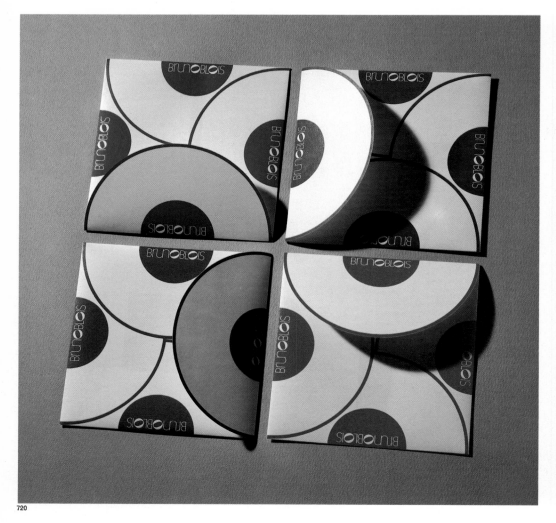

720

721

ARTIST / KÜNSTLER / ARTISTE:

724 Barrie Schwortz

DESIGNER / GESTALTER / MAQUETTISTE:

720 Fred Jordan
721 Charles Goslin
722 Ken Cato
723 Uldis Purins/Jennet Jessell
724 Marty Neumeier
725 T. Suiter/R. Hurtado

720 From a series of carrier bags for a gramophone company. (BRA)
721 "The Atom Bomb." This spray-can for a pesticide made by the Lugo Chemical Co. was especially developed for Spanish-speaking Americans. (USA)
722 A plastic bottle for a washing agent for woolen garments made by Kiwi Australia Ltd. Blue bottle, label in white with blue and red. (AUS)
723 Examples from a packaging series in corrugated cardboard for the Crane Co. china-ware. Design and lettering in blue on white. (USA)
724 This *Creative Education* slip-case contains a reading programme and a cassette that can be played by students during a lesson. (USA)
725 Uniformly designed packaging series for *Rhodes* steel wool. The illustrations, each in one colour on white, show the application spheres. (USA)

720 Aus einer Serie von Tragtaschen für ein Grammophongeschäft. (BRA)
721 «Die Atombombe.» Diese Spraydose für ein Pestizid wurde speziell für Spanisch sprechende Amerikaner entworfen. (USA)
722 Einer Wollstrange nachempfundene Plastikflasche für ein Waschmittel für Wollwaren. Blaue Flasche, Etikett weiss mit Blau und Rot. (AUS)
723 Beispiele aus einer Packungsreihe aus Wellkarton für Porzellanwaren. Design und Schrift in Blau auf Weiss. (USA)
724 Dieser Schuber enthält ein Leseprogramm und eine Kassette, welche die Schüler während der Lektüre abspielen können. (USA)
725 Einheitlich gestaltete Packungsreihe für Stahlwolle. Die Illustrationen in je einer Farbe auf Weiss zeigen die Anwendungsbereiche. (USA)

720 D'une série de sacs en papier pour un magasin qui vend des disques. (BRA)
721 «La bombe atomique.» Bombe aérosol pour un pesticide. Cette bombe a été spécialement conçue pour les Américains de langue espagnole. (USA)
722 Flacon en matière plastique ressemblant à un écheveau de laine: pour une lessive pour les articles en laine. Flacon bleu. (AUS)
723 Exemples d'une gamme d'emballages en carton ondulé pour des articles en porcelaine. Design et typo en bleu sur blanc. (USA)
724 Carton contenant un programme d'enseignement et une cassette que les étudiants peuvent écouter pendant la lecture. (USA)
725 Exemples d'une gamme d'emballages de conception uniforme pour la laine d'acier. Les illustrations en couleurs sur fond blanc montrent les possibilités d'application. (USA)

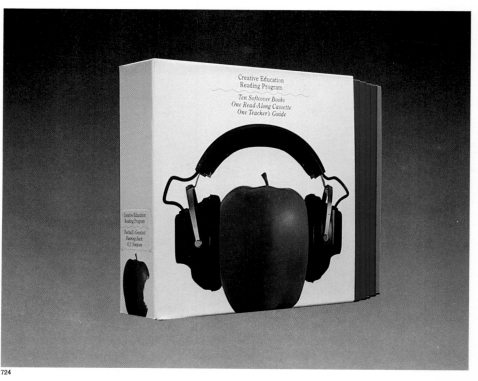

724

722

723

ART DIRECTOR / DIRECTEUR ARTISTIQUE:

720 Fred Jordan
721 Bernard Colonna
722 Ken Cato
725 Ted Piegdon

AGENCY / AGENTUR / AGENCE – STUDIO:

720 Fred Jordan Graphic Design
721 Bernard Colonna Associates
722 Cato Hibberd Design Pty Ltd
723 Gregory Fossella Associates
724 Marty Neumeier Design
725 Design West

725

Paper / Papier: Papierfabrik Biberist – Biber GS SK3, blade coated, pure white 120 gm² and Biber Offset SK3, pure white, machine-finished, 140 gm² / Biber GS SK3, hochweiss, satiniert, 120 gm² und Biber-Offset SK3, hochweiss, maschinenglatt, 140 gm²

Printed by / gedruckt von: Merkur AG, Langenthal (black and white / schwarz-weiss), Sigg Söhne AG, Winterthur (colour pages / Farbseiten)

Cover / Einband: Buchbinderei Schumacher AG, Bern / Schmitten
Glossy lamination / Glanzfoliierung: Durolit AG, Pfäffikon SZ